THROUGH THE LENS OF REALITY

Thoughts from a Maturing Grandpa

THROUGH THE LENS OF REALITY

Thoughts from a Maturing Grandpa

JERRY RABE

Two Harbors Press
Minneapolis, MN

Two Harbors Press
212 3rd Avenue North, Suite 290
Minneapolis, MN 55401
612.455.2293
www.TwoHarborsPress.com

ISBN - 978-1-936198-78-8
ISBN - 1-936198-78-9
LCCN - 2010935512

Cover Design and Typeset by Sophie Chi

Printed in the United States of America

CONTENTS

PART I—LOOKING AT OURSELVES FROM THE OUTSIDE IN

PART III—A DELIBERATE WALK IN THE WOODS

To Diane,
the wind behind my back

INTRODUCTION

*"Who knows whether in retirement
I shall be tempted to the last
infirmity of mundane minds,
which is to write a book."*

—Geoffrey Fisher

Why this book? What do I want to say? And to whom do I want to say this? And why should you take the time to read it?

There is not a single answer but rather several reasons that merge together into a message that I feel, in my heart, is important to be heard. First and foremost, it's a message that I want to share with my kids and grandkids. Along with my wife, Diane, these are the wonderful people I most care about. I am hoping that other people consider the ideas and thoughts contained in this book, but being a realist, I am acutely aware that I am a very small voice in a vast dessert. Yet inside I am hoping that every parent, every politician, and everyone who cares about human existence reads this book because I believe it contains a message that is essential to the survival of society as we now know it.

What exactly is the message that this grandpa thinks is so important? Primarily, it's my thoughts on the biggest questions that we face as human beings—the essence of who we are—and how the answers to these questions are vitally important, both from the standpoint of individual fulfillment and in finding personal happiness. It also deals with a very closely related question: will we progress or decline as a society? I hope this book will cause you to think hard about the beliefs that you hold and which define your essential being. And I most hope that this message will give you an inner sense of security and purpose. And last—and most optimistically—it is the hope that if all of us, as brothers and sisters, have the courage to look deeply into our beliefs, we will see the possibility of a most wonderful path before us, individually and as a society. My hope, as an unknown writer once said, is "that you crawl out on the limb, rather than sit on the porch."

I should caution, however, that my own experience suggests that, at least initially, this will be a very difficult, troubling, and uncertain venture for you. It may leave you feeling naked before it leaves you with the most comfortable set of clothes you have ever worn. I am suggesting that you consider embarking upon a process that may challenge your most defining beliefs; that is not an undertaking to be taken lightly. But it may also be the most important and wonderful decision that you will ever make.

A second reason for writing this book is to give my kids and grandkids, and even my soul mate, Diane, a more authentic picture of who I am, what makes me tick, what goes on inside, and who I am. For some people, I suppose, this would not be an issue. But by nature, I am not a very open person, so before I leave this earthly realm, this is an attempt to let those who are important to me to see me in a more authentic light. I also have a feeling that their reaction might be "we really knew you a lot better than you thought." Good. In fact, I hope this is the case.

The confidence to write this book comes, in large part, from my work experience. Over the years I came to recognize that I was given a unique skill in looking at complex issues, seeing how the various pieces of a complex situation can be brought together into a coherent, understandable, actionable whole. I believe this was my unique offering during my work life, and it allowed me to be valued for an entire work career. I was also a firm believer in the idea that putting your thoughts down in writing is a very effective way to examine critically your beliefs and the views that you hold. Many beliefs seem so logical and right—until you decide that it would be a good self-discipline exercise to put them into writing, and even more so, to then ask others to critique your thought process. It is the most instructive process that exists. It separates rigorous thinking from the casual; informed judgment from unsubstantiated ideology; and ultimately, it separates reasoned thought from myth. It is a process that leads to truth and defines reality.

There is also urgency to all of this. A central thesis of this book is my belief that such things as religious dogma, the environment, financial and economic management, and our notion of what is good and bad, have become monumental issues that will merge into the perfect storm if not dealt with in an informed, thoughtful, energetic way. These are heavy, important issues, all having dimensions that relate to how each of us makes personal decisions.

Much of my thinking on these issues has changed in recent years, and I would like to take the opportunity to share these thoughts and to suggest, on a personal and societal basis, how we might prepare and deal with this as the nation's and world's circumstances evolve. Very simply, it's about the world in which our kids and grandkids will live. A key message of the book is to suggest a way for each of us, individually, to deal with the issues of society, even if—God forbid—society finds itself incapable of dealing with these issues. That is, how can we lead fulfilling, happy lives in what might continue to be a very, very turbulent world? In sharing these views, I am certain that I will be the subject of much criticism. Again, I hope that my family will understand, my friends will not desert me, and where I'm in error, will help me correct my way.

Finally there is, I suppose, the ego factor. The people I admire most are writers and thought leaders. Make no mistake; this grandpa knows he is not in the camp of great writers or great thinkers. In my late fifties I achieved a long-held dream of becoming a pilot and like most other small-plane pilots have dreamt about taking over the controls of an airliner from an incapacitated crew and flying it to a safe landing. In a similar way, this book allows me to tell myself that I, too, wrote a book about something important, making me feel like a member of this "writers and great thinkers" group—certainly not in reality but at least in my daydreams.

I mentioned that my skill is to integrate things, bringing forth a coherent, substantive understanding that folks can grasp. In this book, I doubt that there are any truly new thoughts on any of the subjects. All observations and ideas have been borrowed from others; I confess to intellectual plagiarism. To those people, I want to offer my sincere respect and thanks. My hope is that perhaps I have taken these individual pieces and fashioned them into a whole that is worthy of further thought in today's world.

This book will conclude in a way that may be surprising, given the challenges outlined in the early chapters. I have no doubt that if we have the courage to address reality, both individually and as a society, and to honesty examine the basis for our beliefs, we stand on the edge of the most wonderful, most encouraging era in recorded civilization. We have the incredible opportunity, as a society, to work together on the most critical issues that man and nation have ever faced. And each of us has the opportunity to learn and to grow and to become more complete human beings, to lead fulfilled, happy lives. Each of us has within our reach the ability to become an authentic person, no longer controlled by delusion and unfounded ideology. We can live contently, knowing and accepting the limits of our human capacity to understand the basis for our existence. Only when we achieve that state of being will we have the capacity to truly love each other and ourselves.

Last of all, to Brett, Kendra, Heather, Marlee, Clay, Tirza, and Diane: I hope you see me in this book as someone of whom you are proud. I am not asking for your agreement on any of my thoughts. In fact, it's exactly the opposite: I hope that it encourages you to think for yourselves. You are very special. And for all the other parents, politicians, and those who care about human existence, I invite you to eavesdrop on this message.

With love,
Jerry

NOTES

- You will note frequent use of italicized words and phrases. In most cases these italicized words and phrases are *mine* and, if found in quoted phrases, were often not italicized or written in bold type by the original author. My use of italics is to draw your attention to what I believe is an important point and to help me communicate a key thought.

- To the best of my knowledge the "outside" information cited in this book is factually accurate. The "inside" information—my thoughts and beliefs—are, I promise, honest and authentic. I do not cite specific references or details of the sources underlying the outside information for two reasons: one is that I want you to focus on the core message, to encourage you to begin walking down your own path of inquiry, and that my purpose is not to convince you of any particular fact or ideology. This is a story about how we make decisions in our lives, and references seem to me to foster focus on specific arguments, rather than this core message. The other reason is that most people can now research an issue in a more comprehensive way using Internet search engines or using a library source. This is consistent, I believe, with the fundamental message of this book: that the immense challenges of today's world demand that each of us be proactively engaged in our search for the truths and realities that embed these issues.

PART I

LOOKING AT OURSELVES FROM THE OUTSIDE IN

CHAPTER 1

THE VERY AWESOMENESS OF BEING YOU

"Do not grow old, no matter how long you live. Never cease to stand like curious children before the Great Mystery into which you were Born."

"The most beautiful thing we can experience is the mysterious."

—Albert Einstein

"Most human beings have an almost infinite capacity for taking things for granted."

—Aldous Huxley

It is the ultimate mystery as to why you are here, at this precise moment in time, on this planet called Earth, one person out of 6.5 billion other people, with no one else looking just like you, and certainly with no one else sharing your exact circumstances or your current state of mind or your present feelings. That you are here is against all odds. Because of this apparent miracle, we sense the beginning of the tension between religion and science. And being a very unique individual, a one-and-only, you have to contend with that tension in your very own way: what does it mean to be "you"?

Let's take a mathematical-type look at just how unique your existence really is, because it leads to the inescapable conclusion that, at least statistically, it's close to impossible that you should even exist. But pinch yourself; here you are. It should make you feel not only very special and unique but also very humble. Because of this unique opportunity to be part of the universe's existence, it seems reasonable that you should appreciate and thoroughly enjoy this incredible, awesome, very-close-to-impossible opportunity to experience the wonder of life and the world, even though, cosmologically speaking, it's for a mere speck of time. Because you are so unique and have been so gifted, it also seems reasonable to ask whether this privilege of existence carries with it a responsibility of some measure.

The most widely accepted theory is that the universe is 13.7 billion years old, give or take a bit. It appears to have started with a "Big Bang" an explosion or expansion of sorts of an incredibly dense mass that sent elementary particles and a few lightweight molecules—helium, hydrogen, and lithium gases—and energy every which way. Some of this early matter and energy eventually aggregated, forming the galaxies, of which our very own Milky Way is one. And within each of these galaxies, many, many solar systems formed—the heat from imploding stars providing the energy to create the heavier chemical elements and some of the molecules that became the building blocks of life. Clearly, at least for you and me, the most important solar system formed is the one in which we live, anchored by the life-giving sun that rises from the eastern horizon each morning and sets each night in the west, bathing Planet Earth with its life-generating energy.

Much of our understanding of what has happened to form this universe rests on good science, but a lot of mystery remains that will probably challenge cosmos physicists for centuries, if not forever. As example, the universe is continuing to expand at an increasing rate, which, it can be easily argued, should not be happening. Physicists are now searching for the force that is causing this expansion. At this time we know a lot more about *what* has happened than we do about *why* it happened.

Consider, from a time and space perspective, how unlikely it is for you to be where you are. The Big Bang created many galaxies—cosmologists estimate that there are more than 150 billion of these galaxies in the universe. That's 150,000,000,000 "Milky Ways," each like the heavens I see when I walk out on our cabin dock on a small island in Lake of the Woods before going to bed. And within each of these Milky Way-like galaxies, it is estimated that there are probably 100 billion to 400 billion—or more—solar systems similar to our sun-centered solar system, each with its own array of planets, moons, and asteroids. But here we are, such an incredibly small speck among this vastness. Time-wise, space-wise, mathematical-wise, and logic-wise, our being here is utterly impossible but yet a reality. Using Einstein's suggestion that we look at things like a child, it seems simply impossible that all this—the earth and the universe—could have come from nothing, yet here we are. Our existence is the most profound of mysteries that should keep us all a bit humble and cognizant of our childlike acceptance of the place and circumstances in which we find ourselves.

Our universe, however, is even weirder and more awesome. The stuff we can see—the ordinary matter that the earth and everything on it is made of; the matter the moon and the sun is made of; the stuff cosmos physicists can describe without moving to abstract equations—is only a small portion of what is really out there. It may be only about 4 percent. The rest is what is called dark matter and dark energy. In fact, it may be the dark energy that is pushing the universe to expand faster and faster. Physicists also theorize that there might be many dimensions in the universe other than the four dimensions that most of us can comprehend: length, width, depth, and time. Some of the dimensions theorized even suggest that visible and invisible parts of the universe may co-exist at the same time and in the same space. Imagine another world that does not interact with the world we see, hear, or feel and which might be passing right through the world we do see. All very strange and humbling to the average person's intellect.

On the other end of the size spectrum, there are things that appear, in a deceptive way, to be less mind-boggling, more tangible and here-and-now. Consider the cells in your body. Some scientists have estimated that a baby has on the order of 10,000 trillion cells when it's born, with each cell containing upwards of 20,000 different proteins, plus all the other cellular components. We couldn't even see these cells clearly until devices that produce greatly enlarged images of these structures began to be developed 150 years ago. It gets very complicated quickly when we consider the complex structure of these proteins and all the other biochemical components. The nucleus structure contains forty-six chromosomes or DNA strands, each six feet in length (if you could stretch it out), each chromosome with over three billion letters of coding. If you could stretch out and attach end-to-end all the DNA in your body, it would make a very thin thread long enough to make two trips to the moon and back. And it is the uniqueness of that thread that makes you who you are.

4

How these cells and organ systems and DNA evolved into a human-like being is subject to much controversy and speculation, with the solid fossil evidence pointing in conflicting and diverse directions. What can be ascertained with some degree of certainty is that man began to evolve into his present form about 120,000 years ago. This lineage is known as *Homo sapiens*, our earliest forefathers. We would probably not recognize them if we met them while shopping in Wal-Mart, but they were clearly a different and more advanced species than the Neanderthals, who co-existed with the *Homo sapiens* for a while but who eventually disappeared from the scene. Although they were the species destined to advance, anthropologist have found no evidence that *Homo sapiens* could speak or engage in the kind of activities that we normally associate with modern man until roughly 60,000 years ago.

Sixty thousand years may seem like a long time, but it is a very short amount of time when compared to the age of the earth, 4.5 billion years, or that of the universe, 13.7 billion years. Thinking of our existence in the universe as a percentage of a normal 24-hour day, man did not appear on earth until 2.3 seconds ago. Even after we arrived on earth, it took a long time before man evolved to the form we are now, and only *very, very recently* in the numbers that we have now reached. The significance of this will be discussed later, but for now, the point to take away is that we are not only unique in terms of how we got here, but we are unique in the challenges that now face mankind, challenges that did not exist even less than fifty years ago. *So with this uniqueness, which makes us so special, comes a uniqueness that will demand a level of development, maturity, and clear thinking never before required of man.* Only independent thinking, which this book suggests is your challenge and your opportunity, will solve the issues facing society and provide personal contentment.

Our individual uniqueness has been recognized by many of the great thinkers of the world, who often express this concept in terms of the fundamental rights of all people, every individual. The Declaration of Independence states it well: "We hold these truths to be self-evident, that all men are created equal ..." Inherent in this statement is the notion that each person may have equal but unique thoughts and a voice that must be respected. A comparable statement is contained in the United Nations Universal Declaration of Human Rights, adopted in 1948, which declares "recognition of the inherent dignity and of the equal and inalienable rights of all members of the human family ... that they are endowed with reason and conscience and should act towards one another in a spirit of brotherhood."

The great minds that wrote these statements were saying that there is a universal truth that each of us is unique, that we have an inherent right to think for ourselves, that each of us is special in our own unique way, and that this reality of individualism should be treasured and respected. It also says, in a very clear way, that each of us has a responsibility to use this uniqueness in a way that is considerate of our brothers and sisters, all of whom are members of the human family.

The very awesomeness of being you is the cornerstone of how I want you to read the rest of this book. My hope is that it empowers you. I hope that it helps you recognize that you have been given a very special place in this universe that is all your own, and that you have a responsibility for how you live your very special allotted time here. In the chapters that follow, I will share with you the reasons why I think it is so important that you think for yourself, that you not follow the herd, that you search for your own sense of reality and responsible behavior. I am sharing this message with you because I believe this is the route to true happiness, the living of a life that is fulfilling, and the living of a life that is loving of others. I'm also sharing it because it has taken me so long to learn this reality myself.

Most importantly, because you are unique and special, it's up to you to accept or reject my thoughts and ideas, and perhaps where I am in error, to offer constructive criticism so that this grandpa can continue to mature. If I succeed in making you think, to search for truth, understanding and reality, then this book will have served its purpose.

CHAPTER 2

THE NONSENSICALNESS
OF OUR HUMANNESS

*"The difference between what we do
and what we are capable of doing
would suffice to solve most of
the world's problems."*

—Mohandas Gandhi

*All I care to know is that a man is
a human being—that is enough for
me; he can't get any worse."*

—Mark Twain

"What a splendid head, yet no brain."

—Aesop

To deal effectively with the challenges that mankind faces, it is
essential that we acknowledge a foundational reality: many of the
things that we do as a society are tragically absurd. Much of what
happens on Planet Earth is nonsensical, yet it is all too real. It is
important to look backwards to remind ourselves that mankind
is very capable of—even seemingly predisposed to—engaging in

9

behavior that is senseless, when considered from a distance. Yet we allow this senseless behavior to occur time and time again. And we allow it to occur—and this is what is so surprising—with little thoughtful questioning as to why we repeatedly go down this mindless road.

Perhaps it is the very absurdity of it that dulls our senses. Perhaps our unwillingness to acknowledge this nonsensicalness of our humanness is our coping mechanism. Perhaps it is a sense that man simply does not have control over the tribalism still in his genes. *But it may also be true that we have reached a point in the development of man where this nonsensical behavior has become so risky that it can no longer be tolerated*; if we recognize that the consequences are potentially catastrophic we will begin to acknowledge that this senseless behavior must not continue, and that we have no choice but to look at our place in history through the lens of reality.

What are some of these nonsensical humanness issues that face mankind? Using Albert Einstein's suggestion that we take a childlike approach to looking at problems, it is instructive to pretend that we are looking at the earth from the moon and assess the rationality of some of the things happening on Planet Earth.

• We would see, over essentially the entire span of human life, that war is commonplace and horrendous, in terms of the suffering that it causes its people. We would see wars fought with chariots and swords and spears; wars fought with cannons, warships, and guns; wars fought with tanks, airplanes, and bombs; even evidence of a war fought that ended with nuclear devices having the capability to destroy all mankind. Standing on the moon, one would say, "What an absurdity for this awesome Planet Earth and its inhabitants!" Yet each war has had the support of a large number of people—usually a nation state—and without that support, it could not have happened. Some underlying belief or ideology was advanced and made sense to the people. Our first inclination is to think that this applies to "the other nation's people." But it does not. War mongers exist among us too.

- We would see the people of the earth dividing themselves into religious groups—Muslims, Christians, Jews, Hindus, and others—each claiming to have possession of the eternal truth; each declaring that it is superior to the other in morality and wisdom; each professing to being more righteous than the others in the eyes of God; and at times, each citing dogma to justify the killing and the torture of the other. By definition, this is an absurdity—obviously so, as all can't have unique possession of eternal truth. We are now at a point in history where this has immense and immediate implication. Consider, for example, the books that have been written that predict an unavoidable clash between the Islam and Christian faiths. It is also at the roots of the Judaism versus Islam dogma in the Israel-Palestine conflict.

- We would see a world where the humans view themselves as an advanced, caring, beyond-animal species, but where over one billion of earth's people live in abject poverty, while the others live in abundance; where some feel entitled to good health care, while denying that the less fortunate are also deserving; where some, by the good fortune of birthplace, hold the keys to prosperity and well-being, while withholding those keys from those born into less fortunate circumstances. From the moon, seeing this disparity would be an absurdity that defies the often-cited beliefs in brotherhood and sisterhood. It is the antithesis of what we so strongly confess in the religious dogma we hold. It is absurdity underwritten by the incongruence of words versus

11

deeds, by the hypocrisy of appearance versus action, and by the failure to differentiate image from substance.

- We would see a world where evil is conducted under the banner of "business as usual," rationalized in various ways by those who benefit from this evil and tolerated by others who simply "look the other way." We would see companies that sell cancer; companies that profit from the selling of arms; countries where the populace tolerates the rise of evil dictators who practice genocide to gain power. These are obvious absurdities that would be seen as the nonsensicalness of our humanness by someone from afar. We would see the absurdity and immorality of using religion and deception and the charge of "not being patriotic" to build support for war.

- We would see a world that allows its population to grow at a rate that imperils the ability of Earth to support its inhabitants. We would see a world that is endangering its climate, making it ever harder for the planet to support its inhabitants. We would see governments and their populace unable to muster the will to deal with this issue, even when warned by its own, best-informed, most knowledgeable scientists of the impending peril. We would see a world where thoughtful discussion and decision-making is trounced by denial, ignorance, myth, ideology, and self-enhancement.

- We would see a world that that is undisciplined. We would see a world using its governance energy in a self-defeating way, even though the issues are evident to all. We would see a nation claiming to be strong and prosperous but unable to address its future—budgetary issues, health-care cost issues, fossil fuel energy use issues, and education issues. The philosopher sitting on the moon would wonder how it could be that the adult inhabitants of an earth, who have been so blessed by the earth's splendor and awesomeness of their existence, do not have a sense of responsibility for future inhabitants, even for their own grandkids.

Some will argue that many of these problems are a reflection of our evolutionary development, where survival depended on our ability to compete, dominate, or eliminate a competitor; the characteristic that we often describe as animal or tribal behavior. It has been suggested that tribalism is a humanness trait that is still, to a degree, embedded in our genes. I find this to be an argument hard to refute, yet one that must be addressed if we are to survive and develop as humankind, tomorrow and in future times. The reason is that although we may still be trapped in our tribal genes, we have advanced dangerously far in our technical capabilities. Biological and nuclear warfare are examples of technical capabilities that now have the capacity to destroy much of mankind. And we know that man is still subject to the "beguilement into doing evil." On a positive note, there is indication that there is a growing awareness among world leaders of this condition. But it is also true that the administration of George W. Bush, just a few years ago, was advocating the development of the next generation of nuclear weapons because it was a position that appealed to the militant faction, without there being discussion of what this might mean for mankind at large.

The significance of this, to me, is that tomorrow and future times mean the times of my children and grandchildren. So it is imperative that we now face the reality of the nonsensicalness of our humanness and, as a species, that we grow beyond the absurdity of much of what mankind is now doing. We need to internalize the fact that industrial-age man is a very recent development, with this development creating a new age, an age where responsible decision-making will be essential for the continued well-being of man. It is grossly naïve and irresponsible to say that this is simply the way man is made.

The recognition of these absurdities leads to three important points. First, it points out that, somehow, the decision-making capability of the populace is grossly deficient. We, as a society, nation-wise and world-wise, are making decisions based on tenaciously held beliefs and ideologies of the people. But these beliefs and ideologies lead to decisions that do not make sense. These beliefs and the decisions that follow from these beliefs need to be examined—and in an urgent way. We need to have the character and the courage and guts to recognize what Mark Twain noted over a hundred years ago: "It's not the stuff that we don't understand that gets us into trouble; it's the stuff we know for sure that just ain't so that causes all the trouble." In order to deal with the nonsensicalness of our humanness, we need to examine closely the core beliefs we hold and that form our decision-making. It is like the first step in the rehabilitation of an alcoholic: acknowledge the problem and the hurt it is causing; then there is hope that a positive behavioral change can be made. We need to acknowledge that it may not be the beliefs and ideologies of others that are in error; it may be our beliefs and ideologies that are in error and that are, in fact, nonsensical, if examined with serious, open-minded inquiry. This acknowledgement is the developmental growth—perhaps even the evolutionary growth—of mankind that is required to ensure a better tomorrow … and it will require tremendous courage and fortitude.

The second point is that as awesome as this task may seem—in fact, some will conclude that the task is simply beyond our capability and that the nonsensicalness of humanness will continue because that is simply the way it is—*confronting our nonsensicalness represents the greatest, most wonderful opportunity that mankind has yet faced.*

The idea of putting the well-being of the earth and the well-being of our kids and grandkids ahead of immediate wants and tribal instincts is a notion that far surpasses the precepts held by our nation's founders. It is a cause that could energize the nation, even the world, and make it feel good about itself in a way that most of us have never experienced. It could be the basis for a sense of community and goodwill that would completely overtake the separatism and superiority mentality that is so prevalent in our society and, indeed, throughout the world. We could be part of the most wondrous gift to mankind ever made.

The last point, regrettably, is an acknowledgement that perhaps—just perhaps—mankind will not succeed in dealing with these absurdities, nation-wise or world-wise. We will not succeed because it is simply too big a challenge, too difficult to do, and too hard to secure our nation's commitment, much less the world's support. We will not succeed because we personally do not have the courage for true inquiry. This possibility recognizes that the nonsensicalness of our humanness could continue, that man cannot develop fast enough to prevent his own undoing. That leaves us with ourselves and how we deal with these absurdities in our own, isolated, lonesome way.

That is where your uniqueness becomes all-important. It is then that you and your personal conduct and morality matter, even if many of your brothers and sisters decide not to join your way of thinking. Your comfort and peace of mind will come in knowing that you are being true to your gifts, being true to your sense of reality, and in living a life that shows appreciation for the experience of being part of this awesome world—and even its absurdities. Being an independent, thinking person, doing what you believe is a responsible response to the utterly improbable gift of living in this awesome world, is, I believe, a prerequisite for a truly happy, meaningful, fulfilling life.

Always be true to your inner self, not the herd—that's Grandpa's loving advice.

CHAPTER 3

THE IMMENSE CHALLENGES OF TODAY'S WORLD

*"The ultimate result of shielding
men from the effects of folly is
to fill the world with fools."*

—Herbert Spencer

*"You can't escape the
responsibility of tomorrow
by evading it today."*

—Abraham Lincoln

Much of the "nonsensicalness of our humanness" and the decisions that have resulted have confounded mankind for centuries. It is important to recognize these big-picture problems because they are instructive in setting the context for how we think about today's issues. We must be keenly aware that the decisions we advance today do not lead to similar "absurdities" when viewed from afar and from a more removed timeframe. Our big-picture issues set an overarching direction and perspective for dealing, in an intelligent way, with the immediate, here-and-now problems that we face.

The issues that confront us are many, and they are tightly interrelated, and because they are inextricably linked, it is even more difficult to find the wise-solution path. How we deal with one issue changes the scope and context of how we deal with the other issues. It is also a reality, however, that at the end of the day, we will have arrived at an approach for dealing with these challenges, an approach established by thoughtful thinking and disciplined action ... or by default, we will have continued on a non-substantive course of action that ignores reality and guarantees the decline of our nation and mankind.

My hope is that this discussion encourages us to think independently and clearly; that we separate fact from myth; that we make a conscious effort to focus on substance rather than image; that we garner the courage to address reality. I believe it is instructive, therefore, to look at *a few* of the here-and-now issues that will impact us in a major way in the near future. This perusal will illustrate quickly the immensity of the challenges we face. The way in which we cope with these issues and integrate them into a holistic plan is of paramount importance to the well-being of our nation and its people.

Our perception of the relative importance of these issues will depend, to a degree, on the time frame in which we consider them. For example, I am writing this chapter just a couple months after the 2008 U.S. elections, which saw the history-making election of our first black president, Barack Obama, with the accompanying rejection of the Bush administration and its philosophy and ideologies of governance. It is also the time of the greatest financial problems encountering the nation since the Great Depression. But the challenges outlined below transcend these immediate times and are only *examples* of the depth and breadth of the issues we now face.

A Changing Industrial and Influential World

I am seventy-one years old and during my adult life, I saw the United States as the preeminent power in the world—economically, educationally, militarily, and influentially. We carried the "big stick" in most every conceivable way. Some have argued that this ultimately led to a complacency that was compounded by a large measure of arrogance, particularly among the baby boomer segment, which never experienced the tougher times that our parents and grandparents endured.

During the past couple of decades, however, major parts of the rest of the world have come to recognize the merits of competitive, privatized businesses. China, India, Brazil, Russia, and other countries have begun to move in a deliberate way toward an economic system that retains the broad, regulated organizational structure of a centralized government but combines, in a new way, with the incentives of the free-market system. The economic growth this is generating has created new opportunities and exciting times for the people of these countries, resulting in a positive, invigorating feedback loop that is producing never-before-seen growth rates in the gross domestic product (GDP), the measure of a country's overall economic output. Those of us who have traveled in some of these countries—most demonstrably, China—have seen, firsthand, the contagion of this spirit.

The growth of these economies will very likely continue into the foreseeable future, good evidence being the educational excellence that is now pursued by these same countries as a means to their long-term well-being. China, India, South Korea, Japan, Brazil, and some of the European Economic Community countries

19

are the leading competitors today, but these are only a few of the countries that have entered this very competitive growth curve. Other countries, those in Eastern Europe, for example, are poised to follow this lead in an economically aggressive way. It is not that the United States can no longer be strong and competitive; rather, it's that the economic competition will be great. Our world influence, compared to what it was in the second half of the twentieth century, will be in a slow but steady decline *relative* to other parts of the world, particularly the Asian countries.

This will demand that we change the way in which we conduct our domestic and foreign policy and, perhaps more important, *in how we think about ourselves*. We will need to rethink what it means to be a great, powerful country and the type of image we want other countries to hold of us. We will need to change from a backward-looking mind-set focused on *what we were*, to the more energizing mind-set of what we *aspire to become*. This is the enthusiastic, positive mind-set that characterizes the emerging, highly competitive powers, and it will be necessary for us to develop this same spirit if we want to compete in the future world order.

It is imperative, first and foremost, that we regain our moral standing. This is important not only in how we are seen in the eyes of the rest of the world, but more important, how we see and feel about ourselves. It means a true recognition and practice of the principles "that all men are created equal" and "recognition of the inherent dignity and of the equal and inalienable rights of all members of the human family ... that they are endowed with reason and conscience and should act towards one another in a spirit of brotherhood." If we hope to interact in a productive and mutually beneficial way with the rest of the world, it is critical that we operate with that conviction; it is essential that our competitors see us in that light. The changing global structure demands that we talk with the other 95 percent of the world, not talk *at* them or with a condescending attitude of superiority.

I was born in 1938, and I remember well the years following World War II and the positive, energetic mood that prevailed. Most of the people I knew were poor. Most of them made heavy financial sacrifice for the war effort. But they believed that they had taken part in a good and noble cause, and they knew, without any sense of arrogance or superiority, that the rest of the world recognized this honorable intent. I saw these good feelings have a rippling, energizing effect that led to the greatest growth that any country has ever experienced. I remember well, going to football games and feeling a chill run up my back when the band went on to the field and played the "Star-Spangled Banner." I was truly proud of what this country stood for, and I felt proud and privileged that I was a part of it. The challenge before us—a huge one—is whether or not this can be regained for our kids and grandkids.

To compete economically in this changing global world, we need to recapture the post-WW II "can-do" spirit, the same attitude that now exists in China and other rapid-growth countries. We need to become realistic and tough with ourselves. The "Good morning, America" and "shining city upon a hill" feel-good slogans of the Reagan administration that began during the '80s—what Thomas Friedman calls the "Tooth Fairy" days—were fine, but they were not authentic, and they eroded the foundation of the disciplined, substantive development required to match competitive global efforts. We need the will and capacity to address many issues simultaneously—our educational system (the single most important, foundational contributor to the United States' development), our health care system, the integrity of our banking and financial system, infrastructure development, energy independence, the budget deficit and current account deficit, our social security/retraining structure, defense and home security management, and more. All of this must be done within the context of the environmental issues that face the world and the type of Planet Earth that we want our kids and grandkids to inherit.

I sometimes think this is too tough a subject for a maturing grandpa to think about. But think about it, we must, so that we succeed in creating a promising future for the younger people, a future that allows our nation to compete proudly on the international scene. I do not want our younger people to feel the agony and discouragement of a nation that has lost its way.

A World Pushed Beyond Its Limits and in Need of Tender, Loving Care

Today, the population of the world is over 6.5 billion and growing at a very fast rate, primarily in the very poorest parts of the world. At the start of the Industrial Revolution, only 250 years ago, total world population was less than 1 billion (probably more on the order of 800 million). In the week the United States put a man on the moon—and the week our son, Brett, was born—the population stood at less than 4 billion. Projections vary, but it's likely that the earth will have over 9 billion human inhabitants by the time Brett's now three-year-old-daughter, Tirza, reaches her fortieth birthday.

Compounding this population pressure is the advanced lifestyle and the energy consumption that this lifestyle demands for a better quality of life that all rightfully seek. Most of this energy is derived from fossil fuel combustion, with concomitant production of large amounts of CO_2. There is broad agreement among the best scientific minds—experts from around the world—that this increase in atmospheric CO_2 will result in the warming of the earth to a level never experienced by modern man. The science behind global warming is extremely complex, partly because of the interrelated nature of key variables. Although the science of climate change has many questions and uncertainties, there is broad consensus among highly competent international research organizations that global warming constitutes a significant threat to the world's inhabitants, and that population pressures magnify this risk exponentially.

The population pressure will manifest itself in many other ways. Large tropical forest tracts—for example, in the Amazon region—are being cleared for agriculture use to help feed this growing population, which results in the loss of the areas that are the earth's greatest source of biodiversity—in addition to losing the forests' ability to remove CO_2 from the atmosphere.

Because of the population pressure, water resources are becoming stressed, unreliable, and a source of conflict between nations, states, cities, and farmers. Pesticides and herbicides used to improve production efficiency and increase yields—some bioactive in parts per billion concentration—have become a source of contamination of these waters, concentrating in the aquatic life to dangerous toxicological levels.

Science, by its very nature, in most cases does not lead to exact, bullet-proof conclusions. Instead, it deals with probabilities. The science behind the interrelated issues of global warming and population pressure has reached the "high probability" stage in terms of direction; that is, global warming is very likely happening and will likely get much worse, with some risk that it could spiral out of control within a time span measured in decades. Population pressures are a huge humanitarian concern and, in our poorest of countries, very likely to get much worse. It is true that the exact magnitude and timing of these concerns is not known; but there is substantial probability—whether 20 percent or 90 percent odds—that our grandkids will be living in a world undergoing very significant climate change.

The question, then, to those who have respect for science and to those who believe that it is mankind's responsibility to care for this awesome Earth and the magnificence of life, is what actions do we take in view of this risk? How do we engage the world in this issue? Perhaps more to the point, how do we participate and cooperate with the countries of the world that already have decided that global warming and population pressures are a risk of potentially catastrophic proportions and that coordinated world action is imperative?

We are faced with a challenge that questions our position on the sacredness of life and our recognition of the awesomeness of Planet Earth. It raises the question of respect for science versus burying our heads in the sand, deluding ourselves into believing that our uninformed opinion is as good as the judgment of our best scientists. It is a challenge that places us—individually, our businesses, our nation, and the world—in the crosshairs of a moral dilemma of potentially catastrophic proportions.

How will we respond to this immense challenge? To what degree does it define the essence of our character? Is it possible that we can transform this challenge from a "global problem" into an invigorating global opportunity? It was scholar, writer, and teacher Joseph Campbell who said: "If nothing else unites us, ecological crisis will." This is a very difficult subject for scientists. Scientists are, by nature, not good politicians and often not very good in the public relations field. It is incredibly frustrating to them to have to deal with those who have no appreciation for science and who choose to trust their uninformed intuition or refuse informed discussion.

Here's a very short story about scientific ignorance, simply to illustrate how man's mind, including well-meaning people, resists what it does not understand: My cousin, Dorance Wiebusch, suffered from severe epilepsy. Many times I saw him have a grand mal seizure, which ended with vomiting and unconsciousness. It was frightening to see, and it left him in a dazed state after regaining consciousness. He lived with his parents on their farm less than twenty-five miles from the renowned Mayo Clinic in Rochester, Minnesota. But they never took him there (nor to any other reputable medical center) for evaluation or treatment. Instead, they took him to a traveling faith healer who came to Zumbro Falls once a week and placed his "warm hands" on Dorance to cure him. One time, Dorance's parents heard of another healer in Chicago and drove there, only to find that they apparently did not have the right address. His parents were good, caring people, but they were people who were scientifically ignorant, almost reflexively opposed to real medical science. Only after Dorance became an adult did he finally receive medical care from the Mayo Clinic, with the result that medication was able to control his epileptic seizures completely.

I think of this story every time I hear or read or talk about global warming with those who make the decision to put their trust in fraudulent "experts" and in their own uninformed opinions, rather than addressing the science and coping with the probabilities of the issue. Science is not easy or gentle, and it is usually not totally conclusive, and on occasion, it is dead wrong in its tentative judgments. But the judgments on global warming have been made by extremely intelligent and sincere scientists, and the issue deserves our non-ideological and carefully considered thought.

Financial Stability and Discipline

I'm in my small rental office in Hopkins, three weeks before Christmas, with Minnesota Public Radio playing in the background. The news is not good. The unemployment numbers have just been announced, and they have risen during the past month more than any time in the past thirty-four years. The equity portion of our savings portfolio, which Diane and I thought would allow us to do pretty much what we wanted to do during retirement—like traveling the world—has shrunk by almost half, and we now are coming to grips with the fact that we have to be more careful with our money, and that the carefree attitude toward the world traveling that we have done in past winters may not be possible any longer.

Part of me is angry about the "new" state of our financial affairs. I see it as a result of gross irresponsibility by large financial institutions that I trusted. I am angry at the gross irresponsibility of the Bush administration's needless spending, financed by borrowing money from China and Japan and India, with the idea that we would let future generations foot the bill. I'm angry at the general attitude of the people who seem to think it's okay to build "mansions" but don't want to build schools or factories or roads, or who don't care about the fact that we are not paying our national bills. I'm angry at the lack of discipline, at the lack of our being a responsible people, at the lack of visionary management by many of our largest firms. I'm even a bit mad at myself that I didn't see this downturn coming and, as a result, rode the market down all the way.

But part of me is grateful. I'm grateful because our kids still have their jobs. Grateful because Diane and I still have our health. Grateful for the wonderful family we have. We are all warm and well fed! And with planning, we can still do a lot of things—

maybe even some exotic international travel—if we are a bit more careful with our dollars.

I share these feelings because, in deeper reflection about the current financial and recession issue, my sense is that the personal impact, with its ebb and flow of anger and gratefulness, gets in the way of thinking about this issue in an enduring, substantive way. That is not to say that the personal impact of the financial meltdown is not important; it definitely is. But I think it is critical to the economic health of this nation that we also step out of our personal situation and begin to address the root issues, in terms of financial stability and discipline. By root issues I mean the mind-set philosophies and ideologies that govern the actions that we, as a nation, support and endorse. It will be a difficult task. We will need to examine the role of greed; private reward, coupled with public risk; too-big-to-fail institutions; regulations that protect but do not stifle; the free market versus state-managed continuum. These are big, important "root" subjects; all are embedded with strong ideologies that impede meaningful discussion. And all are important to the economic health of the nation and to the financial well-being of individual people, and it is imperative that they be dealt with wisely.

The Notion of Balance

A fundamental concept that needs a great deal more recognition among people at large is the idea of balance. This notion impacts at least 99 percent of what we do and the decisions we make or support, in all aspects of our lives. Yet very few discussions bring this notion to the forefront in our decision-making. A few examples may illustrate this point:

Taxes, as almost everyone would agree, are an annoying yet necessary element for the conduct and well-being of our nation, our states, and our local communities. But almost never do we have serious discussion of what *level of taxes* delivers the best cost-benefit ratio for our people and society. A great example is the tax level for the state of Minnesota, where almost no one can tell you what the current tax rate is, compared to what it was a decade ago. Instead, we have a governor who gained office entirely on a "lower taxes" campaign mantra. That position may or may not have merit, depending on the much more fundamental question of what level of taxes is best for the overall health of our state. But this does not get discussed. Obviously, the same problem exists at the federal level and at the local level. We argue for "more," or we argue for "less," with little consideration of what level of tax is best for society—the balance point between too high and too low; the balance point between tax revenue and spending. Instead, the issue is controlled by emotion, rather than by substantive, informed thinking.

Balance between the amount of regulation and deregulation of our financial systems is a balance issue that we will, only by necessity, be addressing as a result of the current financial crisis. During the past two or three decades, it has been essentially a deregulation argument, with little serious discussion of the balance point between regulation, which can protect the integrity of the system, and deregulation, which can promote the growth of the system by increasing the level of market place incentive. Because we did not focus discussion on balance, we swung unwisely to the incentive side, only to find that this led us into a financial black hole.

In the same manner, we seem to be unable to have meaningful discussion of the balance point for dealing with terror after 9/11. It becomes a one-sided emotion-based discussion of how we provide a higher level of safety. There is little discussion of what the balance point should be between our actions to prevent further terrorism acts, and the degree to which we are willing to sacrifice individual liberties and to protect the principles upon which this nation was founded and which represent our core being. It becomes a discussion centered on fear, rather than a discussion about the balance between safety and the freedoms we cherish.

Avoiding the discussion of balance is the route to easy, no work, simplistic, emotionally driven answers. It allows discussion and position-taking without being informed. It even allows us to establish personal identity by group association, rather than by thoughtful analysis of the issue. Nowhere is this demonstrated better than in Republican or Democrat party affiliation. For many, finding a reasoned position on an issue is not their focus; instead, it is driven by blind allegiance to the party affiliation they hold. Many others, including Liu and Hanauer in their book, *The True Patriot*, have commented on the problems this is causing our country, pointing out that for many, our loyalty is to party, rather than to truth, reality, and understanding.

This is interesting, in that the notion of balance is so very fundamental in much of nature and in much of what we do. The temperature of the earth is a delicate balance between the physical phenomena that increase warming and those that cool. The blood that circulates in our bodies is a very delicate balance between the acid and base constituents, producing a balanced pH that is critical. We all recognize the balance needed in many aspects of our personal lives, sex being but one example, where there is a widely recognized need between that which provides a basis for love and reproduction of the species, and sexual conduct that represents irresponsible and potentially hurtful behavior. We all recognize the balance needed between work and play; it's a concept essential and innate in our being. Yet we do not recognize the need to find the right balance point in our most important societal decisions.

I think this is true because of three primary reasons: First, it does not constitute exciting, sexy subject matter for the media. Imagine the 6 p.m. news leading off with "the balance point for taxes," versus "the administration has announced its new plan for raising taxes." It would not catch our attention or capture our emotions. The second reason is that a discussion of balance demands in-depth, substantive thinking and knowledge. It's hard, time-consuming work! The subject of balance defies the sound bite. The fifteen-second sound bite allows—even encourages—the holding of simplistic, uniformed opinions. And third, we somehow find more psychological comfort in loyalty to party than in loyalty to the pursuit of truth and understanding.

But not recognizing balance leads to horrible, ill-conceived policy.

Recognizing the Importance of Stability

Stability is the cornerstone of good management. (In some circles, the term durability is used; in others, robustness.) Think about this carefully. It is next to impossible to run an efficient, solid business—the management of a school district, a corporate research laboratory, a home construction business, operating a furniture factory, running a law firm or a hospital—when the budgets and volume of business swings up and down from one year to the next. The ramifications of time period to time period volatility are tremendously negative. More time and energy is spent dealing with the highs and lows of volatility than is spent doing real work and building skills and competence. People and families get hurt. Financial markets flounder. Make no mistake: steady growth, while it may be a bit boring, is the very essence of a well-managed business or a well-governed nation. Conversely, when a business or nation exhibits a high degree of volatility, you can safely conclude that it has been mismanaged. Stability is a crucial cornerstone objective of all good managers.

Paying for What You Buy

A fundamental, substantive change that must be made is to recognize that the nation is *us,* that the culture and attitude of the nation represents the collective culture and attitude of its people. We accept that our nation is running a huge current account deficit—a trillion dollar debt to China alone, a five-fold increase since 2000. That's because you and I have not been paying our bills!

This significance of this deficit has been downplayed by many economists who make the point that this trillion dollars worth of debt to China represents less than 7 percent of our annual GDP, a manageable amount of debt. (That point is debatable in and of itself.) The other argument is that this debt is not a major issue because it serves both countries. It serves China's interest because it provides a huge market for their products, a factor very important to their growth-based economy; it serves our interest because it allows us to enhance our lifestyle and well-being, at least in a materialistic way.

There are two big problems with this thinking. The first is a morality issue. Long term, as the economic status of the United States and China evolves, this debt will have to be repaid, which can only mean that the cost of our living high on the hog will need to be paid for by our kids or grandkids. It has been a guiding principle of our nation—at least, that has been my perception—that we want to leave our kids with a better world than the one in which we spent our allotted days. The nation's use of borrowed funds makes some sense if we believe that the borrowed money is used to invest in productive assets that yield benefits, which the next generation can enjoy as well as ourselves. However, it is hard to make that case with TVs, tires, and purses. The notion of stealing the future from our kids to satisfy our selfishness is morally wrong.

The other problem is that it exposes us to risk. The present economic recession heightens that risk. Most economists, as well as the Obama administration, believe that we need a major stimulus to get the economy back on track. That means printing or borrowing substantial amounts of money. If China gets nervous about loaning us this money, our interest rates will have to go up sharply to entice them to loan us more money. The danger is that it would not take much of an economic jolt to send our fragile economy into a tailspin depression instead of a course-correcting recession (the "D" versus "R," in economist jargon) and importantly, this dreaded economic risk is now under the control of another nation state.

The point that I am trying to make is that we have lost all sense of toughness and discipline in our handling of financial affairs. I chose the current account deficit because it illustrates the connection between the attitude of individuals and national financial policy. Excessive credit card debt, the purchase of homes that we cannot afford, and neglecting to save for the funding of our retirement are other examples of the lack of discipline in the conduct of our financial affairs.

And when we finally have to deal with the inevitable result of this lack of discipline we will interrupt the stability factor that is so important to our financial well-being. Witness the sub-prime banking problem with the spiraling events that have followed, and the economic instability that is tearing at the fabric of our nation's— indeed, of the world's—health. If we are to have stability, we need to develop a "pay now for what you buy" discipline in ourselves, and we will also need to demand this discipline in our policy-makers.

Think Investment, Not Spending

It will be an immense challenge to restructure the nation's budget to meet the demands of today's world. It is an understatement of absurdity to say that the current federal budget (and many state budgets) makes sense in today's world. The budget is so big and so complex and so convoluted that most of us don't try to understand it; instead, we simply rely on the government people to manage it competently.

On the one hand, drastic revisions of budgets are counter to the notion of stability. On the other hand, just "tinkering" with the budget each year, particularly if done over an extended period of time, can easily result in a budget that does not deal with changing times or result in visionary, far-sighted management.

To illustrate this point, it would be interesting to ask people what they believe the dollar amount of the federal budget is and to break this amount into the various expenditure categories. My bet is that very, very few could even begin to get close to the actual amounts involved. Yet this budget represents where our country is going and what we, as a people, believe is important for our future and well-being. Instead, we respond to simplistic, often propagandistic "spend more/spend less" rhetoric, often without sense of how many zeros there are in the number, whether it's millions or billions, or whether the issue is one of significance or sheer bluster. It would be a major step forward, in my judgment, to require that a simple, straightforward explanation of the budget be provided to the people, with an explanation of how this budget relates to the goals and needs of the country. This should be extremely "doable" with today's Internet capability. As an example, few people today seem to be aware of the tremendous amount of under-funded commitments that our government has made in terms of the Social Security, Medicare, and Medicaid benefits promised. This is an exposure estimated at more than $370,000 per full-time worker. Few people today seem to be aware that three-quarters of the federal budget deficit since 2001 has been underwritten by foreign investors. Few people have grasped the real cost of the Iraq War, estimated by some economists, including Nobel laureate Joseph Stiglitz, as most likely being on the order of three trillion dollars.

Simply, our budget is a mess—poorly understood, not reflective of national priorities, and unrealistic and irresponsible from a long-term perspective. This will assuredly come back to haunt us if we do not deal with the issue in a forthright manner. And to be dealt with, the people will have to demand that we, both the person on the street and our government, begin managing our financial affairs in a mature, responsible way. The transition will be painful, but we have no choice because of the decisions and ideologies that we have followed for the past thirty years.

Keeping It Simple and Understandable

Man can make intelligent decisions only when he has the capacity to comprehend the important, controlling factors that enter into the issue being considered. It is easy to become so entwined with details, tangents, exceptions, and trivia that one cannot cope with the essence of the issue. Our tax code is one example. Another example is making a decision on which health care plan to choose. (The Medicare D prescription drug plan is a perfect example.) It has become, for many, so complex that we cannot make a well-informed decision. And, as we have seen recently, our financial institutions have become so entwined with multiple business units and complex products that it becomes impossible to sort through the mess. As Kevin Phillips, a financial reporter, has commented: "Exotic derivative instruments with alphabet-soup initials command national values in the trillions of dollars, but nobody knows what they are really worth." It seems to me that it's fairly elementary that financial institutions would want to know the value of the properties on their books. But because of their entanglement with counter parties and the complexity of their holdings, they do not know.

Even our own lives have become uncontrollable because of the complexity that we have introduced; simply too many things to do, too many things to maintain, too many places to be, and too many responsibilities. It eventually becomes addictive and the norm. And so we find it hard to break away and to get into a space where we can think clearly and focus our thoughts and energy on issues of importance.

With the immense challenges of today's world, it will become imperative that we develop the discipline to demand simplicity so that we can focus on the issues that actually determine our well-being and future. If we do not develop this discipline, we will become a society mired down in its own excessive, compulsive behavior, unable to see the important and unable to manage ourselves to a better future, either for ourselves or for our kids.

Economic Policy and the Free Market

A major challenge forthcoming, when and if we overcome the immediacy of the current financial crisis, is for society to decide how the economic engine of the nation can best be managed. It will be an important decision in terms of our global competitiveness and in terms of creating a more robust system, one that is more stable. This can best be illustrated by citing some of the decisions that we will have to make.

One example is to resolve the question of whether we should allow firms to grow to the point where they are deemed "too big to fail." Can firms that are "small enough to fail" compete in the international scene, or are we faced with the possibility that an economic system that is something less than completely democratic is more effective and is required in order to be competitive globally? If we allow firms to grow to the point where they are "too big to fail," will we be able to profess a truly democratic, free market system, with governmental "sponsors" that come to the assistance of the too-big-to-fail firms but refuse assistance to the smaller firms? What does this mean in terms of the principle of true capitalistic competition?

Another example: to what degree do we regulate hedge funds, private-equity firms, and foreign investment? Where do we draw the line in the sand so that, on one hand, we honor the incentives of a free market, but on the other hand recognize that abuses within the free market can place the entire economy in jeopardy? How do we ensure that these entities operate in a way that is good for society at large?

To what degree do we give the Federal Reserve power over the economy, and how is the nation assured that the Fed operates in the nation's interest, rather than that of the large-money firms and power brokers? And how does power square with the principles of democracy and economic justice?

Like it or not, interested or not, these are major questions that will impact the economic health of the nation in future years. These questions are not immune from politics and from the lobbying power of the large-money firms and their obscenely compensated management group. To arrive at a wise decision on how best to manage our financial system, the overall health of the nation needs to be considered, first and foremost. It will be a major challenge to devise a regulatory policy that assures the health and stability needed. It is a challenge that demands that we set dedication to party and power groups aside and focus, instead, on the well-being of the nation and its people.

When Science by Man Gets Ahead of the Wisdom of Man

A strong characteristic of science is that it is the product of a small number of people. The original thinking in science, the foundation breakthroughs, is probably the product of no more than one person out of a hundred thousand—less than 1/1000 of 1 percent. Furthermore, the "rank and file" scientists who add understanding and reduce this original thinking to practice probably represent no more than 1 or 2 percent of the population. *The result is that major scientific advances are the product of a few scientifically gifted people, but the use and political management of this technology is in the hands and the wisdom of the majority, arguably, by definition, a group of people with average wisdom and intellect.* Interestingly, this is consistent with the notion of the evolutionary development of man. It is to be expected.

Through the nineteenth century, the scientific developments produced were important and often revolutionary, in terms of our understanding of nature, but none had the immediate capacity to destroy mankind or even large segments of mankind. This has changed in a major way. In contrast, the scientific developments of the twentieth century progressed to the point where man now holds the capacity to exterminate human life. In fact—and this is a reality that we must acknowledge—we have made very deliberate decisions and taken very deliberate steps to make this possible. As one example, at one time in the 1960s, the combined Soviet Union and United States thermonuclear arsenal stood at 65,000 warheads. This is far, far more than is needed to eradicate mankind—a rather sobering thought!

There have been changes to this preposterous situation, some for the good and some for the not so good. The former Soviet Union (now Russia) and the United States have reduced this arsenal to something on the order of 14,000 warheads. (The counting of thermonuclear devices is problematic. When numbers are reported by writers, sometimes the number represents ready-to-fire "deployed" warheads; sometimes the number represents deployed warheads plus the warheads in storage; and sometimes the number represents deployed warheads, warheads in storage, and warheads that could be produced, given the quantity of fissile material available. Using this last number, it is estimated that there is enough fissile material, stored in more than forty countries, to build 250,000 nuclear warheads.) The good news is that there has been some effort and some progress in dealing with the preposterousness of these numbers.

The bad news is that more countries are developing nuclear capabilities. The concern is not only that these countries are developing nuclear capability, but that these countries could become the source of a nuclear device for a radical, probably non-state terrorist organization. This bad news also recognizes that science has progressed in other scientific areas, principally the biological sciences, which may result in the development of equally lethal weapons, such as the development of molecularly engineered organisms capable of spreading highly contagious, life-threatening disease.

The challenge that we face is to manage our scientific advances with wisdom and with discipline. The British scientist and author James Lovelock has summarized it very simply by noting: "Our moral progress has not kept up with our technological progress." Or as one pessimistic writer said, "We surely have a lot of killing and savagery ahead of us before we fully civilize ourselves." It would be the supreme irony if man's advances become his ultimate demise. Reality and common sense demand that we address this challenge.

Realistic Foreign Policy

Foreign policy, by definition, is a two-way street. One nation takes an action, then the other nation or nations respond. And this action-reaction cycle continues ad infinitum—always changing, always with newly recognized perspectives. We will see this vividly in the months and years ahead as we recognize that we are in a "changing industrial and influential world." It is an ongoing process that demands the very best in ambassadorship and negotiating skills.

Our challenge in this regard is huge, given the years of the Bush 43 administration: we need to establish (perhaps it's reestablish) the principles that define the essence of this nation—its moral character. No matter the skill of the negotiators, they cannot escape the image that defines the nation they represent. As example, I think we need to very clearly and overtly establish our principles regarding torture. I believe we desperately need to make it clear that we do not invade countries that do not pose an immediate threat; that "preventive warfare" is a repulsive notion to our manner of conduct. It is important that we clearly define what our policy is with regard to the selling of armament to other countries, given the fact that we are currently, by far, the world's largest supplier.

In order to deal with the world, we need to understand the world. We need to understand the people of the world and their beliefs and the basis for their beliefs. A case in point: the Taliban in the Afghanistan/Iran/Pakistan/India region is portrayed and discussed as if it's an entity; it is not. It's a movement, not an organization. People who know the Pakistan country say there are probably fifty separate Islamic groups in the country, each with its own leadership and goals. At best, the only common denominator of the Taliban groups is that they are composed of people on the Islamic right and that they do not want foreigners occupying their country. The effectiveness of policies in dealing with the terrorist segment will depend on how well we truly know and understand the people.

We will need to define our position with respect to the regulation of global financial firms. We will need to define our position with respect to our view on global warming and the concrete, verifiable actions we are prepared to take and our willingness to cooperate with the international community on this issue. We will need to define our position with respect to family planning and women's health issues. We will have to decide whether we are dedicated to making the United Nations an effective organization. We will have to determine how we intend to cope with the Israel-Palestine issue. We will have to determine how we can communicate to the world that we have respect for the dignity of all people.

We will need to define our trade policies and where we stand on the implications of worker's rights in these policies. We will need to establish our image on how we negotiate—fair, honest, and transparent but tough. We will need to address the question of how best to share technology and how to orchestrate the exchange of highly gifted students within the world's leading universities.

It is clear—very, very clear—that "realistic foreign policy" is an area that has many dimensions. It will not be easy or accomplished over night. But in this global world, it is a challenge of immense importance to us and warrants the energies of our very best people. However, the most important first step is to define who we are and what we represent. We will need to merge our desired image with demonstrable action. Our founding fathers discussed this at length and in depth. It is a discussion that needs to be renewed, not only by our government officials but more important, by the people.

Religious Imperialism

In the broadest of views, such as looking at Earth from the moon, there is no greater source of division and conflict than that which can be attributed to religion. For the most part, we are talking about the religious imperialism of the Jewish community, specifically the Zionists, who see themselves as a group that has received special recognition from God and special rights to ancient lands; we are talking about the Muslims, particularly certain sects of the Islamic faith, that believe they have been given God's truth and that it would be better if all the world's people subscribed to their faith; we are talking about the fundamental Christian Right segment of the Christian faith that also believes it has been given God's truth and that they have an obligation to bring others into their enlightenment.

These are hard people to deal with because of their belief that their God-derived truths override any of the points that seem reasonable and logical and just to the people outside their faith ideologies. As a result, real discussion and communication with and between these groups is extremely difficult. In fact, they often see their firmness of position as a badge of courage and a

41

demonstration of the depth of their faith, a stance viewed favorably by their God. The more they deny secular reality, the more they believe they are gaining God's approval. U.S. senator and former presidential candidate John McCain once commented that talking to people with a closed religious mind is like talking to the leg of a table: not much hope.

Given these strong beliefs, the intransient nature of these views, and the mistrust of each other that these faiths engender, it is little wonder that many of the world's most pressing disagreements center on the faith issue. Books have been written that warn the Christians of the Muslim's intent to dominate the world; some regions of the world remember the Christian's attempt to invade their lands, trying to convert the indigenous people to the Christian faith; and the Arabs see the Jews laying claim to lands that the Arab communities held for centuries. Against this backdrop, it is easy to see how wars, religiously based or at least augmented, represent the most pressing risk to world peace.

All indications are that this issue—what I and others have termed religious imperialism—will continue to constitute a major challenge to the future world. Defusing this issue will require the most delicate but deliberative action. For many, because we hold faith views that touch some of these more extreme positions, substantive examination will be a personally challenging and troublesome issue.

Concluding Thoughts: When Myth versus Reality Informs Our Decision-Making

We have many very difficult challenges before us. But undergirding all these challenges is the need to base our decisions and beliefs on reality, not on myths and unfounded ideologies. This is an issue that relates not only to the challenges we face as a nation and as a world but, very importantly and very fundamentally, a challenge that we face as individuals.

The immense challenge that this poses has deep-seated psychological roots. It is disturbing for us to look at the myths that most of us have held for many years; many of us will not have the courage required. The beliefs that we tenaciously hold define who we are; they are the essence of our being. These beliefs give us certainty, without the sweat and agony of serious inquiry. In many cases, these beliefs are the basis for our being accepted into the social groups that are very important to us, a condition to be expected, given that social or group membership has been a powerful element in the evolution of the human species. We are a tribal species. We need each other; we are not a solitary animal. To look at our beliefs and to ask whether they are reality-based or mythology-based is difficult because it holds the possibility that the answer will take us away from acceptance by our friends and the group that shares these beliefs.

It is difficult because we stand to lose our core identity—how we think of ourselves and how we describe ourselves to others. It is difficult because these beliefs have given us a ready-made explanation to the most challenging of questions: why do we exist? What is the ultimate truth regarding our existence? What does death hold for us? How do we cope with evil? How do we live our everyday lives in a moral, responsible way? The myth versus reality question is most closely linked to the religious beliefs that we hold, but myths and unfounded ideologies are also inextricably linked to our political and economic and societal beliefs. It should be easy to see why the ramifications of the myth-versus-reality question are so critically important, particularly at the present time.

Very carefully considering the myth-versus-reality question is not easy, but the rewards are great. It is the right and, I would argue, the responsibility of each of us to do this, given our unique, awesome existence in this universe. The answers at which you arrive will be your own—your very own identity.

It is also the only way that I see our nation, and perhaps the world, emerging from the selfish, chaotic, nonsensical state of affairs that we are in. The future of our nation and the world we leave for our kids and grandkids will depend on the degree to which we seek true inquiry; the degree to which we are willing to challenge the basis of our beliefs. Not questioning these myths and unfounded ideologies leave us a very incomplete, childlike being; we will continue as one who has never matured or become a true adult individual. This is a sad short-change of life. It took Grandpa almost seventy years before he had the courage to look at some of the myths that formed his beliefs.

I'm hoping that you have the courage to do it more quickly. It is the only way that we, as members of society, will be able to meet the immense challenges that face today's world.

CHAPTER 4

EVIL

"All that is necessary for
the triumph of evil
is that good men do nothing."

—Edmund Burke

"Whoever fights monsters should
see to it that in the process he
does not become a monster.
And when you look into an abyss,
the abyss also looks into you."

—Friedrich Nietzsche

Given the awesomeness of our existence and having progressed to the point in time that should represent the most civilized state that evolutionary man has yet reached, it is somewhat surprising that we need to discuss the depressing subject of evil. We do need to discuss it, however, because it continues to be a reality that we must recognize and consciously deal with as we manage our beliefs and actions. It has an individual aspect and a group aspect, both of which have separate dimensions yet are inextricably linked.

When we think of evil we often think of the monster dictator who is quite willing to sacrifice the lives of many to gain more power and status. But that view is too simplistic. Primo Levi, a survivor of Auschwitz, explains it well: "Monsters exist, but they are too few in number to be truly dangerous. More dangerous are the common man, the functionaries ready to believe and to act without asking questions."

It is reasonable to suspect that evil is, to some degree at least, a manifestation of our evolutionary biology, where survival depended upon our ability to compete, dominate, or eliminate a competitor, a characteristic often described as animal behavior, a genetic remnant of our past. This notion implies this is a human trait that is, to a degree, still in our genes and influencing our behavior. I have personal thoughts about this. If we are asked to name the most evil act committed in the history of mankind, the Jewish Holocaust by the German Nazis would certainly be the most frequent answer. If evil has a genetic component, however, this is troubling because I am 100 percent German! So I tell myself that there were the Diedrich Bonhoffers in Germany during this time as well.

In mid-twentieth century, the prime time of my parent's life yet historically not very long ago, the Germans, one of the most advanced nations at that time, liquidated six million Jews. It was a disciplined, well-organized, carefully considered program that had as its ultimate end the incineration of men, women, and children in specially built crematories. This program required the participation—indeed, the cooperation—of many ordinary citizens of Germany. There is a tendency to conclude that all this happened because of the rule of Adolph Hitler. But the issue is far deeper.

Hitler never laid a brick in the crematories that were used; Hitler never loaded the trains that took the Jews to the crematories; Hitler never separated these loads of people into the groups that were sized to fill the crematory machinery for its cycle of death.

Fred Katz, a Holocaust survivor who went on to become a professor of sociology at Notre Dame and Johns Hopkins universities, has studied and written on the subject of evil from his particular perspective—as one who saw his parents and brother not survive. I mention this reference because of its profound, well-founded, and easily understood but often not discussed conclusions.

I share the first of his conclusions by quoting from his writings:

> "I learned that ordinary people, engaged in ordinary behavior, have contributed to extraordinary evil; that every one of us is, on occasion, just a hair's breadth away from contributing mightily to evil; that moral sickness and degeneracy will give us fewer cues about evildoing than will an unemotional look at some quite mundane attributes of our personal and societal makeup ... What is more, the attributes can be known and understood. We need not remain ignorant and impotent against evil."

Katz and other social scientists have looked at the causes— or to use Katz' word, the beguilement—into doing evil. To set an awareness context for the discussion that follows, it may be instructive to outline the five forms of beguilement that, according to Katz, predominate:

• The "authoritarian personality" or "obedience to authority personality" or "loyalty personality," where individuals obey the instruction or accept the conclusion of an authoritarian figure or group position. This is often closely coupled with a form of beguilement, where one can be seduced into evil by the trauma of the immediate circumstances. Katz notes: "This can happen when we find ourselves in a social setting where the immediate circumstances dominate our entire field of moral vision. Here the larger society's values and even our own upbringing that taught us to treat people humanely can be disregarded and new, locally generated values take their place."

- "The packaging of evil: making evil an acceptable commodity to individuals who are not necessarily predisposed to doing evil."

- "Careerism and its potential for creating a person's route to evil: much of it through small, incremental, and innocent decisions."

- "Bureaucratization of evil: moral bankruptcy amid orderliness, when bureaucratic procedures are harnessed for producing evil."

- "Creation of a separate and distinct culture of cruelty: where evil-doing becomes enjoyable and rewarding to a group of people."

Other social scientists have drawn similar conclusions. W. H. Auden said, "Evil is unspectacular and always human, and shares our bed and eats at our table." Hannah Arendt wrote "evil is never 'radical,' that it is only extreme, and that it possesses neither depth nor any demonic dimension." Even Adolf Eichmann, who oversaw the killing of millions in the Nazi death chambers, wrote in his memoir, while in prison, about the aspect of obedience in evil: "Now that I look back, I realize that a life predicated on being obedient and taking orders is a very comfortable life indeed. Living in such a way reduces to a minimum one's own need to think."

These conclusions about evil seem naïve and unsatisfactory as we think about those aspects of human history that are commonly used as our examples and definition of evil—the Crusades, the importation and commercialization of African slaves, the Inquisition, the Holocaust. Perhaps the sharp, crystallized "not us" view we hold of these examples, rather than looking at them from the "beguilement into doing evil" question, is because they occurred a long time ago; they are history, and we see ourselves are as being beyond those times.

The capture and trade voyages of African slaves took place from 1514 to 1866, according to very good records—a span of over three centuries. It was a major, commercial business. Documentation of 30,000 voyages has been uncovered. Many of these voyages were from our mother country, England. Drawings of ships, based on recorded information, show floor plans where hundreds of slaves lay side by side, row after row, as the configuration that optimized ship capacity. Historians estimate that 12.5 million slaves were transported in this fashion.

This economic exploitation of human beings was regarded as legitimate business. Indeed, it was even justified by invoking biblical scripture, where it is inferred that slavery is an acceptable practice, that some members of humankind are somehow inferior to others. Our historical view continues, of course, with the Civil War and the freeing of the slaves, and we are prideful that we have become a more just, humane nation. Clearly, racial discrimination still exists, and not all of our people are ready to render dignity to all, but we took a huge step forward when, as a nation, we voted a black man into the highest office of our land. Katz' comment that "we need not remain ignorant and impotent against evil" rings true.

But evil takes many dimensions and, as Auden said, "unspectacular and always human," and deceptively so. As ordinary individuals, perhaps the most difficult issue to wrestle with is the notion that we are participating in evil when we are aware the evil is occurring but fail to take action to stop this evil. This is the "omission to act" argument. It is this facet of evil that is probably the most pervasive and common to ordinary people. We become supporters and enablers of evil, although not the prime perpetrator. This issue is compounded by the fact that the often insidious nature of evil makes it difficult to know exactly when we have embarked upon an evil course.

I remember a TV panel interview, done in the late '70s, with senior management from the four cigarette companies that dominated the tobacco market at the time. Three of the panelists were the CEOs of their respective firms; the fourth was the company's senior spokesperson. What has stayed in my memory is that all four of these individuals argued adamantly that there was no proof that cigarette smoking caused cancer or any other illness.

What was astounding was that they made this argument in the 1970s, in face of the fact that epidemiological and clinical studies published as early as 1950 indicated clearly that cigarette smoking was linked to lung cancer. In 1964 a landmark report by the surgeon general's advisory committee concluded that there was absolutely no doubt that smoking was a cause of cancer and other diseases. Yet the most senior management of the major cigarette companies, four exceptionally capable people with access to the best scientific information available, chose to lie, very deliberately, to the American people. They did not make the argument that, yes, cigarettes may cause disease, but it's a free country, and people who enjoy smoking have a right to make the decision to accept this risk. Instead, they chose to lie. It is hard to understand how these people lived with themselves, day in and day out, for all those years, knowing they lied about their product and the hurt it caused.

More than 400,000 people in the United States die each year from smoking-caused diseases—that's over 1100 per day, or, in graphic terms, the equivalent of three or four fully loaded jumbo jets crashing each day. Compare these numbers to the 57,000 Americans who died during the Vietnam War, or the 405,000 who died in World War II. Worldwide, an estimated 10 million people die each year from the tobacco products *made in the United States*. I do not know if the CEOs mentioned above ever visited a hospital or hospice to see what lung cancer does to the unfortunate individual or to his family, but my family and I know the devastation firsthand. My wife's brother-in-law, David, a smoker, who I will introduce in the next chapter, died of laryngeal-lung cancer two years ago.

Compounding the monstrosity of the issue is that these companies have targeted the nation's youth. An internal R. J. Reynolds memo read: "To ensure increased and longer-term growth for Camel filter, the brand must increase its share penetration among the 14–24 age group ... which represent tomorrow's cigarette business." To increase the addictiveness of smoking, the nicotine content was increased 10 percent between 1998 and 2004, according to a study by the Massachusetts Department of Public Health. The nicotine content of Marlboro, the brand preferred by two-thirds of high school smokers, rose 12 percent.

The reason for discussing the cigarette business is to raise several questions about evil: Does selling cigarettes in fact constitute evil behavior? Is it senior management that is evil? Are the workers in the company, because they know the implications of the product they are making and selling, also committing an evil act? Is the populace of the United States complicit in this evil? Do we understand the nature and moral character of the CEOs mentioned, who got up each morning and went to work, with the very purposeful objective of selling more cigarettes, knowing very well the horrible health ramifications of that very objective? Do we really understand what drives these people and why they choose to continue with this job? Do we understand ourselves and the decisions we have made with respect to our "look the other way" support of the industry? Do we hide behind the comfort of the modest societal changes made, such as the designation of no-smoking areas?

The positions that we take may well have an evil versus good path, a path that is unspectacular and human, a path where our moral vision is clouded by the immediate circumstances. Certainly, our responses to global warming and population pressures need to be carefully considered so that the next generation does not find it to be an evil path. The way in which we respond to religious imperialism could easily lead us down an evil path, given the certainty of truth that some religions hold. Here, history may be very instructive. I wish I could offer a test for each of us to know when we are going down the wrong path, but that is not the nature of the issue, except for the most obvious of cases. Those, however, are few and not usually the problem. It's the cases for which we make "small, incremental, and innocent decisions" that build into the support required for truly evil acts of history. It is those cases where it is hard to locate the point where we sacrificed our human sensibilities.

You and I may have been part of one of these acts of evil. You will have to decide, but in my judgment, the answer is clearly "yes"—it's the Iraq War. A large number of books have described the decision-making process that resulted in our entering this war, and they provide specific detail of the relentless campaign of mass deception that the Bush 43 administration used to secure popular support for the war; in effect, "the beguilement into evil."

We now know that there were no weapons of mass destruction and that evidence cited by the administration—the yellow cake uranium from Nigeria; the aluminum tubes for enriching uranium; that Iraq was a year away from building a nuclear bomb once it had the fissile material; the "we don't want the smoking gun to be a mushroom cloud"; the discovery of mobile laboratory equipment for producing biological weapons; that Saddam Hussein and Iraq were linked to al-Qaeda's 9/11 attack; that the inspections by United Nations weapons experts Hans Blix and Nobel Peace Prize winner Mohammed ElBaradei were insufficient and wrong in their conclusions—was nothing more than a massive propaganda effort to secure international and domestic support for the war and to obtain legislative acquiescence for the administration's desire for war with Iraq.

Indeed, all the reasons given have been thoroughly debunked. More important, the truth and facts were known by the administration before making its case. As example, technical experts, including Nobel-level scientists, had cautioned that the mobile laboratory and aluminum tubes for enriching uranium were not what the administration was claiming, and that Hussein was not connected in any way to al-Qaeda, an argument that 70 percent of the American people had come to believe as fact because of the administration's repeated claims. All aspects of reality and common sense were ignored by the administration, including the position of the State Department: "Our conclusion was that Saddam would certainly not provide weapons of mass destruction or WMD knowledge to al-Qaeda because they were mortal enemies." Clearly, the policy of containment, augmented by the United Nation weapon inspections, eliminated any "imminent threat" concern. The administration, with our support, passive or otherwise, went to war for other reasons.

The cost and pain of going to war has been enormous, both to this country and to Iraq. Dollar cost estimates by Nobel economist Joseph Stiglitz range from $1.2 trillion to over $3 trillion. This is a huge amount of money when one considers the economic opportunity cost (benefit) that an alternative use of this money could have provided, in light of today's economy and the need for infrastructure investment. One can think about what this amount of money could have done in terms of reducing poverty—*not* in terms of handouts but rather in education, health care and family planning, access to credit, job training, and agriculture business development. To put a bit of dimension behind this, there are about 1 billion people in the world in deep poverty; they do not know what they will have to eat tomorrow. As an alternative use of the resources committed to this war, we could have invested one thousand to three thousand dollars worth of resources per person in poverty to help develop a better, more stable world. Which alternative would you define as "good," and which would you define as "evil"?

The human life costs have likewise been immense—over 4000 United States soldiers killed and 30,000 seriously injured, many with injuries that will change their lives and their families' lives forever. It is not known how many Iraqis have died or been injured, but estimates range from "30,000 more or less" (George Bush's comment in late 2005) to over 650,000, by using epidemiological methodology. In addition to adult military men and women, who constitute the United States soldier count, the Iraqi number includes civilians and children. It is also estimated that over a million Iraqis have fled to neighboring countries and that another million have been forced out of their homes and have moved to other parts Iraq. Many of those having to flee the country are the professional, more progressive part of Iraqi society, leaving a major human resource gap, if and when stability in the country is restored.

In addition to this direct cost and human pain is the damage done to the image of the United States and its loss of moral authority and respect. It affects not only how other nations see us but, probably more importantly, how we see ourselves. The collection of photographs of captives in Abu Ghraib undergoing degrading treatment is the symbol of the character of this war. It is impossible to calculate the ultimate cost to our nation on the world stage.

It appears that the best outcome of our misadventure that we now can hope for is the development of a nation state that is some combination of a Shiite Islamic theocracy and semi-democratic centralized government, one that will very likely have religious ties to the Shiite theocrats in Iran. At worst, we have set the stage for endless civil conflict among the Sunni, Shiite, and Kurds. It has become very clear that the Iraqi people do not want the United States to have an opened-ended presence in their country, and that the people of the United States are tiring of the quagmire and will demand that the Obama administration provide a strategy that allows us to exit the country. This desire of the American people is also driven by recognition that our economic issues demand priority attention, along with our psychological need to relegate an immoral, shameful venture to the past—to put the disgrace behind us.

So why did we travel down this evil path?

It is a question that each of us should ask ourselves. We are unique individuals, each accountable at the end of the day, for our own actions and morality. Sometimes, we will not be able to have any influence on societal morality, but that is not sufficient reason for being passive or for not having taken a stance that reflects our inner being. If we do not do this, we have unwittingly contributed to evil. We have made a decision to "remain ignorant and impotent against evil."

It is instructive to look at the Iraq issue against the causes that Katz delineated. Many of us probably have the "obedience to authority personality," having the inclination to follow our president or our political party affiliation, wanting to believe the rhetoric offered by this identity group. The Iraq war decision was also made at a time where "the immediate circumstances [referring to the 9/11 terrorist attack] dominate our entire field of moral vision." We were also misled by the "packaging of evil," where the propaganda of linking al-Qaeda with Saddam Hussein was used; where we heard the arguments of a horrible dictator having weapons of mass destruction with visions of a mushroom cloud; with aluminum tubes and mobile biological laboratories and yellow cake from an African country and the delusionary vision of being welcomed by flag-waving Iraqi citizens. The decision path was fostered by the "bureaucratic procedures" that the administration orchestrated through Congress to gain arguable support. The venture became one where the "evil-doing becomes enjoyable and rewarding to a group of people," including those of us who watched the "shock-and-awe" show of the invasion on TV, and the president's landing on the aircraft carrier for a "mission accomplished" celebration.

But the fundamental reason why we went to war with Iraq remains a mystery. Perhaps history will eventually dislodge the truth. Was it because of a true, although misguided, fear that Iraq posed an imminent threat? Was it to establish a new nation state in the Middle East that would help stabilize the area and promote democracy by example? Was it because Iraq has the world's second largest oil reserves? Was it because we had a president and an administration that saw a "small war" as a route to secure more power and personal prestige—the "careerism" cause? Was it because there are people who are truly evil and love having the ultimate in power—the power of life or death over others. As Albert Einstein wrote: "It is my conviction that killing under the cloak of war is nothing but an act of murder." Colin Powell's chief of staff, Colonel Lawrence Wilkerson, when discussing the presentation to the United Nations that became the final domino in the argument for invading Iraq, said that it was "the perpetuation of a hoax," that it was "the lowest point in my professional life." Nobel Peace Prize laureate and head of the International Atomic Energy Agency, Mohamed ElBaradei, wrote: "The most dissatisfying moment of my life ... was when the Iraq war was launched. That hundreds of thousands of people lost their lives on the basis of fiction, not facts, makes me shudder."

Evil is alive and well, and it has a very insidious character. Ordinary people, engaged in ordinary behavior, can contribute to extraordinary evil. We need to stand guard, at all times, lest the "beguilement to evil" takes root in our decisions and actions. As a unique, awesome individual, you have this responsibility. It's the responsibility that the sisters and brothers of mankind have to each other, as well as to their own inner integrity and substance and growth as individuals.

May you and I be given the wisdom to see evil and the strength to substitute it with love and understanding.

CHAPTER 5

MY FIRST, BIG, ENDURING MYTH

"The greatest obstacle to discovery is not ignorance— it is the illusion of knowledge."

—Daniel J. Boorstin

"It is worthy of remark that a belief constantly inculcated during the early years of life, while the brain is impressible, appears to acquire the nature of instinct; and the very essence of an instinct is that it is followed independently of reason."

—Charles Darwin

Few of us can explain, in a coherent and substantive way, why we hold the beliefs that we do. Why am I a Roman Catholic, or why am I a Muslim? What is my basis for believing that marriage should be only for two people of the opposite sex? What do I believe, and what solid evidence do I have for believing that

59

the supply-side economic theory is better that the demand-side economic theory? Why am I a Republican and not a Democrat? Why am I a Christian, and why do I profess that this religion is the true religion?

These important examples raise the very fundamental question of whether the beliefs that define us are based on truth and reality or were "adopted" for reasons that we dare not examine, for fear that we may find that facts and careful thought do not support these beliefs. My sense is that we hold many core beliefs that do not stand the test of hard-nosed evaluation; that we have not subjected these beliefs to honest inquiry; that they are not grounded in rational thinking. Indeed, we may even defend the holding of some of these beliefs on the argument that rational inquiry is not a requirement for holding these views; that we have a *right* to these views irrespective of whether they are right or wrong. And so we go on, for decades, without ever submitting our beliefs to serious self-examination. We choose instead to spend our lives in a world of illusion and myth, a world that gives us security and social companionship, and we choose to live among others of same mind who authenticate and reinforce these views. But it also becomes a world that we are afraid to examine for fear that we will lose this security and the sense of life direction and purpose and companionship that it provides.

Over my work career, I found that it was an extremely helpful discipline to defend or examine technical or business propositions by stating, on a piece of paper, the rationale and supporting evidence for these conclusions. Writing down the reasons for the beliefs we hold is often an extraordinary exercise in that it becomes evident that our beliefs might not be as deeply and solidly rooted as we thought. This is particularly revealing when we are willing to state counter views and opposing evidence and explain why these countering points are not well founded or true.

I am not alone in this experience, an example being author Abigail Thomas, who commented that writing down her thoughts was the *ultimate way for her to find truth and clarity.*

There are two very important reasons for looking at whether our beliefs are based on reality or myth. The first is that if we are to be successful in meeting the immense challenges of today's world, we need to deal with reality. In order to solve any problem, we need to understand the problem and the true merits of the proposed solution. A solution that is based on a belief that is not supported by sound thinking will not solve the problem; instead, it will make the situation worse. This poses a very, very difficult issue because it is our human nature to want to dip into our basket of preformed beliefs. We feel confident and comfortable that this is where the answer lies. Mark Twain explained this notion succinctly when he observed: "It ain't what you know that gets you in trouble. It's what you know for sure that just ain't so." If we are to solve the issues before us, we will need to be disciplined and mature and courageous enough to examine our solution beliefs in a thorough, honest way.

The second reason for looking at our beliefs is that this is a critical aspect of becoming a more complete, more grounded person—a person who is truly content in this awesome world and comfortable in his or her own skin; an authentic person. It allows us to see and feel the magnificence of this creation and the interconnectedness of life. I believe it is an indispensable aspect of developing a true religious faith, a faith that acknowledges the wonders of the universe and acknowledges the limits of understanding of which man is capable. It lays aside the need to believe in the unbelievable. Yet myths serve a purpose; they tell a story about our needs, they reveal our superstitions, and they speak to the history of our psychological evolution and the way we deal with the many problems confronting man. Myths and ideologies are instructive, but they need to be considered critically and rationally, and it is dangerous to use them blindly when forming the basis for our beliefs and decisions.

David Brooks, a columnist for the *New York Times*, offers an explanation of why these stories and myths are so important to us:

> "[P]eople have a drive to seek coherence and meaning. We have a need to tell ourselves stories that explain it all. We use these stories to supply the metaphysics, without which life seems pointless and empty. Among all the things we don't control, we do have some control over our stories. We do have a conscious say in selecting the narrative we will use to make sense of the world. Individual responsibility is contained in the art of selecting and constantly revising the master narrative we tell ourselves. The stories we select help us, in turn, to interpret the world. They guide us to pay attention to certain things and ignore other things. They lead us to see certain things as sacred and other things as disgusting. They are the frameworks that shape our desires and goals. So while story selection may seem vague and intellectual, it's actually very powerful. The most important power we have is the power to help select the lens through which we see reality. Most people select stories that lead toward cooperation and goodness. But over the past few decades a malevolent narrative has emerged."

I would like to share the story of a belief important to me that I held for most of my life; it was based, I am now certain, on myth. As the shell of this "myth egg" began to crack a few years ago, I had to ask myself how was it that it took sixty-five years for me to move beyond a superficial evaluation of this important core belief. I am not sure that I can explain this, other than to share the history of how I came to hold beliefs that I never examined. Perhaps this will give you the courage to examine your beliefs sooner than I did mine. I'm going to share this particular story because it speaks very deeply to the idea of allowing myths to form the basis for our beliefs. *This story is about my religious beliefs, but it could just as easily be about political beliefs or economic or worldview beliefs.* I hope you read this story not as a religious faith argument, although that certainly comes through as well, but rather as a story that speaks to the role of myth in our belief development.

*****

Church was always a meaningful factor in my life. My earliest memories are going to Sunday school in a small country church between Oak Center and Zumbro Falls, Minnesota, a church named Lincoln Lutheran Church. I never learned how it got its name, but it might say something about religion and political history getting intertwined, even in that little country church, as I don't recall Sunday school class teaching any Bible stories about a guy named Lincoln.

My mom was close to being a lifetime member of Lincoln, but my dad was raised Methodist, and his paternal grandpa was a Methodist minister. My grandpa Orlin had many stories about his extremely strict preacher dad, and how Grandpa had to sneak out of the house at night to play fiddle in a dance band. I was under the impression that Grandpa Orlin considered church-goers no more righteous or closer to God than non-church-goers, and as a result, church was a rather secondary thing in his life. I thought this was interesting because I always saw Grandpa as having more compassion and decency than many of the "never miss a Sunday" folks at Lincoln. My dad, Mert, apparently inherited most of Orlin's lackadaisical attitude toward church, and so when he and

Mom married it was a small, unimportant decision for him to join the Lutheran tradition at Lincoln.

Rev. Scharlemann, the preacher and accepted leader of his church community, was a rotund, bald, good-natured guy who moved at a slow but thoughtful pace. My understanding is that he was born in Germany and that his dad was a military man. Rev. Scharlemann was the embodiment of the faith we were admonished to seek; he was totally non-materialistic, not at all concerned with tomorrow, and had a deep, unshakable faith that the Almighty was in control of everything. Such was his faith that even if you didn't agree with some of the dogma that accompanied it, you had to admire the peace and contentment that it gave him. He lived in the parsonage, located on the church property—church on the west side, parking lot on the north, cemetery on the south and the parsonage on the east side. I don't believe there was a connection, but this layout led to Rev. Scharlemann and his wife having a large family—eleven kids, if I remember right. All smart, all good singers, and the girls so attractive that I'm sure some of the guys came to church just to fantasize.

Being a member of Lincoln didn't demand much. There was, of course, the Sunday service at 10:30. This was after they discontinued the two-service Sunday morning church service— the early one delivered in the German language, and the second one in the up-and-coming English language. We usually arrived at 10:35 with our hair still wet. To be a member in really good standing, it was important that the wife belong to the Ladies Aid. Furthermore, she had to be able to cook and to fry rich, melt-in-the mouth chicken for the annual summer mission festival and for the lunches after a funeral. Sunday school ran the first half hour of the service, and then the kids came up from the basement to join the rest of the congregation for the sermon. I still remember some of those sermons. Scharlemann was a preacher who took great liberty in his interpretation of the Bible. I wouldn't say he saw himself as a prophet, but it was darn close.

This was just after WW II, and the cold war with the Soviet Union and potential nuclear holocaust was the geo-political issue of huge concern to the nation. Rev. Scharlemann saw in the Bible a prophesy that the Soviets were going to send bombers over the North Pole into the United States for a first-strike atomic bomb attack. His pulpit description of these attacks was vivid: jet-engine contrails, a flight path that crossed Minnesota, wave after wave of Soviet bombers making their way inland. Creatively sprinkled in between some of these descriptions was the preaching of how bad the Jews were and, not much better, the Catholics.

Politics was a subject of substantial interest to Rev. Scharlemann, so it was not too surprising to find him weaving political issues into his sermons. He was a strong supporter and friend of Floyd Olson, governor of Minnesota back in the late '30s. One of the causes that both Olson and Scharlemann supported was the idea that the world would be a better place if it had a common universal language. The idea behind the form of this language was that it should be as simple as possible for everyone to learn. Although it was called the Esperanto language, a term that sounded Hispanic to me, the language was designed to use as many words common to the European languages as possible. All this eventually tied in to the birth of the Scharlemanns' last child, a boy, who would have been a year or two older than me. Mrs. Scharlemann and the reverend had agreed to a name for the new son and, as was custom at Lincoln, to have the baptism ritual toward the end of the Sunday service. The child would be carried to the baptismal font by his mother, accompanied by the father and the sponsors or godparents, usually a man and woman, who would pledge that the child would be taken care of and would received good Lutheran training, should the parents die. So the baptism ritual began, with the dad, Rev. Scharlemann, already up there because he was officiating. It's not known whether it was a spur-of-the-moment decision on the reverend's part or if it was premeditated, but when he came to announcing the child's name before all of God and mankind, he decided not on the name upon which he and his wife had agreed but rather … Floyd Olsen Scharlemann. Story is that Mrs. Scharlemann was shocked and speechless, but in the old Lutheran households, the father was the boss and decision-maker. And Floyd remains Floyd to this day.

Scharlemann's faith in God, however, was never questioned. It appeared to be absolute and unshakeable. The event demonstrating this—one that I will always remember—occurred upon the death of one of his sons; I believe, the oldest. All of the kids, albeit with the normal allotment of troubles from time to time, were very successful vocationally—professors, writers, clergy, business people, and so forth. The exception was the oldest son, who lived nearby with his wife and family. Unfortunately, he had a history of emotional problems, very probably something that today would be diagnosed as a borderline mental illness. At the age of about forty, he died unexpectedly from a massive heart attack. His dad, Rev. Scharlemann, accepted the death completely, saying it was God's will, and far be it from him to argue with God. He officiated at his son's funeral, giving the funeral sermon and conducting the entire service. That's a level of faith and the peace and composure that this faith engendered, which left a long-term impression on me. Faith, indeed, can be strong and mighty.

However, the most important aspect of my experience at Lincoln, and which I feel has relevance in understanding the role of religion in society today, centered on the individual members of the congregation. For the most part, these were farmers and a few small-business people—good, honest, hardworking people, probably averaging dead center on the IQ curve. What I found so normal then (although I don't anymore) was their acceptance of the teachings of the church, without questioning and without serious inquiry. No one in the entire congregation ever asked, as far as I know, where the Bible came from, or who wrote it, or how the books in the Bible got there. No one asked who put them in the order that they are in, or what the other religions of the world were and what they said about God and salvation. No one asked what Luther stood for or what he believed, other than his challenge of the Roman Catholic indulgences sold in the Middle Ages and his writing the little red book, *Luther's Small Catechism*. If there was any debate or questioning, it usually centered on the Catholics and somebody's son or daughter dating or planning to marry a Catholic. That was a big deal, requiring a decision on whether to disown the child or to attend the wedding, and how to cope with the knowledge that any children the young couple might have would probably be damned to hell—a tough realization for the grandparents to think about. I remember my mom being all upset when someone "tactfully" informed her that I was dating a girl from Bellechester, a small nearby town, where almost everyone was Catholic. (She quickly ditched me, so no problem.)

So on what did the people build their faith? The usual path was for a kid to go to Sunday school for a few years, where the Bible stories were told and where we memorized the Ten Commandments and the Creeds. This was followed by a couple of years of confirmation classes. At Lincoln, they were held in the church basement in the morning, Monday through Friday, for several weeks during the summer. Rev. Scharlemann was the instructor. I enjoyed them, in no small part because in order to get to the classes, I got a new Doodle Bug—these were the rage at that time; little red motor scooter with a 1½ horsepower Briggs & Stratton engine, with a top speed approaching 25 mph. Taking off the muffler made it sound even faster. So that was my usual transportation to confirmation class, although on numerous occasions I'd have a mechanical breakdown and have to walk to the nearest farmhouse and call my mom to retrieve me. We read and discussed Bible stories and studied and memorized Luther's small catechism book, with each of us learning enough to leave a favorable impression on Rev. Scharlemann so that he would judge us ready for confirmation. Just before Easter, the final step of the confirmation process was a big ceremony that consisted of a review before the congregation, answering a known set of questions with a known set of memorized answers. Each of us wore a white robe with a flower pinned on for our first bread-and-wine communion following the "examination."

We were now full-fledged Christians; Lutheran Christians, to be precise. We had a religious understanding much like the rest of the congregation. Again—and this is the most germane point—nowhere was there any questioning, much less any discussion, about the source or the validity of this teaching. Sunday school and confirmation class never dealt with that question. We simply "believed." I believed. We just totally accepted the teachings. And why is that? Supposedly, we were dealing with the most important thing of our lives—first and foremost, our eternal destination; secondarily, how to conduct our earthly lives.

I've thought about this a lot in recent years. Speaking for myself, but I suspect the other members as well, my trust in the Lutheran faith and Rev. Scharlemann's teachings were based on a number of factors, with each one tending to reinforce the others.

• I reasoned, perhaps consciously and perhaps subconsciously, that since all the other people in the congregation, including my parents, grandparents, and cousins, accepted these teachings, they must be right. These were teachings that I had heard from my earliest childhood days. In my small world, these teachings had the face of universal truth.

- I assumed that the good Rev. Scharlemann had been trained in the seminary and was, therefore, an expert who would have asked the hard questions regarding validity of the teachings. We trusted him because we were sure that he knew more than we did.

- I also participated in this faith story out of a sense of loyalty. This was loyalty to my friends and family and to an aspect of our lives that was central to who we were. It provided community and, in a sense, the congregation was an extended family.

- I accepted the notion that somehow, by the gracious goodness of the Almighty, I was given the truth, which was strongly reinforced because the entire congregation and circle of family and friends seemed to share this thought.

- It was my impression that the Bible was the entirety of the Christian teachings, and that there was no more information of relevance out there. If I did have questions, it was not clear to me where the answers to these questions might be found. Along with all the others in the church, I assumed that somehow these teachings were, in fact, "inspired," although it was not exactly clear to me how this had occurred.

- It seemed clear that the teachings led to "good," and that even if these teachings were not exactly right in every detail, it represented a belief system and a guidance to conduct that was honorable and right and would lead to worthwhile living.

- I was pretty much convinced that there was a supreme, all-powerful, father-like God "up there," and that through Jesus, our sins were forgiven, and that as long as we believed this, nothing else really was of major importance. By reducing my faith to this simple notion, I could be comfortable, without questioning or trying to understand all the facets of the religious teachings or the mysteries of our existence. It was mentally expedient and convenient.

- And there was the fear, or the intimidation factor—fearful in the sense that if I somehow became a non-believer, I was destined for eternal damnation; intimidation in that I chose not to pursue inquiry myself.

- As an added encouragement, I sensed, probably correctly, that it made me more highly regarded among others in the community. I was a church-goer with a strong faith. It fostered the feeling that I was indeed following truth. It made me feel like a good person. It added to my self-sense of character.

- And last, this was a comfortable faith. Tidy. I had control, at least intellectually if not always in practice in daily life. And it allowed me to not ponder the tough questions of my existence or my beliefs. Rather, my energies could be focused on advancing this faith that was "most certainly true and right."

This is my youth religion story. It served me well in many respects. It gave me comfort and security, particularly when things weren't going well. I carried this faith with me into the army. It was shortly after returning from the army that I made a big, hard change in life; I decided to leave the family dairy farm. But my church faith went with me to college. I remember some of the Sunday services at a church just off the Cornell campus in Ithaca, and the fascinating preacher there, Rev. Snook. My faith was there in our marriage and the first church we joined together, Roselawn Lutheran in Cincinnati, located right in the midst of a community that had become predominantly Jewish. At Roselawn, I became significantly involved in the day-to-day workings of the church, teaching Sunday school, chairing the new membership committee, and serving on the board. And at Roselawn, our children, Brett and Kendra, were baptized.

We followed this faith journey to Minnetonka when I changed jobs from Procter & Gamble to Pillsbury. Our scouting for a new church led us to Immanuel Lutheran church in Eden Prairie; after a year or two we moved to All Saints Lutheran because it was close and easier for the kids to be involved. I did my usual things— teaching Sunday school, chairing the stewardship committee several times, helping form the world hunger group, participating in Bible study classes, serving on the church council board and on the executive committee for many years. Diane taught Sunday school, was a member of the Altar Guild, attended Bible study class, volunteered with Stephen's Ministry, and played in the hand-bell choir.

What's the point of this story? Simply to convey my sense of how most of us decide our religious ties, the beliefs that we hold and which we argue represents truth. I was on that path for most of my life, some sixty-plus years. It was important in shaping my identity and how I looked at the world. It was important to me that Brett and Kendra follow a comparable faith journey. It allowed me to feel that I had a chance in getting into the right place in eternity and that I had a moral compass for my days on earth. My expectation was that this religious faith would accompany me and be part of my whole life; that it would be a continuing, steady presence in my life, something that would offer stability and direction and hope, even if things were not going well; and that it would be with me until the end.

But shortly after retirement, a crack began to develop. The first crack that I could not dismiss was my observing hypocrisy in supposedly strong Christians. It was clear to me that religion, for this group of "Christians," was little more than a front for nationalism. For some, another subset, it was a route to power and prestige. For others, it was a rationale for supremacy—that they were the chosen ones of God, the possessors of truth, giving them the right to see themselves as superior to outsiders and those holding different views. There was an unspoken but clear attitude that they were somehow a bit "better" than those holding different or no-faith views. This was certainly characteristic of the Christian Right. I saw it in some politicians, in some of the TV evangelists and the radio news commentators, and regrettably, I saw this self-righteousness growing in some of my close, longtime friends.

I began to sense that I was seeing a form of Christianity developing, particularly in the fundamentalist Religious Right group, which produced a closed mind; it was a mind that could not deal with sincere discussion about the basis or underpinnings of the Christian faith. I saw a faith that did not seem willing to discuss its authenticity with newcomers to the faith—it was the offer to "just accept our divinely inspired truth," rather than beginning with a discussion such as "Where did these scriptures come from? Who wrote them? Are these biblical scriptures the grand total of ancient scripture? Have there been any arguments made by serious biblical scholars that these scriptures might not be true? Have we offered a reasonable counter-argument that defends our view that these are divinely inspired works in response to scholarly arguments that the scriptures are myth? Has the Christian faith, in fact, produced love and understanding and compassion among its adherents? Why was God performing faith-inspiring miracles 2,000 years ago but not today? If this God is all-loving, why is there suffering"?

A pivotal point began with a discussion with a very close friend, Hans Zoerb, about what I was seeing and feeling. Hans, sharing some of these feelings, told me about hearing an Episcopal bishop speak about some of his misgivings regarding current scripture interpretation. Hans remembered the bishop's name as John Spong. A trip to the bookstore started what has been a five-year journey into the basis of my faith. This journey has been much like peeling an onion. John Shelby Spong's books were instrumental in taking off the first thin layer. This led to many other books by many other theologians. And the more I read, the more questions I had. Layer by layer, I have peeled this faith onion; book by book, I have looked for further insight to the questions that were becoming unavoidable and with answers that were irreconcilable with my earlier beliefs. Slowly, as I peeled the layers away, came the courage to acknowledge my long-term dependency on myth.

For me, that is a strong statement. It did not come easily and certainly is not made lightly. Most Americans say they are followers of the Christian faith. For most of those people, I suspect, to come to a conclusion such as this would be equally difficult and, at least initially, equally troubling. One does not remove the cornerstone of his or her life without tribulation.

A most important point that I want to make is that I have chosen to share my story for the sole purpose of giving you the courage to examine the basis for your beliefs, religious or otherwise. My purpose is not to steer you to a particular conclusion. My belief that we are unique, wondrous beings is a belief that I hold very, very strongly. With this belief comes a corollary belief that with this awesomeness comes a responsibility to think for yourself and to form your own answers to the most important questions of life. My own experience suggests that we can get to these answers only if we have the courage to look at reality. It's a challenging and difficult endeavor because it holds potential for "tinkering" with the very substance of our self-identity, our most inner being.

If you have stayed with me to this point, I suspect you are wondering what my faith status is at this point in my life. In theological jargon, it's something between agnosticism and deism. It's the only faith stance that I can see that is authentic. It is a faith that I feel is realistic in the sense that it does not rest on superstition or beliefs that conflict with the workings of nature and the mechanics of the universe. It is also a faith that recognizes that man is woefully incapable of understanding the mystery of this creation; it is a faith that acknowledges the possibility of an ultimate power that is beyond man's understanding or comprehension; it is a faith that willingly acknowledges an inner sense that our existence is part of something bigger than what we can understand, and that this spiritual existence connects us with each other and with the rest of nature.

Before my brother-in-law, David, died, we talked a bit via e-mail about our faith. I would like to share a note that I wrote to David about my faith story. I share this because it expresses, in different words, where I am.

----original message----
Sent: 08/26/2007 09:45 PM CST
To: David Fowler
Subject: Re: Our Faith

Hi David,

The questions of life and religion were big ones for me too, but interestingly, they started for me about the time I retired, and then the cancer came along [my prostate cancer] while I was in the midst of trying to figure things out. It's a long story but the quick version is that I was a very active Lutheran for 60 some years. I always had some doubts—too many inconsistencies, etc.—but figured some people (preachers, family, etc.) wiser than me must have thought through these issues, concluding that it all makes sense. About retirement time I got to the point where I deeply sensed that a lot of this religion

stuff was almost the antithesis of what one would call Christian values.

So that got me started. Maybe 50 or 60 books and a lot of thinking later, my faith has evolved into a very personal view in terms of what is truth and where I stand with the Creator. For starters, I've come to believe that all the major religions are man-made. Also have come to believe that whatever God is, it's beyond human capacity to understand or comprehend what that is. I even accept the possibility that there is no God; that we as humans are not capable of knowing for sure. Yet my strong intuition and personal belief is that there is a Master of this all...a greater power... and that somehow we are a unique and valued part of this mystery. So although I'm not certain, I personally believe that some way, somehow we are part of a continuing saga after we bite the dust. Coupled with this belief, although with just as many uncertainties, is that doing good vs. doing evil will have something to do with this outcome. It's just too important a part of human existence to be a non-event...unless, of course, there is no God. But that does not feel right to me. So David, I guess I am now an agnostic, but with the needle on the "There Is a God—No There Is Not a God" scale pointing quite a ways toward the "There Is" side—and with the 'There Is' side being a supreme power that is way beyond human capacity to envision, comprehend, or understand.

This whole process and the conclusions I was coming to were uncomfortable after all those hours in church and saying Lutheran/Christian creeds for 60 years, to say the least. But I am now more at peace with my faith than ever before in my life. It's a faith that does not demand believing the unbelievable, the ignoring of big inconsistencies, and having to declare that my religion is truer than someone else's. Yet for me it's a faith that deals coherently with the unknowable aspects of a Supreme Power, with the puzzle of good and evil, and the almost unbelievable fact that we are here, as unique individuals, in this wondrous universe.

I have only a couple of people who I feel I can talk this stuff with. And I hope you don't think I've gone off the deep end. Your note seemed to suggest that maybe you can relate to how people, at least some of us, have pondered and wrestled with this question of religion and life.

Regards,
Jerry

In case you are wondering, David's reply to this note included the comment "I can't thank you enough for your candor. I would have valued wherever you came out. ... The fact that we independently reached conclusions that are almost 100 percent 'aligned' is almost scary!" I appreciated David's comment a lot because I knew it came from a point in his life when he was being very authentic about all important matters. David passed away five months later.

It is not my intent to make this chapter a thesis on why biblical scripture is fraudulent in terms of claiming to be the "inspired" word of God or why Christianity is a mythically based religion, not unlike the other world religions. There are many excellent books by far more qualified authors that discuss the evidence. Instead, I will share in broad scope the reasons that caused me to begin to question the basis of my religious beliefs, with the hope that it may encourage others to look at their beliefs and ideologies in a deeper way. My thinking is that if we have the courage to look deeply into our most fundamental beliefs, we will very likely have the courage to look at the other beliefs that form our decision-making and which will determine the well-being of our children and perhaps the world at large.

So ... I will share with you the path that led me to conclude that Christianity is a mythology-based religion and that scripture is little more than the writings of common man; some of these men very wise, perhaps; some clearly deranged mentally; some very likely attempting to gain power, status, and influence; and undoubtedly all very superstitious ancients.

I was not a serious student of scripture. But then, interestingly and importantly, *almost no one is*. I read the Bible, some parts several times and probably the entire book at least once or twice, during my teenage years. I kept my Bible in my room and read in bed before going to sleep. In my adult life I taught Sunday school, attended Bible study classes, chaired many committees, faithfully contributed a sizeable amount of hard-earned dollars, and went to church almost every Sunday. Generally speaking, I had accepted the church message that scripture was somehow divinely inspired and true. I never questioned, at least not in any serious way, how the church came to this conclusion. Again, interestingly—to make the point one more time—almost no one does!

As mentioned earlier, the first crack that developed was a sense that much of what we were seeing in supposedly strong

Christians—the fundamentalists and the Religious Right groups, for example—was clearly hypocritical and little more than a front or justification for nationalism and self-righteousness. So, in my own and arguably feeble way, I slowly began to recognize that I needed to ask myself some very basic questions about the foundation of my religious beliefs and even more slowly to build the courage to begin the journey of exploration that would follow.

It now seems absurd to me that I could have gone for sixty-plus years attending church, chairing and leading financial drives for the church, going to Bible study groups, urging my kids to become faithful members of the church—and the list goes on—without asking the most elementary question of whether this story is true. Where did scripture originate? Who wrote it? When? Were there other "scriptures" that are not in the Bible? Were there competing religions? What does history say about the development of scripture? How do I reconcile the religion stories with common sense and the obvious? Is scripture internally self-consistent? Does the belief and trust in scripture result in "good" in our lives and in the world at large?

The process of peeling this intellectual onion was not mechanical or straightforward but very iterative. Looking into one question results in looking into another question, a question that may be closely related but sometimes is not. But in an attempt to lay out my journey in a somewhat coherent manner I will touch on the major recognitions, in no particular order, that have led me to the conclusion that the religion that was so important in my life is in fact little more than elegantly presented mythology. I will not elaborate on the details of these points for three reasons: first, each represents subject matter that would warrant a book in and of itself. Second, my purpose is to encourage you to begin your own unique journey. Only by discovering these realities yourself will you gain the confidence and courage to examine the basis of your faith. And third, there are excellent, more authoritative and hence more believable sources. Following are some of the *recognitions* that led me down my path of inquiry:

• Recognizing that scripture is internally inconsistent in detail. There are numerous consistencies, ranging from differing accounts of creation, differing accounts of the birth of Jesus, and who visited the tomb on Easter morning. For me, the importance of this is simply that if scripture is divinely inspired by an all-powerful, inerrant God, certainly the factual details should jibe. But they do not. It is beyond reason to view the Bible as literally true when there are internal inconsistencies of all sorts.

• Recognizing that essential messages of scripture are inconsistent. Is God a kind and loving God, or is he a wrathful God who commands that some less-preferred people be "utterly destroyed." The barbaric God described in parts of the Old Testament is totally at odds with the loving God often cited in the New Testament.

• Recognizing that scripture is full of messages that are clearly at odds with compassion and love of our brothers and sisters—approval of slavery, killing of innocent male children, the giving of daughters to strangers for sexual purposes, and that some groups of people are the children of the devil. Yet this is scripture that many Christians hold to be inerrant and true, inspired by a loving God. This is the scripture that forms the text of the day on Sunday morning service and forms the basis for Bible study. The reason the "avoided" texts are not talked about is because they are indefensible—they survive scrutiny because almost no one has seriously and thoughtfully and open-mindedly read the Bible they profess is God's inspired word.

- Recognizing and dealing in an intelligent way with the stories that are clearly based on superstition and storytelling—the miracle stories, demons being transferred to pigs, burning bushes, donkeys that talk, and a boat that holds all of the animal kingdom during a flood that covers even the world's mountains. These are obviously ridiculous stories if interpreted in any way other than being mythological stories created for a superstitious ancient world.

- Recognizing that the books of the New Testament were all written long after the death of Jesus by unknown authors who never saw or talked to Jesus, and that with unbiased reading (for example, by someone who has not gone to church or who has not gone to Sunday school), these books deliver very different messages, each reflecting the times and geopolitical issues of the day.

- Recognizing that the construct of the Bible is not chronological; that the opening books of the New Testament, the gospels, were written *after* the books written or attributed to Paul, not before, which sets the stage for misleading interpretation and context for Paul's stories. Clearly, the order of the books in the Bible was arbitrarily assembled by man to help create a story written by man. Theologically, this is an important point, leading some scholars to conclude that Paul was writing about his belief in a spiritual, heavenly "Christ" who existed from the beginning of time, not an earthly Jesus born of a woman.

- Recognizing that the books of the Bible were selected by the ancients from many other books in existence at that time, many expressing very different religious beliefs. Some of these have been discovered in relatively recent times. These books show that different groups held widely different views of what the

Christianity faith meant and what constituted truth. Some of these books represent a deep, highly philosophical understanding of man, even more so than what is expressed in the biblical canon.

• Recognizing that man is very capable of strongly believing in absurd, mythological religions. One only has to travel to the southeast Asian countries to see the thousands and thousands of temples built over the centuries. Or one can go to Egypt to see the power of a religious belief, discredited by Christians as pagan myth, which caused tens of thousands of laborers to work for decades to build a suitable burial place, including the famous pyramids, to assure that their god-like king would have safe passage to the eternal world. With this experience of travel, it is easier to recognize that the beliefs of multitudes of people say very little about truth. In the same way, the tens of thousands of churches in our country say very little about the truth of the Christian message.

• Recognizing that it is illogical that a loving God would subject me to eternal damnation for my short life where I questioned the validity of the Bible story—a trillion times trillion-fold punishment for an honest mistake. Is this not cruel and unjustified, particularly when he provided so much contradictory and cat-and-mouse evidence?

• Recognizing that religion is highly manipulative when it says your eternal well-being is dependent on the depth of an unquestioning faith that, in its ultimate fulfillment, becomes an addiction—an addiction that is touted as faith—and that in practice becomes a mind-control process. To this day, serious and substantive individual inquiry is strongly discouraged by preachers and priests. If it were not, the content of Bible study and "beginning of faith" classes would be vastly different.

- Recognizing that the early church had major disagreement with respect to the humanity of Jesus and whether he was equivalent to God and whether the Trinity suggested a polytheistic religion.

- Recognizing that religion and church has become institutionalized; that it has become large and pervasive, with enormous power in controlling thought and worldview.

- Recognizing that organized religion is, in effect, an industry that markets itself to the consumer's quest to find security and meaning in life. It's an industry where ego and the struggle for power and prestige and ideology often seems more important than love. For me, this created further doubt and encouraged more in-depth inquiry as the onion was peeled.

- Recognizing that the Mediterranean region was an area of competing, borrowing, and evolving religions, strongly incorporating elements of the myths of even more ancient, superstition-based religions. Every major story in the Bible has precedence in ancient mythology. Believing that Christian concepts such as virgin birth, baptism, discipleship, and resurrection after three days *is unique* to the Christian story is to be ignorant of ancient history. Many authors have written about the myths in these religion stories, and even myths that bestowed ancient political leaders with divine status. As example, authors Timothy Freke and Peter Gandy noted the following events *common* to these savior mythologies:

  - man is born who is God made flesh.

  - His mother is a virgin, impregnated by God or the spirit of God. The mother becomes "holy."

- The child is born in a cave on December 25, prophesized by a celestial event, with Magi bringing gifts.

- The holy man/child is baptized with water.

- He is declared the Good Shepherd, the Lamb and the Lion.

- The holy man turns water into wine, heals the sick, and does other miracles that confirm that he is Supreme.

- He has twelve close followers who join him in carrying forth his message.

- He dies a sacrificial death and three days later is resurrected and ascends to heaven.

- Through his death and resurrection he offers his followers new life.

- Recognizing that there is no contemporary, historically based evidence of Jesus' existence, even though there were a number of historians recording history during Jesus' time, a point completely at odds with the depth of events described in the gospels. One quick example: Matthew's resurrection story says that "the graves were opened, and many of the bodies of the saints ... were raised ... and appeared to many." Now, that would have generated interest and would be something historians would have undoubtedly recorded. But nothing of the sort is mentioned by the historians.

- Recognizing that the history of the papacy makes the Mafia look like a Sunday school picnic, one humorous example being digging up a deceased pope, dressing him in his robes, propping him up in a chair, and holding court so that he could be condemned officially and properly. This raises serious questions regarding the authenticity and objectives of the oral tradition period during the formative days of the Christian church's development.

• Recognizing that man/humankind clearly has a spiritual and emotional need that religion fulfills, irrespective of whether these religions are true or false. Diane and I have been fortunate to have traveled extensively and the degree to which this statement is true is inescapable when one sees the pyramids and temples and tombs of Egypt, the ancient worship sites of the Incas, or the many temples of Thailand.

A final point describing my journey to the destination point of no longer believing that the Christian religion is true is the simple illogic of God's saying that if you want eternal life, you have to believe that he sent down a son, and that the son died for your sins, and that your believing this is your ticket to eternal life. And because he is God and works in mysterious ways, he will make this known to you in a fuzzy, convoluted way; in a way that all of his other revelations—such as the laws of nature and the science of the wonders of life—are at odds with. It's the miracle stories that you must believe, and which God, for his own reasons and goodness, has given only to "chosen" people and which, although he is omnipotent, he has decided to not give to the rest of humankind.

It now seems strange to me that for the first sixty years of my life, I subscribed to this simple-minded, cat-and-mouse game that the Christian religion suggests, even though we claim that God gave us our intelligence and common sense. In fact, if there is an Ultimate Power or a God, this must certainly be a very insulting response from the most advanced of members of his creation.

In closing this chapter I want to reiterate a few points that I hope were implicit in my personal story. I am not trying to be critical of those who believe in the Christian story. For the most part, believing in the Christian story results in good conduct by good, well-meaning people who are wonderful, caring members of this world. I now view these Christian beliefs as being not well-founded but, in general, not harmful, except for the supremacy and self-righteousness that the Religious Right foments. I was there for sixty years, and I don't view myself as having been a bad person during that time. Where I do draw the line is where these beliefs are used to justify ideologies and actions that hurt other people. In those cases, religion truly becomes evil. It is an easy step for the Christian Right, the Moral Majority, the fundamentalist and the literalists to cross over this line, and this should be a concern to all.

What I wanted to accomplish in sharing my first, big, enduring myth story was not to set forth a thesis to convince you that I am right, although I have to admit that I find it hard to believe that anyone who studies the question with a truly open mind could come to a different conclusion. I believe Bishop Spong was right when he cautioned that "religion is not primarily a search for truth; it is overwhelmingly a search for security." But it is my belief that each of you is a unique, awesome person who must address the question of religious belief in your own lonely way. So my sole purpose is to urge you to examine your own religious convictions carefully, and that by sharing my story, you will perhaps gain the courage that is required. It was not an easy journey for me, and there were times when I felt sad about where the process was leading me. It is not easy to strip away a lifetime identity. It leaves you naked. You sense that you are abandoning your friends and church home. But after going through this turmoil, I have arrived at a point where I feel authentic, stronger in the sense that I see myself as having the capacity to grow, and more comfortable with my beliefs and understanding of this wondrous creation than ever before.

I chose to share my religious belief story not only because of its importance to me but because of the need that we have as individuals and society to challenge many of the myths and ideologies and worldviews we hold if we are to successfully deal with the immense challenges of living in today's world. Verlyn Klinkenborg, author and editor of the *New York Times*, wrote something that I think says it well: "Most of us live easily, almost unknowingly among our assumptions—another word for our ignorance." History is awash with assumptions and false beliefs that have destroyed nations and caused immense human suffering. Somehow, we need to muster the will and courage to examine these false beliefs before they become what controls us.

CHAPTER 6

LEADERSHIP, DECISION-MAKING, AND INDIVIDUAL RESPONSIBILITY

"Leaders are ordinary people
who know where they are
going and have extraordinary
determination."

—Erwin G. Walth

"The love of liberty is the
love of others; the love
of power is the love of ourselves."

—William Hazlitt

"The bravest thing you can do
when you are not brave
is to profess courage and
act accordingly."

—Corra Harris

Meeting the immense challenges of today's world, and for each of us to have an internal sense of being responsible members of the human race, demands that we make wise, well-grounded decisions, and that collectively, we find a way to turn these decisions into substantive societal action. If we do not, the future for our nation and our grandkids is extremely bleak.

This necessitates our dealing with the question of leadership. Where will it come from? How do we make sure that we have leadership in place that is commensurate with the challenges at hand?

The question of leadership has long been argued—does leadership lead, or does leadership follow? Clearly, this is a circular question. It goes without saying that a leader is not a leader unless he or she has followers. Conversely, a societal group joined together by a common cause is a group that will have limited effect if the group does not have strong, competent leadership. My sense is that sometimes societal action is *initiated* by the "followers," and sometimes it is *initiated* by a strong leader who builds a core of passionate followers. It does not really matter how it starts.

What matters is the strength and depth of commitment of the people—the dedicated and passionate followers. In most societal arenas the necessary leadership will emerge when the people demand that an issue be given attention. This is particularly true in a democratic society. Leaders love a cause that they know is of deep-seated importance to the people; one in which the people will support their leadership efforts. We are not short of leaders (read: politicians) who are highly skilled at taking the temperature of the people and responding and leading, accordingly. This is an ego-satisfying experience, and history has proven that we have no shortage of politicians—local, state, or federal—who welcome the opportunity to nurture their ego and power status. This can be annoying, but it is not necessarily bad, because it says that we will always have the necessary leadership when *the people* mobilize behind a cause they believe is important.

Said differently, we have to recognize that, at the end of the day, "we the people" are determining our fate and future. As people, we can make decisions and take action that leads to good, or regrettably, we can make decisions and support actions that lead to human suffering and the demise of a productive, enduring society. Both have been repeated over and over again in the history of the world.

And that, as I see it, is where we are today—at the crossroad. We can make good decisions that will allow our kids and grandkids to live in a healthy, wholesome society, or we can make decisions that severely jeopardize the well-being of the nation and world that they will occupy. We have in our home office a painting that, to me, expresses this dilemma and the decisions we will be making. It shows people pouring forth from some distant place, a colorful, happy, diverse group of people, taking charge of the immense challenges of their time and together, forging a path to a better world. My fervent dream is that this will be us.

Challenging Myth and Worldview

Good decisions—decisions that are well-grounded, thoughtful, non-parochial, and wise—will require that we are strong enough to examine our worldview beliefs and ideologies that have formed our very being. It demands being intellectually honest, not only with others but also (and most important) with ourselves. It will not be easy. It will demand that we dig deeply into ourselves to find out why we believe what we do, and that we are willing to change opinion when the facts and truth so dictates. It means accepting the possibility that some of our positions are based on myth. It means that we may have to gather up the courage to explain to others why we think their positions are based on myth or misunderstandings. It means that, at times, we risk relationships and that, at times, we have the feeling of being disloyal to our ideology group.

Bryan Caplan, a George Mason University economist, speaks very forthrightly about this in his book *The Myth of the Rational Voter: Why Democracies Choose Bad Policies*. He says, "This book develops an alternative story of how democracy fails. The central idea is that voters are worse than ignorant; they are, in a word, irrational—and vote accordingly." In *The True Patriot*, Liu and Hanauer express it a bit differently, saying that the fundamental issue is that many people are more loyal to party or ideology than they are to truth, reality, and understanding—the qualities, they argue, that are necessary for the survival of the nation as we know it. It would not be going too far to conclude that this often describes those who are far-right wing Republicans and those who are far-left wing Democrats—those who put their identity with party ahead of the effort that it takes to understand an issue and form an unbiased, fact-substantiated opinion.

Just as it's hard to set myth aside, the same is true for most of the decisions we make, because it is a human compulsion to make our decisions dovetail with our worldview without subjecting this worldview to examination. Stephen Davis, a professor of philosophy, in discussing religious believers versus non-believers, said, "The non-believer's position is probably convincing to the non-believer, not primarily because of the evidence or arguments in its favor but because it is entailed by the worldview he or she accepts—there is no such thing as bare, uninterrupted evidence or experience, and so the way one evaluates the evidence one sees depends to a great extent on one's worldview—all people interpret their experience within a philosophical framework."

What these writers underscore is that it requires extraordinary discipline and courage to examine the context or basis of our beliefs and that these beliefs influence our decision-making. But that is exactly what is needed for us to make thoughtful, wise decisions; to not have the courage to dig deeply within ourselves is to risk making the wrong decisions and to risk the future of our children.

"Sticking to principles" is often viewed as a positive character trait, but it is easy to see an inconsistency between "sticking to principles" and the willingness to change position on a belief or long-held worldview. This can be a problem but it is less so if our "first order principle" is to seek truth and understanding, with the focus on making the best decision possible. We live in a world where decisiveness, speed, simplicity of the message, and unwavering consistency are valued, often, it seems, more than is the search for truth and understanding. Decisiveness and consistency are certainly valuable management characteristics, but they can be horribly detrimental characteristics if they lead to a bad decision; a bad decision is usually worse than no decision at all, as it only means getting into problem territory more quickly and with more pain.

Fear

One of the biggest challenges we face in decision-making is fear. That is not to say that fear is an unjustified factor in our decision-making. Rather, it's that fear is often irrational, and its importance overstated or understated. Even more dangerous is that some leaders use fear as a tactic to gain support for their policies and decisions, irrespective of whether those policies and decisions are wise, well grounded, and based on truth.

The psychology underlying fear is not in my portfolio of skills. But one does not have to be a clinical psychiatrist to see how the issue of fear plays into our decision-making. It is extremely important that "we the people" demand—from our political leaders and from ourselves—an honest, rational appraisal of fear in our discussion of issues and in our decision-making. We need to acknowledge that fear can drive our emotions and that these emotions can lead to irrational and ill-founded decisions.

How, then, do we deal appropriately with fear? I believe the way to deal with it is to make it an open subject of discussion, acknowledging the reality, in as quantitative and descriptive way as possible. There is almost always an emotional component to our decisions that we need to recognize and control; if we do not acknowledge these emotions and manage them accordingly, they will lead us to making very inadvisable decisions. Those who cannot make a case for their arguments may use fear deliberately as a manipulative tactic when their position is at odds with fact and rational thinking.

Some of the greatest leaders in the world have recognized the danger of irrational fear and have vigorously cautioned the populace not to allow it to replace solid thinking. Franklin D. Roosevelt urged the nation's people not to succumb to "nameless, unreasoning, unjustified terror." One of Winston Churchill's most remembered messages was that "the only thing we have to fear is fear itself." Former U.S. Secretary of State Madeleine Albright, in assessing our national conduct, cautioned against fear by pointing out that "we have been told to be afraid so that we might be less protective of our Constitution, less mindful of international law, less respectful toward allies, less discerning in our search for truth, and less rigorous in questioning what our leaders tell us. We have been exhorted ... to embrace a culture of fear that has driven and narrowed our foreign policy while poisoning our ability to communicate effectively with others ... *fear is an unwillingness to think seriously about alternative perspectives.*" The danger of fear is a timely subject, because as author Fareed Zakaria has cautioned, "We have become a nation consumed by fear, worried about terrorists and rogue nations, Muslims and Mexicans, foreign companies and free trade, immigrants and international organizations." It will be hard for the populace to make sound, thoughtful decisions if they are making their decisions in the climate of fear, as described by Zakaria.

Fear was the justifying factor in selling the Iraq war by the Bush administration. It took root in the emotions of many people who envisioned the image of a mushroom cloud over an American city. Political columnist E. J. Dionne Jr. has commented on this story:

> "A band of reactionary terrorists [referring to the 9/11 perpetrators] whose actions reflected the weakness of their position were raised up to world-historical status. They were 'totalitarians,' which suggested they represented a threat as powerful as those embodied by Hitler and Stalin. They were the 'Islamofascists,' a sobriquet that credited them with battling under the banner of a coherent, modern ideology, when in fact they are inspired by a ragtime jumble of ideas rooted in the medieval past. Osama bin Laden's commitment to reviving the power of the old Islamic 'Caliphate' was taken to be as real as the danger of Soviet troops pouring across the old East German border of Hitler occupying Czechoslovakia. The new 'global war on terror' was endowed with the same coherence as the old Cold War."

As we now know and as Dionne concluded, "It was a dangerous and self-defeating set of illusions." Irrational fear and, particularly, the exploitation of fear are extremely dangerous in our decision-making and a tactic based on cowardice.

Fear is an appropriate and justified response when danger lurks. But it can also be used by the unethical and immoral to justify actions that reasoned and thoughtful decision-making would condemn. It can be insidious in nature because it spreads and breeds and takes on a life of its own, unrecognizing fact, logic, and the higher qualities of human character.

Principles

Decision-making, which for most of us means little more than establishing the stance that we are going to take on a particular issue, is not easy. Most serious subjects are, by nature, complex and multifaceted in terms of the many things that need to be considered, and these factors often are at odds or in tension with each other. Many times the information that we have is incomplete. The other major issue is that all our judgments are colored by the experiences we have had and the worldview that we have formed. This presents an especially difficult problem because in order to come to the best decision, we may have to change our position as we learn more and as we listen to the arguments of others. Human ego makes this difficult.

So what character qualities guide us in the difficult task of decision-making? Two are crucially important. Interestingly, they will not only help us in making good decisions but they also simply make us better, stronger human beings who are more comfortable and secure in living in our own skin.

First, we need to seek truth. If we are truly in search of making the best decision possible, it is lethal to start with the idea of defending a predetermined position. This is, however, a very human starting point, and it takes courage and discipline to set aside the views we hold, even for a brief period, while we listen to and make an effort to understand an alternative position. Far more energy should be spent in seeking truth and understanding as we search for the right decision. Fortunately, and sometimes surprisingly, a decision often becomes self-evident once we have done a better job of establishing truth and developing a comprehensive, factual understanding of the issue.

Second, we must be totally honest regarding the facts and information on the issue. Far too often we see spin, the defense of ideologies and distortions of fact, at the heart of the decision-making process. For "we the people," this is an insulting attempt to steer us to a predetermined decision. When it becomes obvious that honesty has been breached, the issue of honest communication, rather than just the decision itself, needs to be addressed.

The reason this is critical is that *good decision-making is a process, and dishonesty destroys that process*. As an example, when the Bush administration lied to the nation about the evidence for going to war with Iraq, the issue was not that the evidence was manufactured but that there was a lack of honest communication between the administration, Congress, and the people of the nation. It is a difficult subject to bring up because it carries a strong message about character, but it is the essence of our nation's making good decisions. So the issue of honesty needed to be dealt with in a very forthright manner, rather than being swept under the rug. If the evidence is factual and honest and the situation is discussed authentically, then everyone will be able to focus their energies on making the best decision possible.

Sincere communication—whether between a husband and wife, between two countries, or between a president and the people of the nation—is not possible without a sense that both parties are striving to be honest. The results of the alternative—real or perceived dishonesty—are obvious and therefore, we need to be tough enough to address the issue in a forthright manner when it occurs. A liar needs to be called a liar. Lies should never be left to fester and to create further mistrust.

Reality

All decision-making represents an issue that is set in one's context. It is important, therefore, that we examine carefully our perception of the context that embeds an issue. It is easy to have an overriding goal that becomes so important to us that we fail to consider the reasonableness of that goal in broader context. One aspect of this is often called the "unexpected consequences" of our decision-making. We may accomplish a more immediate objective but with long-term consequences that we will regret. Coming from the business world, I have seen this many times; a common example is cutting a particular cost to help short-term financial numbers, even though this jeopardizes long-term business health. Making decisions that give us short-term comfort but cause problems long term is a very common occurrence, both in the lives of individuals and in business, but given that we so often lose sight of this important point, it should be at the forefront of our decision-making process and should always be given deliberate and careful consideration.

We also need to give thoughtful attention to the issue of wish fulfillment. This means taking a position or making decisions that support or build on wishful thinking, rather than rigorous consideration of the issue. This is important, as it is very easy to make decisions that support myth when closer examination would question the reality of that myth. Example: perhaps democracy is not a realistic possibility at the current stage of development of a third world country. Because of our wishful thinking, we may be inclined to support decisions that give the noble idea of democracy more weight than is appropriate for that country's stage of development.

The opposite is equally true. Wish fulfillment can cloud our perception of reality in terms of denying reality. The global warming issue—where we will be making potentially critical decisions near term, either by thoughtful deliberation or by default, deciding to do nothing of significance—is an area ripe for wishful thinking, in terms of hoping that global warming is not a substantive issue. It will take courage and discipline to base our decisions on reality and good science, rather than wishful thinking. Conversely, we need to be careful to not base our decisions on seeing goblins that are not real. To date, the former appears to be the bigger danger, given the fraudulent, pseudo-scientific organizations and individuals who are attempting to create doubt about the scientific underpinnings of those who are the true experts in climate change. We have been there before, with the tobacco companies' deliberate effort to deny the scientific reality of the danger of smoking.

A rather unique problem when dealing with major, difficult decisions is the tension between optimism and reality. Most of us want to hold an "optimistic" view, whether on an economic issue, a health issue, or some other significant issue, but this view may not jibe with reality. This makes for a messy, hard-to-resolve problem, given our natural dislike for intractable issues. We like to be a forward-moving people. But at times we need to face the fact that we are making a decision that simply is the best out of a set of bad alternatives. Clear recognition and communication of this situation is critical.

Hard Work

In most areas of decision-making, we expect that the decision-maker is knowledgeable and that he has done his homework. Interestingly, we do not seem to place this expectation on ourselves when we take a position on key societal issues. In part, this is a logical conclusion, given the fact that our individual position constitutes an extremely small fraction of the total decision-making process.

The problem that arises, however, is that if a large portion of the decision-makers are relatively uninformed, the ultimate collective decision may not be based on consideration of facts and thoughtful thinking. Instead, the decision will probably reflect the effectiveness of thirty-second sound bites and a gut feel for how well this decision dovetails with our worldview. Charles Pierce has written a thought-provoking book on this subject, *Idiot America*, the conclusion of which notes "the Gut is a moron ... a roiling repository of dark and ancient fears."

From the beginning, our country has wrestled with trying to assure that knowledgeable people make the important decisions. In the beginning, only land owners were allowed to vote on national issues, the premise being that this was a prudent, although not perfect, screening tool to assure that the people were competent voters. This philosophy was ultimately rejected in favor of the one person/one vote philosophy, which was determined to be the most just and competent way to make national decisions.

It can be argued that if we feel we are entitled to participate in decision-making then we, as individuals, have the responsibility to become informed on the subject of interest. And if we are not prepared to put in the work required to become reasonably well informed, we should, as a conscientious, responsible person, allow the decision to be made by those who have worked to become informed. Certainly, in many other areas of decision-making, we do not hesitate to take this position; for instance, when we obtain medical treatment, we often defer the major decision-making responsibility to someone more knowledgeable than we are.

Obviously, this is a very subjective area and most of us would claim, particularly since we have adopted the one person/one vote philosophy, that our personal level of knowledge on a particular issue is probably better than many of the others who are involved in the decision-making process.

But that does not reduce the danger that some of the most important decisions are made by people who are poorly informed and who base their decisions on myth and misinformation. A solution that I endorse—although it will be far from perfect and certainly insufficient—is that those who share this concern do everything possible to get the populace more involved and more knowledgeable of the major issues facing us by using public radio and TV, the Internet, the printed media, and schools, and by encouraging these channels of information to give the challenges that face the nation more attention and to become more demanding of truth. Our nation and the future for our kids and grandkids are at risk if we are not successful in finding a better path to good decision-making.

Ideals Reflecting the High Road

A last point on good decision-making is to argue that we always strive to take the high road. This means that our deliberations and ultimate decision should always reflect a respect for others. Embedded in these deliberations and decisions should be clear evidence that we believe in the dignity of all people. Any sense of superiority communicated in our decisions will ultimately prove to be damaging, not only to those we have degraded but even more so to ourselves. No decision that says that we have unique possession of truth, particularly religious truth, will be received in a constructive way by those we say do not have the truth. Disagreeing is very different than expressing superiority. The former is usually not a problem; the latter is always a problem.

Madeleine Albright has explained ways in which this happens:

"We have developed a dangerous lack of self-awareness. No nukes, we say, while possessing the world's largest arsenal. Respect the law, we demand, while disregarding the Geneva Conventions. You're with us or against us, we declare, while ignoring the impact of our actions on Turkey and the Middle East. Hands off Iraq, we warn, while our troops occupy Baghdad. Beware China's military, we cry, while spending as much on defense as the rest of the world combined. Honor the future, we preach, while going AWOL on climate change. We need to do a better job of seeing ourselves as others do...people put themselves in our shoes and expect us to act with confidence ... but true confidence is shown by a willingness to enter into difficult debates, answer criticism, treat others with respect and do our share or more in tackling global problems."

Former senator George Mitchell says it in a similar way:

"We must recognize that power and principle are mutually enhancing and must be bound together firmly. For too many people in the world, our power and our principle appear to be divergent. Our power must always be deployed in a way that is consistent with our ideals, for it is our ideals that have always been the basis for our influence in the world. We were a great nation before we were a powerful nation, when we were still 13 states clinging to the Atlantic seaboard, because of the principle articulated in our charter documents. That is what makes us great."

It is clear that the decisions we have made have been disrespectful of the people of other nations, damaging severely our ability to work together. When we lose sight of these ideals, when we show disrespect for others, we lose the essence of what we once stood for. My message is that "we the people" have to take responsibility for not passing on this loss of character to our kids and grandkids. Truth, honesty, humbleness, and strength of character—these are qualities that I'm hoping will be restored within our national being and once again become the essence of who we are. I urge you to be tough and to be demanding in this endeavor to restore character; it is the foundational essence of leadership and the essence of wise decision-making.

PART II

THE CHALLENGE:
SEEING ISSUES THROUGH THE
LENS OF REALITY

CHAPTER 7

ISSUES AND MYTHS DEMANDING REALITY

"We don't see things as they are, we see things as we are."

—Anais Nin

"Most human beings have an almost infinite capacity for taking things for granted."

—Aldous Huxley

"Each of us makes his own weather, determines the color of the skies in the emotional universe which he inhabits."

—Fulton J. Sheen

Dealing effectively with an issue demands that we understand the substance of the issue. If we do not understand the problem, the likelihood that we will find an appropriate answer is remote. In fact, we often make the situation worse. This is true for business

105

issues, for personal issues, and for the major societal challenges we face as well. Nothing in successful problem-solving is as important as clear, accurate, unvarnished understanding, and nothing prevents the finding of an effective solution as much as an inaccurate, misdiagnosed understanding, or distorted view of the issue. It is astonishing, then, that we are so quick to base our position on an issue, based on very weak information and lack of understanding and that we spend so little energy in studying the roots of the problem.

David Brooks has referred to a "new body of thought" that challenges what he calls the "classical model" of decision-making. The classical model assumes that people are generally orderly and rational in their behavior. But according to Brooks, observations do not support the theory that our decisions are based on the classical model. Rather, he suggests, one has to recognize a different picture of human nature: "Each person's mind contains a panoply of instincts, strategies, intuitions, emotions, memories and habits, which vie for supremacy. An irregular, idiosyncratic, and largely unconscious process determines which of these internal players gets to control behavior at any instant ... we pick out those bits of data that make us feel good because they confirm our prejudices."

I agree with Brooks, and he has described it well. I do take exception with the notion that this represents a new body of thought; it is, in fact, as old as mankind. What may be somewhat new, however, is recognizing that some elements of our misguided decision-making is not only rooted in the biased judgment and prejudice of which Brooks speaks but also that our decisions are rooted in long, broadly accepted myth and unsubstantiated ideologies. In fact, this later element may be a stronger, more important factor than biased judgment and prejudice for many of the most important issues facing mankind. Clearly, these two points are inextricably linked—Brooks may even argue that they are one and the same. And as a practical matter, both will have to be recognized in order for us to make thoughtful, wise decisions.

A good example for illustrating the amalgam of Brooks' concern of biased judgment and prejudice, and my concern of myth and unfounded ideology, is health care cost and health care availability—a subject of intense, heated debate. This is a very important subject, given that our nation is currently on an unsustainable financial course, but the cost of health care is a subject that actually carries less emotional baggage than some other issues (for example, the religious implications embedded in the Israel-Palestine issue). Nevertheless, the health care problem is still plagued with an immense lack of factual understanding and recognition of realities.

Many people still believe that the United States has the best health care in the world. Factually, it does not. We are behind many developed countries in essentially every measurable quality parameter. We lag behind in life expectancy at birth, infant mortality rate, postpartum care, preventable death, cancer survival, diabetes care, asthma management, and most other objective measurements. The only quality parameter where there is evidence of better care is that the insured have quicker access to care, although there is equal evidence that this does not translate to a better health care outcome.

When discussing the subject of the forty-five million-plus who do not have health insurance, one commonly will hear people say that they simply go to the emergency room to get their care. They do get emergency treatment; it was made federal law in 1986 under the Reagan administration that emergency treatment cannot be denied to anyone brought to an emergency care facility. But they get little preventive health care, the care that has the highest cost benefit of all health care. The uninsured have more sickness, die sooner, and live their lives without the comforting assurance of knowing they have one-on-one health care with a trusted physician.

Compared to the health care systems of other developed countries, our cost is excessively higher. Example: we spend over 16 percent of our gross domestic product (GDP) on health care. France, which has a universal health care system built on private and government insurance, spends less than 11 percent but provides superior care. According to Dutton V. Dutton, who has studied the French system, their costs are the equivalent of $3,500 per person per year, while the United States cost is $6,100 per person. (Other sources show the U.S. cost as high as $8,000 per person.) Regardless of our ideologies on health care, it seems absurd that we have no substantive understanding on what makes the French system so cost-effective; the reasons for this huge cost and quality disparity are not understood by the decision-makers who, at the end of the day, are the payers of this health care—that's you and me. Instead, we talk about death panels and socialism and made-up numbers. It seems as though we don't want to know for fear of the understanding and conclusions that such a study would provide.

And if our egos and prejudices are too big to accept learning something from the French, we can choose from a number of other countries—there are several. We could look at the Swiss system, a private system with no government-run insurance plan but a system that provides universal coverage. The cost of the Swiss system is 10.8 percent of GDP. Or we could learn from the Japanese health care system, a universal system that utilizes an insurance pool concept, which costs them about 8 percent of their GDP.

This information might indicate that a competitive, private system carries a very large cost (for example, marketing and administrative costs that competing private insurance companies incur), and that instead, a Medicare system, with its universal-type administration can be extraordinarily cost-effective. Medicare's overhead is 1.5 percent in comparison to 13 to 16 percent for the private sector health care organizations. Private sector health care organizations also have an estimated profit in the order of $40 billion per year. One might reasonably compare this to the $54 billion cost that would be incurred to provide universal health care to the forty million-plus who are uninsured.

To date, the people of our country have not demanded— nor have they been provided with—a factual assessment of the economics of health care cost or an explanation of how and why the health care systems of other developed countries deliver superior results. And all the while, we are being devoured by health care cost, with a trajectory that indicates it will get much worse.

The question that we have to ask ourselves is *why*, on such an important subject, we have made our decisions with such a lack of information and understanding. Instead of demanding a solid, substantive understanding of the health care subject, we are willing to listen to political, intellectually dishonest, non-substantive points. One quick example: we often hear that our costs are extraordinary high because of malpractice insurance and lawsuits and the defensive medicine practices that may result. Although relevant, this constitutes less than 4 percent of our health care cost issue, a significant but not controlling consideration. We have to ask ourselves why we have not had essential, fundamental discussion on how to revamp a health care system that pays for procedures rather than wellness. We have to ask ourselves why we have not had substantive discussion on the high cost of end-of-life care for the elderly, and how we balance morality and our conscience with the wisdom of expending large amounts of health care resources on those who are nearing their end of life.

My point is not to draw a conclusion on the merits of one health care system over another; it's that even on a subject so important to us individually and to the nation's long-term financial well-being, we have chosen to bury our heads in the sand and to bind ourselves to ideology that is deficient in fact and understanding. It is hard to see how we can make high-quality decisions, given this lack of rigor and discipline. Absurdly, we are already tinkering with various health care system proposals without having these facts or understanding. Imagine if we all sent a note to the senators and representatives of our respective states: "We want a substantive, factual, impartial assessment of health care cost and quality and the alternative systems that nations use to deliver heath care." Rest assured, leadership would follow, once they knew we were demanding substance rather than TV sound bites.

Once we understand these facts on alternative health care system costs, we can begin to deal with the softer but equally important issues, such as the willingness of the people to consider a major change in health care funding; the role of company-paid health care in keeping our industries competitive in the world market; possible long-term, unintended consequences of reducing the competitive structure of private health care insurance; the question of providing continuity of health care in a society where employees now change jobs several times in their career; and the question of whether it is the mark of an advanced nation that all its members have access to quality health care; the question of what this means in terms of being a caring society, and the image we have of ourselves and the image we present to the rest of the world. It would be amazing if we found out that these benefits are achievable, at affordable cost, with good decision-making.

In an earlier chapter I shared my faith journey. My purpose in doing this was to show how strongly and influential myth can become in terms of controlling our worldview and our decisions. It's a "been there, done that" story of my accepting myth as reality. Gregory Bateson, a behavioral scientist who studied addiction, described how this addiction eventually controls the person; that when it takes root, it will "bankrupt the epistemology of 'self-control.'" Adherence to religious myth can reach the point where thoughtful, rational decision-making becomes subservient to literal interpretation of mythology and subservient to fact and reality. Some of the most important issues and decisions that we will make in the near future have this as a factor that must be dealt with. It is in the center of the fanatical Islam concern, in the abortion issue, in the Israel-Palestine issue, and in many other subjects of debate.

I hope to encourage rigorous thinking about the role that such factors as factual understanding, fear, and religious myth play in our decision-making. It demands that we have the courage to look at what we believe and to examine the reasons for these beliefs. Doing so, I believe, is an absolute prerequisite to seeing the reality of these issues and to enable us to make decisions required for meeting the immense challenges of living in our world, today and tomorrow. Having the courage and discipline to look reality in the face raises each of us up to a higher level. Aside from its societal importance, this is also a key to individual happiness and contentment. Please give it your deepest consideration.

CHAPTER 8

CHARACTER: AT THE END OF THE DAY, ALL WE HAVE

"He is not great who is not good."
—Shakespeare

"Try not to become a man of success. Rather, become a man of value."
—Albert Einstein

"Nothing is so strong as gentleness, and nothing so gentle as real strength."
—Ralph W. Sockman

Character is perhaps the one word that describes, more than any other, how favorably or unfavorably we are held in the eyes of others. This one word speaks to whether we can be trusted, the one word that describes the kind of people we want to do business with, and "a person of character" is perhaps the one phrase we would most like to have as our epitaph. So … how would someone from the outside looking in describe your character or the character of our nation? And is it really that important?

Dictionaries have a hard time coming up with a concise definition of character. Webster's gives the word thirty-seven lines of definition. A few of the phrases that stand out are "features that make up and distinguish the individual; the aggregate of distinctive qualities; marked by conspicuous traits; moral excellence and firmness." My sense is that this is a word that has a gut-level meaning for most of us. We feel that we know character when we see it. It's an intuitive yet educated feel that is surprisingly right, much of the time.

What seems clear is that "good character" represents the sum of many separate actions and decisions that we have made. It takes a while to earn the "good character" image. It's an assessment that is not generally conferred without substantial thought and evidence that has accrued over time. It's different from likeability or having a nice personality. It's more substantive and enduring and is most notable when it has withstood severe test.

What also seems clear is that while character is hard earned, it also can be quickly lost. One specific action or decision or mistake can slice the heart out of a good character rating. This is not necessarily illogical. We sometimes face a litmus test—tests that are not administered in the real world very often. So our response, when faced with a difficult situation, becomes very revealing, and it is usually lastingly informative.

This chapter will focus on the issue of character and look at how our decisions ultimately establish our "character" image, whether individual character or our nation's character. The premise is that character carries immense importance, that it represents a "soft" power that is critically important to our effectiveness and well-being. The antithesis is when decisions are perceived by others as based on arrogance and self-centeredness and thus become very detrimental to our ability to deal with the challenges we face.

Over time, the character of a nation, particularly a democratic nation, becomes the summation of the character of the individuals. In a sense, we are back to the question of whether leaders lead, or whether leaders follow. Ultimately, leaders follow, because a leader simply cannot lead without followers. The reality then, is that the character of individuals and our national character are inextricably linked. Our individual decisions not only establish our personal character, but eventually, the collective character of individuals is the character of the nation.

This may seem very obvious, but it is a linkage that we violate routinely. For example, we personally may find it very difficult to lie; we are afraid that if we are found out, it will damage our character. Therefore, most of us set a pretty high standard for ourselves in terms of wanting to be viewed as a trustworthy, honest person. On our personal hierarchy of character qualities, honesty is placed very high on the list. Yet we do not hold our elected officials to this standard. We are quite willing to "look the other way" on the honesty issue if we find some other qualities in the candidate that confirm a prejudice or ideology that we hold. Because the issue does not affect us in a personal sense, we are willing to make a decision on someone else that we would not make for ourselves. It should be no surprise, then, that we end up with leaders who have a lower honesty character than that which we find appropriate for ourselves. We have, collectively, made a decision that honesty is not of major importance.

We often form a comparable opinion on the character of an entire nation—is it a nation that can be trusted or not trusted? Is it a nation that respects human rights, or is it a nation that disregards the well-being of the individual? Is it a nation that has concern for all of mankind, or is it a nation that is self-centered, with little regard for the rest of the world? We form this judgment of character, quite logically, on the overall conduct of the nation.

The character image that we hold becomes a nation-versus-nation comparison—no faces are needed. It's as if one nation on the map is speaking to another nation on the map, without real people being involved. It could be argued that if real life people are not involved, the personal character of these people is not particularly relevant. But that is not the whole story.

Regardless of the depth of dialogue or magnitude of a negotiation—whether a neighbor-to-neighbor discussion deciding the best variety of tree to plant between the two houses, a major business collaboration between two companies, or a discussion between two nations to develop a mutually advantageous trade policy—there will always be individuals who look into the eyes of other individuals. How the character of a participant is perceived by another participant is critical. And ultimately, it is the character of these individual people, judged as reflecting the will of the masses, that establishes the character of the entire nation. There is no way that a country can be perceived as having "moral excellence" and good character when the country's representatives and leaders are not perceived as having good character. When a nation's leaders are judged as deficient in character, but the populace still claims that the character of "we, the people" is honorable, it becomes a hypocrisy and inconsistency in the eyes of other nations. This may be difficult for us to acknowledge, but the reality is irrefutable: the character of the nation is inseparable from the character of the people.

I have chosen three topics upon which to center discussion of the importance and the multi-faceted nature of character: poverty, human rights, and honesty. There is an unlimited number of topics on which the relevance of the character issue could be discussed, but I hope that these three will suffice to illustrate why character needs to be a central consideration when making our most important and far-reaching decisions.

Poverty

Roughly one-sixth of the world's inhabitants—nearly one billion people—live in what is considered to be extreme, or "absolute," poverty, which is defined as those having an average income of less than one dollar per day. These people seldom know where their next day's meal will come from. They are chronically hungry, usually do not have safe water to drink, and do not have access to basic health care. Shelter is usually dilapidated shacks, at best, with no basic facilities, such as toilets. Education of the children is unaffordable.

The extreme level of poverty in which these one billion people live should not be confused with being poor. Close to half of the world's people are considered poor, but they generally have sufficient food and live under conditions where their basic needs are met. Nor does it include those who live in what sociologists term "moderate poverty," which is defined as living on one to two dollars per day and having the bare minimum of resources to meet basic needs.

These *extreme* poverty conditions result in eight million deaths per year, over 20,000 per day. Using an airplane analogy, this would be comparable to fifty plane-loads of people dying needlessly per day. About three-fourths of these deaths are kids— six million per year, or 15,000 per day ... or thirty-five large airliners filled *only with kids*, crashing each day. Most do not die of starvation; instead, they die from systemic weakness, including diseases contracted from others, or, often, from contaminated water, diarrhea, lack of basic medical care, and other factors that result from lack of food, sanitary living conditions, and the most basic of health care services.

The world's countries, at large, have addressed the inhumanity of this condition with some success. It's estimated that in the early 1980s, the number of people living in extreme poverty was approximately 1.5 billion, compared to 1.1 billion some fifteen years later. This indicates that it is possible, with committed effort, to reduce significantly the extreme poverty numbers. With this as incentive, the United Nations initiated the UN Millennium Project, with the goal of halving the numbers in extreme poverty by 2015. Most experts agree that this is an achievable goal, *given* sufficient support and commitment from the world's nations and from concerned people.

These "concerned" people are those that Webster's defined as having "character." These are the people who have a broader sense of perception and the strength of empathy—*the capacity to see the interchangeability of circumstances.* People of character are willing to feel the hurt of others, to look it in the eye and to do something about it. Character is a quality that demands we set aside self-absorption and self-centeredness and feel the world from the position of another's situation. We all have this capacity, as we all know what hunger, dignity, love and warmth, companionship and security, hope, and health mean—but not all of us have the courage to engage this capacity. Instead, we choose denial and blindness to a situation that enslaves one-sixth of mankind.

Most of these people, many of them kids, are in this extreme poverty condition because of luck of the draw. They live in poverty because of the country or region or circumstances into which they were born. They are there because of drought, civil war, corrupt governments, and the fate of being caught in a vicious cycle of deprivation that makes escape impossible. Jeffrey Sachs has made the observation, "When a society is economically dominant, it is easy for its members to assume that their dominance reflects a deeper superiority, rather than an accident of timing and geography." Nothing in this assumption could be farther from the truth. Poverty-stricken people have innate capabilities and desires that are comparable to those living a prosperous life. But they do not have the means to escape the tenacious cycle of poverty.

Sachs, a Columbia University economist who headed the United Nations Millennium Project from 2002 to 2006, has identified five specific elements that, when adapted to the circumstances, produce proven, sustainable results: (1) increased agriculture production, (2) establishing basic health care services, (3) education and vocational training, (4) electrical power availability, and (5) clean water and sanitation facilities.

It is common perception, however, that efforts to break the cycle of poverty have been ineffective; that large sums of money have been spent but have never produced sustainable results. Paul O'Neill, former Secretary of the Treasury, is reported to have said, "We've spent trillions of dollars on these problems, and we have damn near nothing to show for it." It is important to note that O'Neill was not against efforts to reduce poverty but was saying that the job had to be done more effectively. The reality is also that we have not been spending very much money on poverty alleviation programs, and we have never developed or supported programs that have the resources and management competency commensurate with the task. The belief that we have been making such an effort is a cruel misperception.

International dialogue among the developed nations, going back more than three decades, set a funding goal of 0.7 percent of GDP of each nation for foreign development and poverty reduction aid, a goal that then-president George W. Bush confirmed the United States was committed to on several occasions. To date, our nation has not come close to delivering on this commitment. Our giving is less than 0.2 percent, near the bottom of the contribution rate of major developed countries. It is interesting to note that our foreign aid rate was 2 percent of GDP after World War II, a rate that forces a comparison of our capacity to our will.

Governmental Assistance to Poor Countries
Percentage of GDP

Norway	0.95
Sweden	0.93
Netherlands	0.81
Ireland	0.54
France	0.39
United Kingdom	0.36
United States	0.16
United Nations Target	0.70

Much of our thinking about the role that the United States plays in poverty alleviation is based on wishful thinking, myth, and self-delusion. We do not deal with the poverty issue in an *informed, mature,* and *responsible* manner. Following is an example for each of these hard-nosed words:

With respect to being *informed*, the degree to which we misjudge our contribution level is astounding. In one study, the respondents indicated that they thought about 15 percent of the federal budget was spent on foreign aid. In reality, it is about 1 percent of the federal budget (not to be confused with the percent of the nation's GDP noted above). Our perceived giving level is a myth that has persisted for ages.

The degree to which we often refuse to take a *mature* attitude to the issue of poverty can be illustrated by sharing a personal story. I was a member of the world hunger committee at our church. We were planning for the annual World Hunger Sunday service, and the idea of handing out a small "hunger" bank for home use had taken root in the committee. The approach suggested was to have each child assemble a small, cardboard bank for home use. I liked the idea, in general, but I was a bit concerned that the use of small, cardboard banks made the focus of world hunger a children's project, not a serious adult issue. I did a bit of research and found that we could obtain a low-cost but very nice-looking ceramic bank that much more clearly said "adult." I proposed that we make World Hunger Sunday an adult-focused event and that we do this by distributing "adult" banks in church, rather than cardboard banks for the kids. I lost the argument. We were not prepared to make the issue of feeding the hungry a mature, adult issue in our church.

The degree to which we do not deal with poverty in a *responsible* way can be illustrated with another church story, a story that has been repeated, I suspect, many times in different churches. It's the story of a church youth group with several adult chaperones, choosing a poverty-stricken area in Mexico and taking a bus to the site, where they spent ten days. Each morning they would have an hour-long prayer session, then help to build a school for three or four hours (even though there was a 20 percent local unemployment rate), visit the area's orphanage, join in a traditional "poor people's dinner," and close the evening with a sing-along. And, at the end of ten days, they boarded the bus for the trip back home.

Let me be clear that I do not object to this type of venture. It's a great experience for the kids and increases their awareness of the living conditions of millions of people. What I find disturbing is that it is a fraudulent exercise in terms of our thinking that we have "helped the poor." Dealing with poverty in a substantive, meaningful way is a difficult assignment that demands serious, sustained, committed effort. As Bill Gates has said, "These are intense, complex issues." To treat poverty as a summer trip, a fun adventure, is either disrespectful of the issue or ignorant of what poverty alleviation really means. The seriousness of poverty demands that we get real.

It is often argued that our governmental contribution rate is misleading; that our contribution is much greater when we include our exceptional level of private funding. To counter the "stingy" accusation, a former Bush administration spokesperson once reported that for each dollar of governmental aid, there are two additional dollars provided privately ($16 billion from our government, and $35 billion from private American aid). Scrutiny of these numbers indicate, however, that the $35 billion included such things as the $18 billion that immigrant workers were sending back to family members living outside the United States, as well as the value of scholarships given to foreign students to attend U.S. colleges. These were bogus, deceptive numbers, yet they are numbers that those who refuse to deal with reality prefer to believe. Organization of Economic Cooperation and Development (OECD) numbers for the year 2003 estimated that our governmental rate was 0.15 percent, and that the private rate added 0.06 percent, for a total of 0.21 percent, or that private giving is less than one-half the governmental-derived sources.

Alleviating poverty is a complex, difficult, multi-faceted issue. Many efforts with good intention have not been successful, but the substantive, competently managed programs have produced favorable results. Poverty is not solved by handouts or charity or by creating dependency. Real poverty alleviation is in education, business development, infrastructure development, access to credit, family planning and health care, and hard-nosed governance. It is beyond the scope of this book to discuss, in depth, the elements or management systems that make a program effective—or for that matter, the level of financial commitment appropriate for our country.

I hope I have made the point that poverty is a daunting struggle for existence for almost one-sixth of the world's people—people who have the same feelings and needs as you and I. And the corollary is that if we have character, individually and as a nation, we will face this reality, look it in the eye, and answer the question of how are we responding and what are we doing in a meaningful way. I do not believe, for one second, that we can claim to have "character"—the moral excellence and firmness that Webster's describes—if we do not have the strength and courage to address the reality that extreme poverty has enslaved a billion of our fellow Earth inhabitants. Not only will we feel this lack of character in ourselves, but others will also sense it. It will be sensed individually. And it will be sensed as a nation.

Human Rights: Torture and Detention

It is interesting the way in which we sense character. Many years of experiences (remember, I am seventy-one!) have convinced me that most of us will eventually come to the same conclusion regarding our assessment of someone's "character." Where we differ, substantially, is on how long it takes us to get to that conclusion. Two people that I know well are much faster at forming an accurate character assessment than I am (I eventually get to the same conclusion, but it takes me much longer).

One of these people is Diane, my wife. Many times, if we are meeting a new person, either for a business reason or socially, I will ask her what her feeling is about the person. I have learned over the years that she will, more often than not, be right in her assessment. I wish I had that innate skill. It would have helped me immeasurably during my work life.

It would also have helped a whole lot in my selecting a financial advisory team after we retired! A member of the investment advisory team was substantially less than competent … and more than a tad short on character. We absorbed a substantial financial loss before I fired him. We decided to ask our estate advisor (also one of the team) to also be our investment advisor. He had met Diane's character test, and we have had an excellent, trusting relationship for many years; he is a man I have come to respect and admire. After all these years, you would think I would have learned to listen to her character assessments sooner!

The other person is my old car-pool colleague and long-time friend, Jay Morgan. He is really quick and almost always right when judging character. To cite one example, I remember the case of a new managerial level hire at Pillsbury—I'll call him Mr. X. A couple of months went by, and Jay and I both got to know the guy, mostly on a casual, over-lunch basis. On the way home from work one day, I commented that Mr. X seemed to be an upright and smart individual and seemed to have what it takes to be a good manager. After an extended pause and with a slight frown on his face, Jay replied that he had come to a much different conclusion: that the guy was mostly fluff—he lacked substance. As fate and corporate life would have it, I found myself later reporting to Mr. X. As usual, Jay was dead-on; the guy proved to be all fluff and even of questionable honesty. Fortunately, Mr. X decided to leave the company, and I moved on to report to Katy Ghiasi. Katy, an immigrant from Iran, is a gifted manager, intelligent, and tough, yet very caring; a person with character and substance. Jay and Katy are both very good friends to this day, both with character and abilities that I truly admire, and both have the courage to look reality in the eye. These are the kind of people who exemplify true character. They are the kind of people our subconscious moves to when the word "character" is used.

When I think of character on a broader basis—our nation's character, for example—I invariably think of my teenage years. I remember very well how I felt about our country. Perhaps some of these feelings were misplaced, but I saw our nation as a nation of people who were truly exceptional in what they stood for— morality, commitment to doing good, a sense of equality for all humankind, integrity. I remember vividly how I felt when the band took to the football field and played the national anthem at our high school football games. I was extremely proud and grateful for being a part of a nation "marked by conspicuous traits"; "with moral excellence and firmness"; having the courage, the substance, the toughness to act with honor, regardless the circumstances.

And I knew I was not alone in that feeling. That was a sense of national character that had been earned. It was based on the sacrifices all made during the WW II era. All of our families seemed to have contributed to this cause, and I remember that we were poor because of it. My mother made dresses for herself and my sister from patterned feed sacks. I remember that I got two shirts each fall, different colors but with the same pattern, and those were my shirts for the school year. We farmed with out-of-date, obsolete equipment because no modern farm equipment was made. I remember how happy we were when we were finally able, after the war, to get a new tractor. I remember when I was finally able to get a new bike from Sears. (They didn't have the right handlebars for it but were able to ship it with a mismatched set of "girl's" handlebars.) After a while, Grandpa Orlin was even able to get a new Hudson car, although it arrived without front and rear bumpers. To make the car available to the customer, Hudson bolted on 2 x 6 boards that served as temporary bumpers and shipped replacements when enough steel became available.

Perhaps I'm rambling, but this is what character means to me, both from a personal, individual viewpoint and from a national point of view. It's about our substance of being. It's about truth, and sacrifice, and respect, and all those hard-to-describe things.

But yet, these are all the things that we feel and know to be terribly important.

As I write this, it is February 4, 2009. We have just elected a new president and are still trying to count the votes to see who the elected senator from Minnesota will be. We clearly have an abundance of problems—a major financial recession and banking system meltdown; the question of how to disengage from Iraq; the global warming issue that we can't seem to address; the sense that we are losing our capability to compete effectively in the emerging global economic order; a feeling that our long-prized capitalistic philosophy might not be able to cope with the looming deficits; the feeling that we will be passing on a future for our children that is not nearly as promising as what we were given.

But these concerns are not what worry me most. A far bigger, far more fundamental concern is the feeling that we have lost our character.

This is not just my concern; many others have expressed the same concern. It has been sensed in many ways. A common refrain is "We seem to have lost direction," or "We seem to be going down the wrong road," or "We seem to have lost our way." The challenges that we face are huge. But I am certain they are manageable if we have confidence and character—character to look at reality, to be honest and thoughtful, and the character to act. Without renewing our character, it is difficult to be optimistic.

What has happened? What could possibly have transpired during the past several decades that raises the question of whether we have sufficient character to face our challenges, to endure? Have we simply gotten fat and lazy? Have we really changed? Is it a one-way path?

My belief is that there is not one specific reason or societal factor that we can point to that has caused this loss of character. We can, however, identify specific examples where loss of character is apparent, and by looking at these examples, we may be able to identify the qualities in each of us that manifest themselves in the totality of "character." A few of these examples are big enough that they may, in fact, constitute a significant portion of the cause of our sense that "we seem to be going down the wrong road." They may be so significant, in terms of being a cause of this malaise, that we need to deal with them before we have any hope of changing course. One cause could be our knowing that we are using our resources in a way that is not sustainable in the longer term; another cause could be our knowing that we are not dealing with the question of global warming and its possible impact on our children; another cause could be that the concept of pre-emptive war, as advocated by the Bush 43 administration, lacks a moral foundation. The question before us is whether the decisions we have been making on such issues reflect "character" of moral excellence and firmness.

To *illustrate,* I'd like to look at an issue that, in my judgment, represents a distinctive or conspicuous quality of a nation that does not have "character." This is the subject of torture and detention, something that I would never have imagined would become an issue for our nation when I was listening to the band play the national anthem at the Lake City football game as a teenager. But our nation somehow rationalized the use of torture, and it is now a mark of our character, individually and most certainly nation-wise, and we have to deal with it.

Torture is not a new subject to our nation, or for that matter, to the other nations of the world. All civilized nations have dealt with it in a thoughtful, deliberate way. Torture was already prohibited by George Washington during the Revolutionary War. So the guidelines are clear.

There are a number of agreements and statutes that define acceptable conduct when faced with the question of permissible

127

treatment of prisoners and detainees. The most well known is the Geneva Convention, which has been followed for more than a half century by more than 190 countries, including the United States. The language of the Geneva Convention regarding torture is very clear in its intent—it prohibits "violence to life and person, in particular murder of all kinds, mutilation, cruel treatment and torture," and it prohibits "outrages upon personal dignity, in particular, humiliating and degrading treatment." In all past situations, waterboarding (or simulated drowning) has been clearly judged as torture that is prohibited by this Convention.

It is perhaps instructive to note the degree to which we believed this important and the depth of our conviction. In 1994 the United States ratified the international Convention Against Torture, and in our testimony to the other countries in the United Nations, we said:

> "Torture is ... categorically denounce[d] as a matter of policy and as a tool of state authority. ... Every act constituting torture under the Convention constitutes a criminal offense under the law of the United States. No official of the government, federal, state or local, civilian or military, is authorized to commit or to instruct anyone else to commit torture. Nor may any official condone or tolerate torture in any form. No exceptional circumstances may be invoked as a justification of torture. U.S. law contains no provision permitting otherwise prohibited acts of torture or degrading treatment or punishment to be employed on grounds of exigent circumstances (for example, during a 'state of public emergency') or on orders from a superior officer."

Article 2 of this Convention, ratified by our government in 1994, states that "No exceptional circumstances whatsoever" can be used to justify torture, and it makes specific note that this prohibition of torture includes "terrorist acts," "threat of war," and "public emergency," along with the more usual situations, such as declared war.

To emphasize our commitment even further, Congress passed the War Crimes Act of 1996, making it a felony to violate the Geneva Convention, and specifically prescribing the death penalty to anyone who violates the Convention, if that treatment results in the death of a prisoner or detainee.

Pretty clear. Pretty firm. The farm boys in the bar in the back of the Oak Center General Store—boys who had no college degrees but were professors of common sense—would have said, "Torture is immoral—shouldn't take a law to say so." This is who we are; our American personification of "moral excellence and firmness." These are easy-to-understand terms that we have always believed to be a good definition of character. And we always had the sense that other nations would admire this firmness. The Oak Center boys were proud of their nation's character.

Shifting gears, but only slightly, *habeas corpus* has been described as one of the civilized world's most sacred and ancient liberties. It can be traced back in common-law countries, such as Britain and the United States, as being a cornerstone of human rights since the medieval age. The essence of habeas corpus is that it recognizes a human being's fundamental right against unlimited imprisonment without a charge being made; it recognizes that anyone being brought to trial has the fundamental right to see and challenge evidence used to support the alleged charge; and that evidence obtained by torture is held to be unreliable and therefore, invalid.

There are few things as fundamental to our sense of justice and to our sense of character as the principle of habeas corpus. When my mother was alive and I took weekly trips to Lake City to see her in the nursing home, I drove past the Fort Snelling Veterans Cemetery. Invariably, I thought of all those who had given their lives to pass on to us the ideals that made this nation exceptional, including the ideal of habeas corpus. Habeas corpus has been a sacred concept of human justice since our founders declared that King George III was denying this right to the colonies. They said so in the Declaration of Independence, and they said they were willing to die for this right. Retired Admiral John D. Hutson said it well: if we deny this right to others we "will have changed the DNA of what it means to be an American."

But that is what we have been doing.

In fact, our Congress, under pressure from the Bush 43 administration, passed what has been called the Military Commissions Act, which says "unlawful enemy combatants"—an accusation and designation that is very arbitrary—do not have right to habeas corpus. It gives the president absolute power to decide who is an enemy of the country and to imprison those people indefinitely *without* charging them with a crime. Legal scholars are in disagreement on whether this affects the right of habeas corpus for the citizens of the United States. In one place, the Act refers to "alien unlawful enemy combatants"; in another, it simply refers to "unlawful enemy combatants" *without* any explicit exclusion of U.S. citizens. A writer from *The Economist* calls it the "stuff of nightmares." A *New York Times* writer wrote that there are "too many moments these days when we cannot recognize our country." As the subject of torture has unfolded, it is now apparent that the main reason for the former administration's pressure to pass this bill was an effort to establish a basis for arguing retroactive immunity, should they be charged with war crimes.

I do not intend to cover the Guantanamo Bay and Abu Ghraib issue in detail here. Many others have done it better and more authoritatively than it would be possible for me to do. It will suffice to simply point out that prisoners have been held for years without charge at Guantanamo Bay, some of them as young as thirteen years old. Some were incarcerated at Guantanamo through an Afghan "bounty-seekers" system, whereby one Afghan could turn in another Afghan, hardly a process that speaks to justice in a tribal country. Some come from countries like Bosnia and Zambia. There was no tribunal system in place to make judgment on whether these people were, in fact, terrorists and whether or not they were dangerous. Some have been sent to other countries—extraordinary rendition—for interrogation by countries known to use brutal torture techniques. Many are denied the right to see the evidence of the charge against them. Many have never been formally charged.

The Bush administration made several legal arguments, including an attempt to redefine torture and to argue that the Geneva Convention does not cover non-state enemies. The argument has also been made that terrorists represent a different form of threat that demands, for security reasons, that we employ interrogation techniques not previously considered.

This later argument has been refuted by essentially all experts in interrogation and by virtually all military leaders. Not to make light of a serious issue, but it is of interest to note Mark Twain's comment: "To make them confess—what? Truth? Or lies? For under unendurable pain a man confesses anything that is required of him, true or false, and his evidence is worthless." Donald Gregg, who was national security advisor to Vice President George H. W. Bush from 1982 to 1988 and worked for the CIA for thirty years, wrote about a South Vietnamese colonel who routinely tortured prisoners, "producing a flood of information, much of it totally false," and that "the key to successful interrogations is for the interrogator—even as he controls the situation—is to recognize a prisoner's humanity, to understand his culture, background, and language. Torture makes this impossible."

Aside from failing to listen to the advice of all the experts, one would hope that the Bush 43 administration had some recognition of the likelihood of creating more terrorists because of the inflammatory images conveyed via the global media (recall the photographs from Abu Ghraib and Guantanamo run, day in and day out, on the Middle East TV channels). One would hope that someone in the administration would have done the quick calculation that if there are 1.5 billion Muslims and that if these pictures motivate only one out of every 10,000 to cross the line from moderate to extremists, that will produce a flow of another 150,000 extremists. Former Secretary of State Zbigniew Brezezinski has written: "The undiscriminating American rhetoric and actions increase the likelihood that the moderates will eventually unite with the jihadists in outraged anger and unite the world of Islam in a head-on collision with America." The boys at the end of the bar in the Oak Center store had enough common sense to know that you are going to lose a lot more by beating on a hornet's nest than you are by treating it with some respect— irrespective of whether or not you like hornets.

For the realist, how to treat terrorist suspects is a rather straightforward issue. First, use the justice system in place for dealing with the terrorist suspects. Demand that it be rigorous but honest. It's a system that has worked reasonably well for a long time. It's a respected process. Second, don't encourage and permit activities that play into your enemy's hand, like mistreating or torturing prisoners, treatment that has good odds of being documented by someone with a digital camera. And third, the most critical, remember the importance of character. One can only speculate on the psychological motivation that caused the United

States to engage in torture, a decision that political journalist Joe Klein described as being a "callous, despicable act."

The torture of detainees has created a huge mess. And because we are members of a generation that has made a mockery of the American standards of justice and due process, the character of each of us, individually, has been tarnished.

As of this writing, President Obama has announced that a special commission will be formed to determine how to deal with the closing of Guantanamo, and he has announced that the closure of the prison will occur within a year's time. Two of the closure issues will be difficult to manage: how to identify the dangerous from those who are not a danger but were simply caught in the web of being in the wrong place at the wrong time; and how to bring the truly dangerous to justice. The illegal and abusive policies of the Bush 43 administration have made it difficult to have evidence accepted by a legitimate court of law, and hence, it will be difficult to bring the truly dangerous to justice.

These are big, difficult problems, but by using common sense, we will find a way to deal with the prisoner question. And we will, I believe, repeal that part of the Military Commissions Act of 2006 that denies habeas corpus to arbitrarily selected people. Legal experts have suggested a fairly straightforward process: first, begin a transparent review of detainees; second, repatriate those who have no charge against them; and third, try the remainder in Federal Courts where cases involving national secrets have been dealt with in the past.

In my judgment, however, there is a larger issue that will have a far more significant impact on our future and our sense of who we are—our character—both in terms of how we see ourselves and how we are viewed by the rest of the world. How we move forward will determine if we can reclaim the image of being a country with character.

It is clear that the Bush 43 administration committed war crimes, and unless this is acknowledged and dealt with in some definitive way, the character of the nation will remain tarnished. This will be difficult, given the political ramifications, and it would be a severe distraction from the serious issues, including the current financial recession, that now confront the country and which need our undivided attention and bipartisan cooperation. A route that has been suggested is for the president to issue pardons to those who have never been charged with a crime, accompanied by an acknowledgment to the world that we have made a grievous error of character, that remedial action is being taken, and that for the good of all, we need to move on.

Character has many dimensions and is measured in many ways. The 9/11 tragedy presented us with a defining test, and we failed. We had an opportunity to demonstrate to the world and this generation of Americans that we can stand tall, even when facing difficult issues and unchartered waters. But we allowed cowards to determine our posture, demonstrating to the world that when this nation gets a bloody nose, the notion of justice and due process gets thrown out the window. Where were American citizens while it was happening? How did we allow fear to trump courage? Can we get off the canvas, brush ourselves off, and tell the world that we made a mistake and that we will not allow it to happen again?

Honesty

If you conducted a poll that asked people for one word that best defines character, the overwhelming response would be "honesty." Webster's does not need many lines of text to define honesty: "A fairness and straightforwardness of conduct; adherence to the facts; a refusal to lie, steal, or deceive in any way." One of the synonyms given is "integrity." Based on Webster's, honesty is not a hard dimension of character to understand.

I can still remember the first time I got caught lying. A bit of context: I was born in Zumbro Falls, Minnesota, on May 5, 1938, in the second house from the highway to Rochester on Main Street (the only real street in Zumbro Falls). This was the house of my mom's parents, Fred and Maggie. Times were tough, with the country still coming out of the Great Depression. My mom and dad eloped to Iowa to get married because she was pregnant with me. Since they had no money and no place to live, they moved in with Fred and Maggie. My dad worked at the local feed elevator, tended bar, and worked on the public works highway project between Oak Center and Zumbro Falls. My parents were dirt-poor and not able to afford a hospital delivery, so I was born in their bedroom.

Fred and Maggie rented the lower level of the house from the owner, a dirty, disheveled old man, Barney Clark, who lived on the upper level. A couple years later, my grandparents were able to buy the small, one-level house next door, and this was their home for many years and the place of many of my childhood memories. Barney Clark's house had a flower garden, surrounding a small goldfish pond beside the driveway. One summer evening—I was maybe five or six years old—I stole one of the goldfish, took it "uptown" and showed it to the grocery store lady. I told her I had "found" it. Of course, before I got back to my grandma's house, the grocery store lady had called my mom. My defense was to continue the lie about finding the goldfish—too young, I guess, to comprehend the improbability of the tale I had made up. The real reason I stole the fish was because I didn't like Mr. Clark.

The point of this story is that lying is more than just not telling the truth. There is almost always a deeper story behind the lie. Often, there is a psychological element that plays an important part in our decision to lie. We lie not to get ourselves out of a jam but to build an image or to justify an ideology, or in my case, simply to "get even."

One Wikipedia contributor describes some of this very well: "Honesty is the human quality of communicating and acting truthfully related to truth as a value. This includes listening ... means stating the facts and views as best one truly believes them to be. It includes both honesty to others, and to oneself and about one's own motives and inner reality ... acknowledges his mistakes."

Another Wikipedia contributor describes it this way:

> "There is a widespread confusion about honesty ... it's at the moment when one willfully disregards information in order to benefit (such as to justify their action or beliefs) that one shows whether [he is] interested in the truth or whether [he has] a lack of respect for the truth, which is dishonesty, regardless of whether [he mislabels] it stubbornness or conviction ... furthermore, the more dishonest someone is, the less likely [he is] to understand honesty and to characterize [his] behavior as wrong. The understanding that honesty requires an unbiased approach to the truth and to evidence ... collides with ideologies of all types. This would explain why honesty ... has failed to become a cultural norm. Ideologies and idealism inherently exaggerate and suppress evidence in order to support their perspectives."

Another Wikipedia contributor speaks to another dimension of honesty—emotional honesty: "Emotional honesty means expressing your true feelings. To be able to be emotionally honest, we must first be emotionally aware ... it takes emotional awareness, self-confidence, even courage to be emotionally honest." The importance of this point is that there is a very real difference between factual honesty and emotional honesty—that sense that the person has shared not only the facts as he best understands them, but that he also has shared his innermost feelings in as honest a way as possible.

Honesty is a two-sided issue. On one side, there is a benefit—a positive result, a good outcome, an improved situation—from our telling the truth. Few problems will be solved if we do not address them in a truthful way and look at the reality of the issue. After a full career of working in corporate America and managing many people, I have but a small number of learnings that I put in the "extremely important" and "always right to do" basket. One of these is the value of being completely honest with people. Subordinates will almost invariably accept what you tell them, usually with sincere appreciation, if it is done in total honesty and with constructive intent. I have been absolutely amazed at how well subordinates accepted my thoughts on corrective action when delivered with honesty. I have been equally amazed at how my superiors accepted bad news when I explained the issue with complete honesty, including not only the hard facts but also acknowledging that I had made a wrong decision, based on gut feel. Honesty is simply something that brings out the very best in people; it is the strongest trust-building action there is.

On the other side—the downside—is the harm that can be caused by dishonesty. It's the side that we see so often and which is so regrettable, simply because it doesn't need to be. Thomas Paine, in *The Age of Reason*, said it well: "It is impossible to calculate the moral mischief, if I may so express it, that lying has produced in society. When a man has so far corrupted and prostituted the chastity of his mind as to subscribe his professional belief to things he does not believe he has prepared himself for the commission of every other crime." This phrase hit home when

I thought about the cigarette company CEOs and the "mischief" their dishonesty caused.

Matt Groening's fictional character Homer Simpson makes a germane point, one we too often forget. It is a simple but far-reaching and powerful point because it speaks to those of us who accept (who do not challenge or confront) those who are not telling the truth: "It takes two to lie. One to lie and one to listen."

In that respect, an argument can be made, much like the accomplice to a crime, that we are also guilty of dishonesty when we permit dishonesty to go unchallenged. We often, and with a fair degree of rationality, respond by saying this is primarily the responsibility of two forces in our society, Congress (or the "government") and the media, and that individual challenge is simply ineffective, usually a waste of our limited time, and without a sense of what specific steps we should take to challenge this perceived dishonesty. So we roll over. Yet in doing so, we allow things to happen that should never, ever happen.

We now know, with certainty, that the Bush 43 administration gained support for the Iraq war based on repeated dissemination of information that, at best, "willfully disregarded information in order to benefit" (such as to justify their actions or beliefs), or even worse, that they knew were bald-face lies. Many authors, a number of them from the inner circle of the Bush administration, have described the details of this deception far better and far more authoritatively than I can. So I will recap the "mischief" that this dishonesty has dealt:

The result has been over 4,000 of our soldiers killed, and 30,000 seriously injured. Although a deliberate decision was made not to count the Iraqi casualties, estimates are between 100,000 and 650,000 men, women, and children killed or severely injured. Over two million Iraqis have been forced out of their homes. The dollar cost that we have incurred is estimated between $1.2 to over

$3 trillion. After six years (at the time of this writing), the future of the country remains questionable and where our departure will be on the basis of declaring the condition of the country "good enough." This means our actions will have produced either a Shiite Islamic theocracy or, at best, a semi-democratic centralized government, with guarded hope that civil conflict between the ethnic fractions does not erupt when we leave.

The story of how we got there is numbing when we consider the "willfully disregarded information" that the Bush administration used to gain support for this "mischief," as well as the evidence that has come forth that shows that the desire for war with Iraq began the day Bush 43 entered the White House. The topic list that describes this dishonesty is long: the Downing Street memo; uranium from Africa; aluminum tubes for fissile material concentration; mobile biological laboratories; Greenspan's statement that oil was the reason; the neo-cons "America Dominance" working papers; shock and awe message; curve-ball intelligence; anthrax stockpile; the Jessica Lynch story; the projected war cost; the mushroom cloud over a U.S. city; "fight them there or fight them here" fear; the UN weapon inspector Hans Blix refutes; the untruthful link between 9/11 terrorists and Saddam.

This is not the nation that created feelings of pride when the band played the national anthem at the high school football game. This is not the nation for which those under the white crosses at Fort Snelling Cemetery died. We can, perhaps, simply bow our heads and decide to move on. But the stain is not easily removed; it's deeply embedded in our sense of inner self. We are not the nation of character that we thought we were. And because it "takes two to lie. One to lie and one to listen," there is also a loss of character in all of us, individually, who allowed this "mischief" to happen.

Character

Character—so precious. Something we want to take to the grave. Something we should think about whenever we make decisions, particularly those of far-reaching importance. You have the capacity to make "character" part of who you are; to ensure that when people think of you, their minds immediately tell them, "This is a person with character, and I admire and trust this person." We can't control the character of the nation, but we can control our individual character, and in that sense, we have an obligation to do whatever we can to give our nation character. It will take courage ... but most things of importance and value do.

CHAPTER 9

ABORTION: THE COST OF DISTRACTION

"A conclusion is simply the place where someone gets tired of thinking."

—Arthur Block

"Man often applaud an illusion and hiss the real thing."

—Aesop

Few nationally debated issues have been as polarizing as abortion. It has become the symbolic, defining issue for many of the Far Right. This group sees the issue as the defining test of morality and a measurement of the depth of their religious faith. In their view, the abortion issue trumps all other issues, and "pro-life" is the first door that a candidate must pass through for any further consideration of having sufficient stature to hold office. Strong feelings.

Diane was born and raised in South Dakota, and her mom and dad were solid stock of that state. South Dakota was their home, and to them, the people of South Dakota represent the finest example of what being a good citizen means. They have a true love for their state, and it shows—not in a boastful way but in a way that shows loyalty and a visible thankfulness for the land they call home. Good folks. And I'm happy that our kids have South Dakota genes in them.

It surprised me, however, when a few years ago the abortion issue rose to a main-street, high-decibel debate. The best I could tell, half of the state wanted a near-absolute ban on abortion; the other half saw the issue from the other side of the fence. And in '06, the abortion issue ended up on the ballot. It surprised me, because I saw South Dakota, although conservative by nature, as having a strong realistic bent, perhaps not as progressive as some but with the common sense and pragmatism of people who have dealt all their lives with the realities that farms and small towns and prairie life demand. So I was surprised to find that these terms seemed to describe only a bit over one-half of the people—at least when it came to the abortion issue.

As the election loomed, I wrote the following good-neighbor letter:

March 13, 2006

Governor Rounds
Office of the Governor
500 E. Capital Ave.
Pierre, SD 57501

Dear Governor Rounds:

Being a neighbor, I have watched your state in its actions regarding abortion prohibition. It is a sad, sad affair and certainly does not speak well of the intellect of the people of the state of South Dakota.

I very much share the position that we should do what we can to eliminate or certainly reduce abortion as much as possible. I too believe that a moral, caring society should not kill its unborn.

Any true student of the abortion subject knows how this can be accomplished, and that it can be accomplished. It is a straightforward answer that has been proven around the world. And anyone who is willing to spend a small amount of time on the subject can learn the facts.

The only effective way to reduce abortions is to provide women who do not want to become pregnant with the knowledge and means for preventing pregnancy. Taking away individual rights is not the answer. And creating unwanted kids in not the answer. I know of no woman who has deliberately chosen the path of becoming pregnant with the plan to end it with an abortion.

It is not my intent in this note to discuss the issue in depth, but I will quickly point out that the countries that have made abortion illegal have the highest rate of abortion, and the countries that have the lowest rate of abortion are those where abortion is legal—but almost never used. **Those countries, of course, are the countries that deal with sexuality, family planning, and birth control in an open manner, with access to the information by all the people in their society.**

What your state is doing is taking away the focus on what would be truly effective in reducing abortions. It may be driven by some sort of a self-righteous show by your constituents, or it may be driven by stupidity. In either case, it is a tragic move because we will now lose more time in developing the way to be truly effective in reducing abortions. You and your legislators should be ashamed of this political stunt—if that is what it is—or of your lack of knowledge of the subject—if that is what it is.

Sincerely,
Gerald Rabe

CC: Representative Ramstad, Senator Dayton, Senator Coleman

I never heard back from Governor Rounds. In 2006, the bill, declaring a near-total ban on abortion, was defeated. A revised pro-life bill, containing exceptions for rape, incest, and high-risk pregnancies was presented to the South Dakota people in 2008; fortunately, it too was defeated.

Legality

It would perhaps be instructive to discuss the legal aspects of the South Dakota bill, as it is representative of the pro-life movement. The first point is that the bill would not be enforceable because the Constitution of the United States has been determined to confer a pro-choice right to women. This interpretation is, in essence, in the custody of the Supreme Court and, at least for the time being, rests on the Roe versus Wade decision of 1973. State law would not have power over the Supreme Court Roe versus Wade decision, so the South Dakota law would have been judged unenforceable and unconstitutional in the court of law. My sense is that because this is a straightforward legal issue, the real motivation among the knowledgeable advocates of the pro-life bill was to bring the issue to a higher level of national attention. It also appears that the "national awareness" motivation was not shared in a forthright manner with the South Dakota people.

Pursuing the constitutionality subject a bit farther, let us take a closer look at the Roe versus Wade decision. All the overturning of Roe versus Wade would do, legally, is return the regulation of abortion to the individual states. Therefore, assume for the moment that South Dakota made abortion illegal, but Minnesota continued to be a pro-choice state. All a South Dakota woman would have to do, after making a very difficult personal decision, is drive to Minnesota for the procedure. This is almost never discussed, and it represents a reality that the pro-life advocates do not want to see brought into the discussion. Simply put, recognizing the individual state's-rights point messes up a very tidy opportunity to demonstrate their righteousness and religiosity.

Learning

Ignoring reality distracts and detours us away from the opportunity to reduce abortions effectively—severely so. Not only are the pro-life advocates ineffective in their "make it illegal" efforts, but they also cause more abortions by diverting our efforts away from programs that are effective. *These are the family-planning programs that have been proven, worldwide, to be extremely effective in reducing abortion numbers.* These programs produce results relatively fast, much faster than programs designed to improve societal conditions usually do, and they are very cost-effective. If reduction of abortions was the real motivation of the pro-life group, they would put their energy toward making family-planning services available to all women.

The effectiveness of making family planning and discussion of sexual issues a key component of health care and societal responsibility has been proven to be dramatic. Several European countries have been extremely successful in this respect, and they are excellent models for us to consider. The rate of abortions (I'm using 2003 numbers to get apple-to-apple comparisons), measured as the number of abortions per 1,000 child-bearing–age women per year, is as follows:

Region	Number of abortions
Worldwide	29
United States	21
Progressive European Countries	
Belgium	7
Germany	8
Netherlands	9
Switzerland	9

Nearly half, 49 percent, of the pregnancies in the United States are unintended; four out of ten of these unwanted pregnancies are terminated by abortion. During the course of their life, about one-half of all the women in the United States have an unintended pregnancy, and about one-third will have an abortion. A significant portion of these abortions are among younger women, 20–24 years old (33 percent of the total abortions) and teenagers (17 percent).

Never-married women constitute about half of the abortions. Abortion numbers are also highly skewed towards the poor: Women below the poverty line have an abortion rate four times the rate of women comfortably above the poverty line.

Between 1973 and 2005, there were slightly over 45 million abortions performed in the United States. This translates to about 1.2 million abortions per year in our country. The rate has declined slowly, from about 29 per year per 1000 women in 1980, to about 19 per 1000, currently. The decline was most substantial during the Clinton administration, dropping from about 27 to 21 during the eight years of his presidency.

These are startling and disturbing numbers. Many of us see human life, including fetal life, as something that is very special and very awesome. It is an aspect of our wondrous existence that, I believe, should compel us to treat the subject with utmost thought and care. I am reasonably sure that this feeling is broadly held and transcends religious orientation. It speaks to our sense that life is sacred and that our conduct should reflect the profoundness of this belief.

Sex Education

To be responsible to the subject of abortion and the profoundness of life, we need to deal with reality. A logical starting point is acknowledging that sex is a fundamental aspect of human existence. Studies indicate that nine out of ten Americans have premarital sex. Aside from the question of whether it's right or wrong, I believe that meets the definition of "normal." Among the teenage set, over 60 percent have sex before they are eighteen. The numbers in Canada and Europe are comparable.

What is different is that United States teenage girls are four times as likely as German girls to become pregnant, nearly five times as likely as French girls to have a baby, and seven times more likely to have had an abortion than their Dutch counterparts. Another striking difference is that the sexually transmitted disease rate among teenage boys in the United States is many times higher than the rate among European boys.

The right-wing fundamentalists have argued hard that the answer to the resultant teenage sex issues is to promote an abstinence-only program. They would ban comprehensive, fact-based sexuality programs as a component of school education, even though these programs teach responsible behavior undergirded by clear understanding of sexuality and reproductive biology. Study after study has shown that the abstinence-only approach does not work. There is even evidence that it might be counter-productive.

For example, all reputable scientific studies show that teenagers who take a virginity pledge—a feature common in many abstinence-only programs—have their initial sexual experience at the same average age and with as many partners as those not involved in abstinence-only programs. Some studies, such as a recent Columbia University study, show that abstinence-only programs may be counter-productive: virginity-pledge takers used birth control 64 percent of the time, compared to 70 percent for those who never made a marriage-only sex pledge; among boys, only 40 percent of those who had pledged used condoms, compared to 59 percent for the non-pledge group. A University of Washington study indicated that teenage girls who receive comprehensive sex education are 50 percent less likely to become pregnant than those enrolled in abstinence-only programs. Abstinence-only programs appear to be somewhat effective in producing guilt and denial but totally ineffective in actually reducing sexual activity.

United States

One of the core family planning programs in the United States is the Title X program. This is a federal grant program run by the Department of Health and Human Services. It deals exclusively with family planning and reproductive health. Through the program, contraceptive supplies and services are available to all who want and need these services but who are not financially able to obtain them through other means.

It is not a large program by federal standards. Its current funding is less than $300 million per year. Services are directed primarily toward low-income women, with women above the poverty line paying part of the cost, according to a graduated fee scale. In 2006 the program provided family planning services to about five million women.

By comparing pregnancy, birth, and abortion rates of women with access to family planning services to those not receiving these services, it can be shown that the Title X program and other public-funded programs have prevented 1.3 million unintended pregnancies per year. These pregnancies, had they occurred, would have resulted in over 630,000 abortions, more than 530,000 births of "unwanted children," and 165,000 miscarriages. Title X alone is estimated to have prevented almost twenty million unwanted pregnancies since its inception in 1970. It is interesting to note that the Title X program costs, for a full year of operation, are less than we are spending *each day* in Iraq.

What is so often not understood is that the federal Title X statute that originated and regulates this program explicitly prohibits any use of funds for abortion services. The closest link that Title X has to abortion, if one can reasonably call it a link, is that a pregnant women must be provided information and counseling about all relevant options, including infant care, foster care, adoption services, and legal abortion options.

Nevertheless, opposition from the Religious Right and social conservative groups has been strong, and funding of the program has not kept up with the inflation rate. This is true even though the program saves three dollars for every dollar invested and contributes significantly to the well-being of our nation in terms of preventing unwanted pregnancies and the high abortion rates that result from the unwanted pregnancies.

International

An even more far-reaching effect is the "global gag rule" imposed by three of our presidents—Reagan, George Bush, and George W. Bush—as payback for the political support from the social conservative group. In brief, this is an executive order policy that requires foreign organizations that receive U.S. Agency for International Development (USAID) family planning funds to agree that they will not "perform or actively promote abortion as a method of family planning." This includes agreeing that they will not provide information requested by a pregnant woman on legal abortion options that are provided by other organizations in her country. It also stipulates that the recipient organization cannot use its own funds or funds obtained from other sources to provide this information while receiving USAID funds.

It is interesting to note that United States-based groups are not subject to this policy because it would be considered unconstitutional. It is also interesting to note that if USAID funds are provided to a foreign organization for non-family planning services—a hospital or clinic, for example—there is no funding restriction or "gag rule," even if these organizations are involved in abortion services.

It is also a fact that while the gag rule is presented politically as an anti-abortion measure, it is also an anti-family-planning measure. The end result is that the rate of unplanned and unwanted pregnancies goes up, and then, as is always the case, the number of abortions to terminate these pregnancies goes up. But the social conservative group likes the "gag" rule. Puzzling, isn't it?

The effectiveness of family planning in lesser-developed countries is well known, well studied, and well documented. A study in Turkey, for example, showed that in one participating hospital with the focus on providing post-abortion counseling, the number of women using birth control rose from 65 percent to 97 percent after one year of the program's existence. The number of abortions at that hospital dropped from 4,100 in 1992 to 1,709 in 1998. Nationwide, the abortion rate has decreased from 45 abortions per year per 1,000 women, to 25 per 1,000 in 1998.

Russia was a country where birth control was not readily available, but couples wanted small families. Abortion became the means for having small families, with many women having repeated abortions. In an effort to reduce the abortion rate, Russia implemented a family-planning program. The program indicates that family-planning services can reduce the abortion rate fairly fast. In 1990 about 19 percent of the women used contraceptives, with an abortion rate of 109 per year per 1,000 women. Four years later, contraceptive use had increased to 24 percent, with a reduction in the abortion rate to 75 per year per 1,000 women.

In Hungary, the use of contraceptives has increased from 20 percent several years ago to 69 percent today, with a corresponding decrease in the abortion rate, from about 70 per year per 1000 women to about 35 per 1000 today. Eastern European countries, as a region, have reduced the abortion rate substantially, from about 90 per 1,000 in 1995 to 44 per 1,000 in 2005. Clearly, family-planning programs work.

Our next-door neighbor, Mexico, is an example of the success of family planning. This is surprising to many, given the common perception that Hispanic couples choose large families. United States family-planning aid to Mexico (USAID family-planning program) was discontinued in 1999, and since that time, the family-planning program has been run by the Mexico Ministry of Health. In 1977 the fertility rate for Mexico was 5.25 children per woman. Today, the fertility rate is 2.21. United Nations experts have estimated that without family-planning services, the population of Mexico today would be over 170 million, compared to the current population of 108 million. Without this family-planning focus, the number of abortions and the number of people living in poverty would be far greater. This again speaks to the point that to achieve a meaningful reduction in abortion numbers, making family-planning services available to all women is a far more effective use of resources than are the passionate efforts to make abortion a criminal offense.

Currently, about 60 percent of the world's women live in countries where abortion is legal, with the number increasing. One reason for this is the recognition that legal restrictions on abortion do not reduce its occurrence. Another reason is that in those countries where abortion is illegal, the abortions are usually performed under unsafe conditions by unskilled practitioners. Some studies indicate that up to 95 percent of the abortions in Africa and Latin America—countries where abortions, for the most part, are illegal—are done under unsafe, high-risk conditions.

Decision-Making

What does all this tell us about our decision-making process with respect to the heated, controversial issue of abortion? What does it tell us, in a broader sense, about our willingness to address reality? What does it tell us about our ability to cope with challenging issues in a truly effective way?

The abortion issue demonstrates the danger of the "price of distraction." It has been proven, beyond any reasonable doubt, that the number of abortions can be reduced dramatically when family-planning services are made available. I have talked to medical sociologists at the University of Minnesota Medical School who simply shake their heads with an air of disbelief when the question of how to reduce abortions is discussed—their response is "sex education and family planning; keep women who do not want to get pregnant from getting pregnant." This view is shared by all experts in the field.

This "price of distraction" is, in my judgment, morally reprehensible. Given that the facts are so readily available, it is difficult to believe that it results from ignorance. Yet it continues. Imagine if we all joined in a concerted effort to make family planning a health care service that was available to every woman. Imagine if we approached the subject in a factual, honest way that recognized the sexuality and reproductive biology of the human species. And imagine if we approached the subject with the attitude that the women who face the very difficult abortion decision are caring human beings who agonize deeply over their situation; that we not attempt to pass ineffective laws that dehumanize and criminalize these women. Within a fairly short period of time, the abortion numbers in our country could be at the level of the European countries that have dealt with the issue in a far more open, factual way. As they would say in Oak Center, it ain't that hard to understand.

So what is the underlying source of the beliefs and ideologies that lead people, probably well-meaning people, to expend huge amounts of time, energy, money, and passion to the notion that it is "good" to pass laws (or rescind laws, as the case may be) that make abortion illegal? The evidence is there, for anyone who wants to see it: this does not reduce the number of abortions but only results in the abortions being done under hidden, unsafe conditions. The evidence is also there, for anyone who wants to see it, that the number of abortions can be reduced substantially, at low cost, by making family-planning products and services available to all.

My suspicion is that the "make abortion illegal" advocates are driven by two ideologies. The most important is a religious-based ideology, meaning that the right-wing, fundamentalist-oriented Christians see their actions as an expression of their faith. But it is a faith that demands burying your head in the sand. This gets very close to the "blind obedience" view discussed in Charles Kendall's book, *When Religion Becomes Evil*.

The second reason that is closely related, and probably a companion motivation, is that these people see themselves as moving to an elevated moral status because of their activism in the pro-life movement. This gives them far more satisfaction than any real reduction in abortion numbers—obviously so, because there is no real reduction in numbers. The bogus "morality movement" for these people generates a far greater buzz than a common-sense, pedestrian-but-effective family-planning program.

Another possible explanation is ignorance, the result of simply not putting in the effort to understand the subject in any depth, and following the uninformed herd.

My primary objective is not to convince anyone about a specific view but to encourage us to enter into better decision-making by asking ourselves why we believe what we say we believe; to establish a higher level of truth and understanding of the issues that will be major challenges in our near future. As Arthur Block cautioned, we need to be careful that our conclusions are not simply the place where we got tired of thinking. We certainly owe this to the coming generation.

CHAPTER 10

FUNDAMENTALISM, THE CHOSEN AND THE SUPERIOR

"It is not fair to ask of others what you are not willing to do yourself."

—Eleanor Roosevelt

*"Fixation on the written word
is a form of idolatry.
It mistakes the garment
for the naked Truth.
It confines the living insight within
the concepts of the past."*

—Freke and Gandy

The chapter "My First, Big, Enduring Myth" was a difficult one for me to write. Most of the people that I know, some of them very close to me, view themselves as good Christians. The "Enduring" part of the chapter's title is there to remind me that I was in this camp most of my life. But layer by layer, during the past seven or eight years, I have come to the conclusion that traditional Christianity is a myth-based religion. There may be a God, but the God of the Bible does not exist. I no longer believe that Christianity represents truth. In fact, very much the opposite: it stops us from the pursuit of real truth.

When I share my story, I realize that I am also saying those who are followers of the Christian tradition are following a false religion. I realize that this is much more than simply saying that I see things a bit differently; it's an assertion that Christianity is no more true than the pagan religions of earlier times. It's saying that whatever traditional Christianity believes just isn't so—that in reality, it is a collection of ancient mythical stories.

This has troubled me. It has troubled me a lot. I do not want to anger people or to damage my relationship with the many good people who profess the Christian faith, particularly family members and friends. Because this was causing endless personal turmoil, I had to deal with the issue. It took me a long time but I finally have come to the decision that it is more important to me to be authentic than it is to be liked or respected, although my fondest hope is that it can be all. Another aspect of this conclusion is the hope that those who disagree with me will not forget that I spent the first sixty years of my life believing what they believe. I've been there, and I think I understand why they are there.

The major aspect of my conclusion to move forward and to share my story is that my whole purpose in this book is to urge you to think for yourself, and to urge you to seek reality and truth in your decision-making. I share my stories and thoughts, not so much to convince you of my views but to share with you the process and path that resulted in my change of views about the Christian faith. For me to do anything less would mean that I am being deceitful with the people who mean the most to me. But still, the thought of slaying sacred cows, particularly in something as personally important as one's religious beliefs, is troublesome for me.

A final comment with respect to your reactions to my faith story is that although I believe Christianity is a myth-based religion, I feel I have a strong spiritual center, stronger than what my former Christian faith gave me. I am sure that those who profess the traditional Christian beliefs will not be able to understand that we can have a profound faith that is centered on a sense of awe, a recognition and acceptance of our utter inability to comprehend or understand the wonders of our existence. My faith says that, as mortal human beings, we simply cannot hope to understand this aspect of our being, but there is sacredness in our capacity to understand love, security, family, generosity, purpose, and all other life needs that human beings share. It is a faith that is humbling when one's perspective includes seeing beautiful works of art and music, the love and compassion of those who help the less fortunate, a mother's love of her child, and what we see when we allow the wonders of nature and our existence to penetrate our very being. It's a way of saying that the melding of agnosticism and humanism and deism is a faith, a faith that is the closest to truth that man is capable of comprehending or articulating. It is the only faith that I can find that speaks to the uniqueness of man and withstands inquiry from all sides.

Sam Harris, even though a self-professed atheist, says, "There is no denying that most of us have emotional and spiritual needs that are now addressed—however obliquely and at a terrible price—by mainstream religion. And these are needs that a mere understanding of our world, scientific or otherwise, will never fulfill. There is clearly a sacred dimension to our existence, and coming to terms with it could well be the highest purpose of human life."

The purpose of this chapter is to look at a certain aspect of religious faith—*fundamentalism*—that has become an important part of not only Christianity but also the Islamic faith. It is an aspect of religion that has become extremely dangerous to the world. As we face the immense challenges of the future, this is an aspect of religion that cannot be swept under the rug. It is, as Charles Kimball, an ordained Baptist minister, pointed out, a face of religion that has become truly evil and dangerous. Seventeenth-century philosopher Blaise Pascal said it very bluntly: "Men never do evil so completely and cheerfully as when they do it from religious conviction."

Kimball has pointed out that when religion is viewed in a very narrow way, it often becomes the cause of major problems, rather than producing good. He goes on to describe a more enlightened view, using the thoughts of Joseph Campbell, perhaps the best-known scholar of mythology. Kimball says:

"For Campbell, the messages communicated through the mythological traditions of the world—from tribal cultures to the great world religions—are all about being alive, the thrilling mystery of existence. They teach us how to live a meaningful and moral life as an individual and in community. The sacred stories that have nourished and sustained human beings combine historical information with symbolic imagery. Those who simply dismiss sacred stories as untrue miss the point. Demanding historical veracity as a prerequisite for truth is another kind of tunnel vision. To do so is to mistake poetry for prose."

This is what Campbell called the "song of the universe."

The word "fundamentalism" is a relatively new term, not even in some dictionaries until 1950. The term is used in several ways but in general, it means strong adherence to any set of beliefs, even in the face of evidence that contradicts that belief. It is a mind-set that allows one to strongly defend entrenched positions and beliefs that are inconsistent with the laws of nature and which defy a reasoned, logical argument. The "fundamentalism" that we most need to be concerned about, as professor of theology, religion, and culture at Kings College London Alister McGrath defines it, is "a religious fundamentalism which *refuses* to allow its ideas to be examined or challenged." This is a mind-set which, as the Webster's Thesaurus notes, allows one "to have opinions formed without due knowledge or examination." It's the mind-set of those who claim that religious truth demands acceptance of scriptural infallibility, inerrancy, and literalism.

It is this literalism and absolutism that leads groups of people to believe they hold the truth and to believe that all other religious views are based on bogus mythology or the ranting of some sorely misled and ultimately damned individuals. It is a very coercive religion, in that it teaches, explicitly or by the message of fear, that to examine the precepts of this faith is, in and of itself, an acknowledgment of lack of faith. This is the deep-seated fear often described as the "egg shell fear"—the fear that if one examines the basis of one's beliefs, a crack will be found, leading to a layer by layer, piece by piece, questioning of the basis of one's faith. We tell ourselves that this is not what God wants; we may even fear that we have succumbed to the alluring voice of the devil. We tell ourselves, very likely with the encouragement of a preacher or priest, that faith built on a rock-solid foundation that shuns all doubt is the depth of faith we should seek. We fear that our whole identity, not to mention the "promise" of eternal life, is at risk if we begin a path of real inquiry. We cannot look, for fear of what we will see. And if we do peek, it is with the purpose of authenticating beliefs already held, rather than with open-minded inquiry.

This is also the point where the solidity of our belief that we hold the "truth" begins to make us dangerous. At this point, we have entered the cycle of seeking only positive reinforcement. Some would call it the growth of faith. Our circle becomes those who think and believe as we do. These are the people with whom we identify. And they reinforce and authenticate our view. We begin to develop an us-versus-them view. We begin to see those who hold different religious views as not being given God's true word; somehow, by the "grace of God," we have been "chosen" to be the holders of the truth. We study scripture and find verses that support our beliefs, and verses that speak to the erroneous views of the "others." We begin to develop a sense that those holding these erroneous views are unworthy. We see them almost as enemies because of their efforts to spread their false religion. When strife and conflict occur, we pray for our soldiers, but not theirs. We ask for further blessing of our Christian nation and our more noble efforts, but not theirs. We have reached the point of supremacy and arrogance. It has become part of us. And we have gotten to this state of being by convincing ourselves that we have the truth.

But do we?

What I have described is a description of the Religious Right and other fundamentalists of the Christian faith. We could change a few words—for example, changing Koran for Bible, and Muslim for Christian—and we would have the Islam counterpart. Muslims are perhaps even more dogmatic in their view of having truth than the Christian group. But each believes it holds the truth, and each asks questions of the other that they will not ask of themselves. And each is unable to examine, in a sincere and authentic way, the basis for their believing in the literal truth of their scriptures and traditions. And each finds justification for their actions of condemnation of the other and acts of violence against the other.

As I shared earlier, there were many reasons for my growing unease about the foundation of my Christian faith, but probably the strongest reason was the hypocrisy of the fundamentalists—they do not practice what they preach. Gandhi summarized it vividly: "I like your Christ; I do not like your Christians. Your Christians are so unlike your Christ." Because of this unease, I found the courage to peel away the basis of what I had professed to believe for sixty years. It has been, for me, an iterative study process, one in which I've recognized, as many scholars have said, that history is not only about what has happened but—often more important, *why* it happened. And in religion the "why" has an inescapable psychological content. Sam Harris was right when he said that we all seem to have an emotional and spiritual need. It is part of human nature and is clearly observable throughout the history of mankind. The psychological aspect cannot be ignored. It is real. Very real. It is no wonder that Kimball's book, *When Religion Becomes Evil*, begins with the statement: "Religion is arguably the most powerful and pervasive force on earth."

The significance of the fundamentalist movement is that we have a perfect storm in the making: from one direction, a growing segment of the Islam religion—the radical extremist—believe they have absolute truth and that it is their command from Allah to bring the world to this truth; killing of the infidels is justified. From another direction, the fundamentalists—a segment that has grown in recent years and which is a sizeable portion of Christians—believe they have absolute truth and that almost any action (preemptive warfare or simply denying dignity to the Muslims) is justified behavior. From another direction, the hardliners within the Jewish faith, the Zionists, believe they are the chosen people of God, and that he has given them a level of importance and a special piece of the earth, with little regard for the indigenous people who inhabited these lands. With this umbrella of "righteousness" pervading the public arena, it is possible for immoral leaders of any of these fundamentalist groups to gain support for even the most evil of decisions. That this can result has been proven over and over again throughout history. One need look no farther than the Crusades, or the Inquisition, or 9/11, or those who claim to have God on their side in all that they do.

Many scholars, theologians, psychologists, and lay folks who are concerned about dangers that these groups pose are attempting to understand the underlying psychological factors that lead an individual to fundamentalism. Chris Hedges, an experienced war correspondent and, in earlier days, a Harvard Divinity School graduate, speaks to this:

> "The moral certitude of the state in wartime is a kind of fundamentalism. And this dangerous messianic brand of religion, one where self-doubt is minimal, has come increasingly to color the modern world of Christianity, Judaism, and Islam. Dr. James Luther Adams, my ethics professor at Harvard Divinity School, used to tell us that we would end our careers fighting an ascendant fundamentalist movement, or as he liked to say, 'the Christian fascists.' He was not a scholar to be disregarded, however implausible such a scenario seemed at the time. There is a danger of growing fusion between those in the state who wage war— both for and against modern states—and those who believe they understand and act as agents of God."

Hedges discusses other aspects of the fundamentalist mind and those who are trying to bring others into the fundamentalist fold—Christian, Muslim, or other:

> "The conversion is supposed to banish the deepest dreads, fears, and anxieties of human existence, including the fear of death. This is the central message we are told to impart to potential believers. But along with this message comes a disorienting mixture of love and fear, of promise of a warm embrace by a kind and gentle God that yearns to direct and guide life of the convert ... and also of an angry, wrathful God who must punish nonbelievers ... this control, while destructive to personal initiative and independence, does keep believers from wandering back into the messy situations they fled. The new ideology gives the believers a cause, a sense of purpose, meaning, feeling of superiority, and a way to justify and sanctify their hatreds. For many, the rewards of cleaning up their lives, repairing their damaged self-esteem, and joining an elite group and blessed group are worth the cost of submission. They know how to define and identify themselves. They do not have to make moral choices. They are made for them. They submerge their individual personas into the single persona of the Christian crowd."

Hedges, while citing Christian fundamentalism in this discourse, sees a similar psychology in fundamentalism of other faiths, particularly Islam and Judaism.

Bishop John Shelby Spong says that a "major function of fundamentalist religion is to bolster deeply insecure and fearful people. This is done by justifying prejudices. It thereby provides an appropriate and legitimate outlet for one's anger. The authority of an inerrant or infallible Bible that can be readily quoted to buttress this point of view becomes an essential ingredient to such a life. When that Bible is challenged, or relativized, the resulting anger proves the point categorically." It is extremely difficult for these "insecure and fearful" people to consider the evidence and arguments that the Bible, albeit a beautiful book with many truths, is a mythological-based book.

Even Charles Darwin, often ostracized by the Religious Right and fundamentalists, has been misunderstood with respect to his understanding of our existence. It is true that Darwin rejected the literal reading of scripture, concluding that the Bible is "no more to be trusted than the sacred books of the Hindoos, or the beliefs of any barbarian." He knew the God of the Bible to be mythology, but he did not argue the sacred, the unknown, the mystery of what set the universe in motion, the possibility of something divine that mortals would, for lack of a better term, call God: "The safest conclusion seems to be that the whole subject is beyond the scope of man's intellect ... every man must judge for himself, between the conflicting vague probabilities." He was troubled by the idea of reconciling a loving supreme power and the immense amount of suffering throughout the world. But in the end, he concluded that the only reasonable conclusion he could draw was "I don't know."

Examining the basis for our beliefs is not easy; when the subject is broached, most Christians immediately respond defensively. Jeffrey Bennett, an astrophysicist and author, notes that "Revolutionary change is never easy [and looking at the possibility of changing one's religious beliefs is certainly revolutionary]. Clear as the case might seem to us now, many of Galileo's contemporaries put up fierce resistance. Some refused to look through the telescope for fear of what they would see." Likewise, most Christian fundamentalists are reluctant to examine the authenticity of scripture for fear of what they might discover. Fundamentalists tenaciously resist inquiry because, as Joe Klein has pointed out, "facts are powerless in the face of mythology." For the fundamentalist, mythology provides more psychological comfort and security, albeit false security, than does the search for facts, truth, and reality.

The fundamentalist religion that is of most concern to the people of our nation is, of course, Islam, specifically that segment of the Islam religion that subscribes to the idea that any means of conversion or death of the infidels is justified. Kimball's work suggests that there are five warning signs of when religion has the potential to do evil: (1) when that religion holds the claim of having absolute truth, (2) when the religion is given blind obedience, (3) when the religion holds that there is a specific "time" for some aspect of their faith to happen, (4) when the end justifies the means, and (5) when a "holy war" is being advocated. These are symptoms that we have seen in the Islamic faith, particularly among some of the most fundamentalist elements of the faith.

And so, what do we do?

There are certainly many facets of how to reduce the danger that the Muslim terrorists present to the world. Helping them develop an improved economy where there is employment opportunity, helping them rebuild their education institutions, and treating them with dignity are, without doubt, needed changes in order to reduce the Muslim terrorist threat in a major, sustained way. But in my opinion, there needs to be an accompanying movement from our side, and that is to challenge, in a sincere, respectful way, the most basic tenets of the Islamic faith. We need to say that we believe their faith to be a mythological faith (as it is with Christianity and Judaism). Certainly, Islam's a faith with some beautiful and wise teachings, but it still is a faith that is not a revelation from God.

Right now, this is a 500-pound-gorilla-in-the-room issue—we all know how we feel but we don't have the courage, or maybe even the honesty, to be truthful. Yet I'm sure that it represents a very core belief when we talk with our Muslim neighbors. I believe it would change the dynamics of our conversations immensely if we were truthful and if we demonstrated the courage to share one of our foundational beliefs—that their claim of religious truth is false. Anything else is simply allowing evasion of the core issue and attempting to treat the symptom rather than the disease.

But this approach also places a tremendous burden on ourselves, for if we challenge the authenticity of their faith, we will have credibility and respect only if we apply the same examination to our most dominant faith, the Christian faith.

Sam Harris has recognized this issue:

> "If religious war is ever to become unthinkable for us, in the way that slavery and cannibalism seem poised to, it will be a matter of our having dispensed with the dogma [fundamentalism] of faith. If our tribalism is ever to give way to an extended moral identity, our religious beliefs can no longer be sheltered from the tides of genuine inquiry and genuine criticism. It is time we realize that to presume knowledge where one has only pious hope is a species of evil. Wherever conviction grows in inverse proportion to its justification, we have lost the very basis of human cooperation."

Harris goes even further, arguing that the moderates—those who still see themselves as Christians but do not subscribe to the tenets of the fundamentalists—are equally to blame: "Unless the core dogmas of faith are called into question ... religious moderation will do nothing to lead us out of the wilderness."

I would summarize this chapter with four points: The first is that the claim of having absolute truth by the Christians, the Muslims, and the Jews runs headlong into each other, and constitutes an immense risk to the well-being of the world. The second is that we must look at ourselves—Christians, for the most part—and ask ourselves whether our faith is mythology-based rather than an inerrant revelation of God. With serious inquiry, most will come to the conclusion that the Bible is mythology-based; that it is the word of man, not the word of God. The third point is that to deal with the Muslim fundamentalist terrorism issue in a lasting way demands that we challenge the foundational beliefs that justify their actions. And the fourth point is that in order to do this with any degree of honesty and integrity, we need to ask ourselves—the Christians and Jews in our country—the same question. This would be a revolutionary move but one that could begin to transform the world, reflecting the growth of humankind beyond the vestiges of our tribalism and superstitious past.

Admittedly, the idea that we could do this seems so farfetched that to declare it an absurd notion may be appropriate. Yet I see movement in parts of Europe where this notion might not be judged absurd. I believe more people are traveling down the path that I walked, questioning the faith that they once accepted without substantive inquiry. And I see more people with their spiritual home grounded in the sense of awe of our existence.

Each of us will have to decide for ourselves whether we have the courage to examine the basis for what we believe. It is a decision that will be made either by thoughtful inquiry or by continuing down our faith path without asking any questions of ourselves. We will decide whether our beliefs can withstand sincere inquiry, or whether we want to live our short time on earth in an eggshell.

CHAPTER 11

THE ECONOMIC MESS, DEFICITS, AND A VISIONARY BUDGET

*"There will come a time when
you believe everything
is finished. Yet that will be the beginning."*

—Louis L'Amour

*"Any fool can make things
bigger, more complex,
and more violent. It takes a
touch of genius and
a lot of courage to move in
the opposite direction."*

—Albert Einstein

*"If everybody is thinking alike,
then somebody isn't thinking."*

—George S. Patton Jr.

What a mess!

It's Thursday afternoon, February 19, 2009. The Minnesota Public Radio news says that the Dow Industrials are down 30 points. Good news, nowadays! For over a year and a half, we have been watching a systemic erosion of the vaunted United States of America economic system. It was a slow, steady erosion for many months, which raised questions about the sustainability of our economic path, but most of the financial pundits (and folks like me) had an underlying confidence, albeit a somewhat uneasy confidence, that moderate course correction would allow the downward curve to flatten out, and in due time, the economy would resume an upward movement. We couldn't even decide whether or not we were in a recession.

The first overt awakening, at least among the masses that pay little attention to the fundamentals of our economic system, was a rapid increase in the price of oil and the cost of filling-up the family sedan at the pump. That caused a debate about repealing the law that prevents drilling in the Arctic National Wildlife Refuge, a debate that has little impact on our petroleum supplies, other than confirming our ignorance of economic and energy issues. But the debate was illustrative. It reflected our profound lack of discipline in managing our financial affairs, a lack of discipline that is probably only possible because of a refusal to look at things through the lens of reality and understanding.

And who is it that would be so unenlightened?

Well, it looks like it's most of us. It clearly included the 2000–2008 administration which, regrettably, proved to be morally bankrupt and incompetent in most every facet of management and leadership. And it includes the airwave media that delivers only what they believe the people are interested in hearing. It includes the print media, which no longer engages in serious investigative journalism. It includes our Congress, which exhibits a lack of responsibility and vision that is almost beyond comprehension. But most important, it includes us lay folks who were enjoying life and who were putting our trust in party and ideology, rather than summoning the courage and energy to seek truth, reality, and understanding.

So a societal climate was created. We are numb to any sense of reality—almost all of us. Home prices will continue to go up; always have—the delusion, some say the "Kool-Aid" that we kept drinking. The stock market will continue to go up. Deficits don't matter, be it the budget deficit or the current account deficit (even former Vice President Cheney proclaimed "deficits don't matter"). Why save when the better savings account is the asset appreciation of a house, or a cabin, or even a nicely maintained Cessna 172 airplane (I was not far away from that one). President Bush, in his usual wisdom, argued that we needed to move to the "ownership" philosophy by converting Social Security from a savings concept to an investment concept, citing the low bond returns versus the high returns of the equity market. Businesses were also drinking the proverbial Kool-Aid—the successful business of tomorrow would be built around "knowledge centers," the inventors, the entrepreneurs, the financial hubs. Let the rest of the world compete for the lowly low-cost manufacturing jobs. Business ethics were redefined to mean "if it's not illegal, it's morally okay." Greed is simply the "American capitalistic system at work," so make as much as you can in any way that you can, because that's the underlying, motivating driver that propels the economy.

It was fun while it lasted. Big houses. Turn the appreciated value into an even bigger house. High-horsepower cars. Flying clubs. Cabins. Big lake fishing boats with GPS navigation. Granite countertops. Adventure trips. Ah … those trips. Big trips. Trips to exotic places with a "small group of twelve to sixteen people" to experience raw adventure. East Africa safaris, Panama and the Embera Indian communities, Cambodia's Angkor Wat and

Tonle Sap Lake, the Caribbean Islands, Egypt's pyramids and Jordan's Petra, Thailand's floating markets of Damnern Saduak and the River Kwai, family trips to a Mexican all-inclusive resort, China and Tibet, Peru's Machu Picchu and Ecuador's Galapagos, Argentina and the Antarctica. What educational, eye-opening experiences. We loved perusing the glossy overseas-adventure travel brochures that came weekly. We even loved the planning, getting the vaccinations required for these third-world places. We loved the phone calls with our travel friends. We talked about how fortunate we were to have these experiences. And we assumed it would last.

And all the while we watched the account deficit grow. We watched the equity market grow. We watched the house and cabin value increase by double-digits each year. We watched the tax cuts for the rich, but no one was challenging the dubious trickle-down, supply-side economic theory that legitimized the income disparity these tax cuts created. We watched the national debt grow at rates never before seen. We watched consumer debt grow, also at rates never before seen. We watched our future liabilities—Medicaid, Medicare, Social Security—grow to levels that defy common sense and the ability to pay, leaving the problem to our kids to figure out. We saw the issues of the world like adolescents see a high school rivalry. Our energies focused on the Democrats winning or the Republicans winning, depending on our "loyalty" and ideological strips. We endorsed the idea of "spend now," rather than invest for the future. The issues would take care of themselves if we had the right party in power—it was an easier and more comfortable position to sell to ourselves than rigorous, fact-based thinking and having to address the tough issues of reality that result from hard thinking. A *Vanity Fair* writer saw a "unique combination of ideology, special-interest pressure, populist politics, bad economy, and sheer incompetence" bringing the nation to a historically dangerous juncture. David Brooks, expounding on the role that unfounded ideology plays in our conduct, asked "how so many people could be so stupid, incompetent, and self-destructive all at once." Some saw it as the "fat and happy" syndrome; others, like author Tom Friedman, could only conclude, "Dumb, dumb, dumb."

On Thursday night, September 18, 2008, things changed very abruptly. The slowly progressing, chronic but ultimately debilitating disease of being naïve and irresponsible reached a vital organ. The patient turned critically ill. And alarmingly, the disease was found to be very contagious. The patient is now, months later, still in critical condition. Some in our societal family have not yet accepted the depth of the news—the patient is in danger of not surviving, at least not in a way that will resemble its former self. At best, if recovery is possible, it will most likely take years of rehabilitation. Societal family life will be changed, probably forever, because of our foolishness.

The inflection point on September 18, 2008, will be a date later noted in history with far more significance than is sensed today. It will be viewed as a historical turning point, not so much because it defines an abrupt historical event but because it was the point where years of irresponsible management behavior reached a breaking point—Malcolm Gladwell's symbolic tipping point.

On that night of September 18, Secretary of the Treasury Henry M. Paulson Jr., and Chairman of the Federal Reserve Ben S. Bernanke called an urgent meeting with the president of the United States and a small group of the most important, powerful members of Congress. The message was shocking: the United States banking system was on the precipice of collapse. The nation's credit system was frozen. Attendees report that the room was enveloped in a silence of disbelief: *The mighty United States economy was facing imminent meltdown.*

The issue that became the straw that broke the camel's back was the decline in the value of housing, affecting particularly the sub-prime market. Irresponsible lending practices had created mountains of loans with little or no down payment, often to borrowers who were marginally credit-worthy at best. The great and powerful institutions that processed and repackaged and resold these loans had drifted off into a world where reality and common sense and responsible behavior had given way to unmitigated greed. To assuage the guilt of this behavior, risk-evaluation models were built by the "quants," statistician-type folks, to show that the risk of these loans defaulting was nil. Risk models were built with key variables based on the history of market-place variation, but basing the magnitude of this variation on short-term market-place history, where the variation was atypically small, essentially guaranteed a bogus risk assessment. But this produced the risk assessment that management wanted; it served their purpose. The bogus risk assessments legitimized greed, allowing smart men to abandon common sense and principled management.

The issue is far, far more complex than what I have described. In fact, the September 18 meeting on the banking crisis was, I would argue, a secondary effect, a crisis resulting from other far more fundamental problems in our financial behavior. The underlying causes are many, but three factors are most significant.

First, during the past few years we have, in effect, been *stimulating the economy* to an extraordinary degree by drawing huge sums of money from our homes via refinancing. Estimates for the years 2005–2007 are in the range of $500–700 billion. On top of that, we had a current account deficit of another $300 billion or more. *Together, this has been the equivalent of a trillion dollar per year stimulus package, with a very high efficiency of spending ratio accompanying this infusion.* Because consumer spending has become the major driver of our economy, with upwards of 73 percent of our economy dependent on consumer spending, this was a controlling factor, albeit temporary, in the illusionary prosperity of our economy. Because the individual consumers were making the spending decisions and, in effect, deciding the allocation of national resources, we saw houses getting bigger and bigger and very little being invested in infrastructure or long-term economy building efforts, such as improved education.

The second factor producing the artificial prosperity bubble was the extraordinary profits of our corporations. Corporate after-tax profits rose to over 10 percent of GDP versus the historical average of 6 percent. Unlike the 2001 dot-com bust, where price per share ("P") rose to unreasonable levels, it was the annual earnings per share ("E") rising to unsustainable levels, a far more insidious movement that could not be sustained. With the resultant P/E ratios looking so favorable, the market value rose accordingly, without the appearance of unreasonable valuation. Many of us saw 15 percent per year gains in our equity portfolios, adding to the all-important psychological "wealth effect." We knew it would not last—15 percent yields can't last—but we were not prepared for the rapid 50 percent loss that occurred.

The third factor in the cause of the financial meltdown was lack of common sense regulation, a lack of recognizing the common sense *balance point* on a continuum anchored on one end by a totally unregulated, competitive, free-market system, and on the other end by a totally regulated system that stifles competition and innovation.

There are many elements within the deregulatory climate that contributed to the meltdown, but three "decisions" are of particular importance. One was the 1999 repeal of the Glass-Steagall Act which, until repealed, had prevented commercial banks from engaging in investment banking activities. In Oak Center terms, the old-fashioned savings-and-loan bank collected the money on the first floor, with high-risk investment banking on the second floor, and with greed-motivated management on the third floor running the whole shebang. Not smart. Not wise.

Another regulatory element was the Commodity Future Modernization Act which, by federal law, said that derivative securities were no longer subject to any regulation (inserted on Christmas Eve 2000 into the annual appropriations bill by former Senator Gramm). With this deregulation, securities debt offerings exploded, creating an unbelievably tangled mess of paper assets of unknown value.

The other regulatory element, perhaps the most important contributor to the meltdown, was the 2004 waiver by the U.S. Security and Exchange Commission (the SEC) on the debt to net-capital leverage ratio that the banks were required to maintain. The ratio required, since 1975, was 15-to-1 or lower. (International standards are more on the order of 10-to-1.) In 2004, however, the SEC approved a waiver from this regulation for five large security firms: Goldman Sachs, Merrill Lynch, Morgan Stanley, Lehman Brothers, and Bear Sterns. (Do these names ring a bell?) It is of interest to note that the push for an increase in leverage ratios was led by the chairman of Goldman Sachs, Hank Paulson. Very quickly, within three or four years, these banks increased their leverage ratio from less than 15 to an astronomical 30- or 40-to-1. It was a strategy that made a lot of money fast. But at these levels of leverage, a depreciation of only 3 or 4 percent in the underlying value of the assets, can lead to insolvency

Things began to unwind slowly, then faster and faster. And it has been brutal. And scary. The irresponsible financial and moral management of our nation during the past decade had come home to roost. Warren Buffett has noted: "The world almost did come to a stop." His comment was not a joke. The day after Lehman filed for bankruptcy, Chief Executive Mohamed El-Erian of PIMCO (the world's largest bond firm) told his wife to "please go to the ATM and take as much cash" as she could. He feared that the banks might not open. And today, February 19, 2009, we are in a very, very dangerous situation.

There are several ways of looking at this danger. One way is the straightforward danger of entering into an economic spiral, one that keeps feeding on itself, which cannot be interrupted. This is the situation where the thoughtful decisions of each individual, while appropriate and right for that individual, collectively become increasingly detrimental to the economy at large. It is a situation where each short-term decision may be appropriate, even necessary, but the long-term effect may be disastrous. I know a bit about this phenomenon; it's called the "death spiral" in the corporate world. I was part of the Pillsbury decline and watched the "death spiral" of a once-great company. It ain't fun, and it ain't pretty. A lot of families and good people got hurt.

Another way of looking at this is in recognizing that we have a governance system that no longer works. We will have to face the possibility that other more centrally controlled economies may be stronger from an overall competitive standpoint, and we will have to face the question of how we adopt to regain competitiveness. The other part of our governance system that no longer works is the people part. As I write this chapter, I am beyond disgusted, at this critical juncture of our nation's well-being, to see partisanship given priority over finding a way to resolve this economic mess, a mess that our government's irresponsible, ideologically driven behavior has created.

To look at this issue further, we will have to address the question of what this all means in terms of the standard of living for the people of our nation. This question encompasses a lot: on a personal level, I wonder if Diane and I can continue to travel. What does it mean in terms of how the resources and energies of the nation are used (smaller houses but new, competitive factories)? What does it mean in terms of investment in education so that we have the scientists and engineers and professionals needed to compete in the global market? What does it mean in terms of moving to sustainable financial behavior in our trade balance and in our federal budget? Very, very importantly and a near-term question: *how do we transition from an asset-based economy to a savings economy without sinking the ship en route?* How do we deal with foreign-relation issues while in the midst of these economic challenges? And how do we factor in the energy independence issue and environmental issues and the health care issue?

In an earlier chapter I tried to capture a sense of the immense challenges of living in today's and tomorrow's world. The economic crisis is a biggie. And it's a present challenge, not just something that we old-timers can pass on to the kids to figure out. We are in it together, and we need to make decisions together. It also means that we need to face reality together. And it may mean that the future that we create, by design or by default in our decision-making, will be quite different than what it is now.

As I write this chapter, President Obama, less than one month in office, is leading the rebuilding effort. Diane and I had a dinner-table discussion about these efforts last night. I am of the opinion that the proposals the administration has made are as sound as any I can envision, and I am, to use the old phrase, cautiously optimistic, short term. But I believe the medium- to long-term odds of success are no more than 50/50—a tough opinion to share with my kids and grandkids. But the hole we have dug is so deep that transition to a sustainable, healthy economy will be extremely difficult. My concern is that the long-term solutions will require changes that are beyond our capacity to acknowledge or accept. Diane is less optimistic, even about the short term. Her concern is that we have a Congress that is incapable of governing and that the partisanship that we have seen in the past few weeks is a clear indication that the people in Congress do not sense the severity of the issue, nor do they have the quality of character to put the nation's interest ahead of their own parochial interests and ideologies.

The new administration's short-term "get the economy moving again" plan has three elements. The first is the stimulus plan to reignite consumption, a $787 billion plan. The second is mortgage relief for at least some of those who face foreclosure or have mortgages beyond their ability to manage, roughly a $75–275 billion plan. The third is a program to restore the health of the financial institutions, managing the resolution of the toxic securities they hold and thereby restoring the credit flow required for normal commerce. This effort was initially funded during the last days of the Bush administration, with a total of roughly $700 billion allocated (the TARP program). About half that amount has been spent, but as yet has not unlocked the system, primarily because valuation of toxic assets has not being resolved. As of this writing, the intricacies of the banking financial system are being studied and the mechanics of the President Obama/Treasury Secretary Tim Geithner plan are still being developed.

The overall Obama economic plan is like walking a tightrope over Niagara Falls in a 50 mph cross wind—from the standpoint of transitioning from the short-term stimulus program to an economy that is financially disciplined and has mid- and long-term sustainability. It is a plan that demands the consumer to spend lavishly and save little, short term—the consumer behavior that got us into this mess—but then transition to a sustainable, healthy savings economy mid- and long term.

This will require nothing short of revolutionary change for our nation and for the people of our nation. It will require us to change what we describe as values and how we view material assets. It will require cooperation and bipartisan support for a non-ideologically driven effort. It will, in all likelihood, change the character and image of our country, including how others view us and how we view ourselves. If we are successful, it will be because we have found a way to work together, with our loyalty being to reality and understanding, rather than to party and ideology. This could be the greatest opportunity that we have ever faced as a nation, and it could be the most wonderful adventure for the people of our nation.

But do we have the will and the character? Are we capable of acknowledging that as a nation, we may be on the road to failure with status-quo management of our economy? Or does simple-minded partisan behavior, driven by primal genes, keep us from addressing reality?

Our answer to this question is important. And it's important for a couple of reasons. First, if we succeed as a nation, it will undoubtedly require commitment and sacrifice and understanding from all of us. If we do not succeed, and there is very real risk that we will fail, given our lack of governance competency, we need to prepare—*as individuals*—for that possibility. The tide of the nation may not be there to lift us. We will be left to our own ingenuity, character, and preparation to carry us through the nation's decline. My strong recommendation is that we—you, family, friends, Diane, and I—prepare for both. Your own preparation will not be for naught in either case, so it makes sense for you to make decisions that buy you insurance if the nation does not have the capacity to get its act together.

Throughout this book I have hammered on the point that our future will depend on our capacity to look at the issues we face through the lens of reality, rather than basing our decisions on mythology and ideology. Looking at issues through the lens of reality means being informed as well as having the internal courage to set aside ideologies and examine the issues with a fresh mind. In the "My First, Big, Enduring Myth" chapter, I shared the hardest challenge that I have faced in terms of having the internal courage to set aside a long-held belief and to examine the subject with fresh, open eyes.

I mention this because it may take a comparable level of courage for some people to examine their economic and political ideologies. If we think of a friend or an acquaintance and ask ourselves what characteristic most strongly defines that person, we will often think of their economic or political views as the qualities that speak to the essence of that person. So it does not seem unreasonable to me to conclude that the economic and political views that we hold are comparable to religious views, in terms of the degree of tenacity and importance that we attach to these beliefs. Said more explicitly, it may be as hard for us to examine our economic and political views as it is to examine our religious beliefs. John Kenneth Galbraith, the noted economist and social scientist, spoke about how hard it is for leadership to face reality: "The threat to men of great dignity, privilege and pretense is not from the radicals they revile; it is from accepting their own myth. Exposure to reality remains the nemesis of the great—a little understood thing." Bottom line: if the nation is to look at reality, it will be because of us little people, the individuals who are grateful for what this nation has given us and for our strongest wish of being able to give our kids and grandkids the same gift.

Some of the greatest minds of our time see our nation at a very critical juncture. John Bogle, the founder of Vanguard Group and certainly one of the keenest minds on economics and finance, believes the very survivability of our nation, as we have known it for over two centuries, is at risk if we do not change our sense of what constitutes moral behavior and the beliefs or ideologies that we hold regarding our nation's financial and economic system. And he is not alone. Former Senator David Boren opens his book, *A Love Letter to America*, with: "The country we love is in trouble ... we are in grave danger of declining as a nation. If we do not act quickly, that decline will become dramatic." David Walker, comptroller general of the United States from 1998 to 2008, compares our financial mess to the circumstances that ruined the Roman Empire: "Rome fell for at least four reasons, and please listen carefully: A decline in moral values and political civility at home, overconfident and overextended military, fiscal irresponsibility by the central government and inability to control one's borders."

Clearly, our nation's financial and economic system is one of the immense challenges that we face, and the decisions we make will—almost certainly—determine whether we leave our kids and grandkids with a nation of opportunity and hope, or we leave them with a nation of decline and despair. With this being on the line, it would be an act of utter irresponsibility not to address the issues forthrightly and to make the best decisions we are humanly capable of making. Following are examples of some of the issues that we need to address. They are heavyweight issues that will demand wise, thoughtful consideration and will determine the future of our nation.

A Biggie: the Foundation

I might as well start out with the most fundamental, most contentious question we face: Is the U.S. free-market capitalism system capable of being a competitive system in tomorrow's global world? The financial crisis that we are experiencing is not one that originated overnight but is a manifestation of management issues that, some will argue, have been accumulating for the past three to four decades. But it has brought the "foundation" question to a head: We are closer to system failure today than at any time since the 1930s.

During the past decade we have also watched the exceptional economic growth in countries that have developed a modified form of the capitalistic system, countries such as China, Russia, and India. Clearly, the old state-controlled socialism and communism systems were not competitive with the free-market, capitalistic system. To become more competitive, these countries have developed an economic system that combines capitalism with an element of central government control. Different terms have been used to describe this hybrid economic concept. Dave Kansas, in *The End of Wall Street*, terms it "authoritarian or autocratic capitalism." Stephen Roach, Morgan Stanley Asia chief, has commented, "What we are seeing is that the Chinese command-and-control system can actually work more effectively than other market-based systems in times of economic stress."

I raise this issue to open the door and to encourage a more fundamental discussion of our financial and economic system philosophies. David Brooks, in addressing the issue from a Democratic versus Republican view, cautions his Republican party: "If the free-market party doesn't offer the public an honest appraisal of capitalism's weaknesses, the public will never trust them. Power will inevitably slide over to those who believe this crisis is a repudiation of global capitalism as a whole."

Personally, I *strongly* believe in the concept of a free-market, competitive economic system. But I also see it as a point on a continuum, anchored on one end by the pure socialism concept, and anchored on the other end by a free-market system that has no regulation or central control element. The relevant question, then, is where on this continuum is the balance point that maximizes the economic well-being and stability for our nation? The best point on this continuum for China, given its state of development and culture, is very likely not the optimum point for our nation. But arguments that do not go beyond "conservative" versus "liberal," or "free market" versus "controlled market," or "socialist" versus "democratic" are naïve and uninformed and will not solve the problem. To the contrary, it will assure further decline.

My argument is that we need to target a position on this continuum that is based on solid thinking and reality, rather than arguing a purely ideological position that results in our not being competitive with other more pragmatic global players. For example, one manifestation of this continuum issue is the question of how to balance the use of our nation's resources and energies. During the past two or three decades, we have seen a very high level of our resources invested in ever larger homes to satisfy individual wants, as opposed to investment in our infrastructure and in human capital development (education and worker-skill development). Nationally, this is not a survival strategy. A second example is the movement to offshore manufacturing of a large portion of our material goods—electronics, clothing, appliances, toys—leaving the United States without a competitive manufacturing environment and with the stage set for almost a certain account deficit and the need for a high level of borrowing from foreign countries to pay for our consumption of these products. It also makes the current financial crisis more difficult to resolve. We do not have a manufacturing sector that can readily absorb workers. Beware our entering an economic death spiral.

Bottom line: we will need to make an important, foundational decision on whether the free-market system provides sufficient "invisible hand" control for a vigorous, stable economy or whether a stronger element of central control is needed to assure long-term direction and competitiveness. This is an exceedingly important, far-reaching issue. It is an issue that is dangerous to our economic well-being because it is an issue that we may not have the courage to address.

Regulation: The Control of Greed

The farm boys at the end of the bar in the Oak Center Store understood greed. Of course, it seemed reasonable to believe that everyone did. It didn't take much common sense or understanding of human nature. So when Alan Greenspan said, "I made a mistake in presuming that the self-interests of organizations, specifically banks and others, were such that they were best capable of protecting their own shareholders and their equity in the firms," it was hard not to ask the question of whether Mr. Greenspan has enough common sense to come in out of the rain.

Somehow, Greenspan, and many others, forgot to consider the human psychology that drives Wall Street. Jack Welch, the legendary past manager of General Electric, made the point emphatically during an interview on Charlie Rose's show, that one has to understand that the guys (and very likely, a few gals) on Wall Street are there for one single purpose: *to make money.* His message was that if you don't understand that, you don't understand anything about the Wall Street businesses. Chris Hedges describes greed as "the God-given American freedom to exploit other human beings to make money." This is the first thing to understand. It should not be hard.

The second follows, rather logically: With unbridled greed, some reasonable level of regulation just might be needed. Just maybe! If the Bear Stearns manager's compensation is determined by the volume of mortgage loan business his company does, you can safely bet that Bear Stearns' managers will find a way to increase the amount of loan business done. So will Citigroup and Lehman Brothers. And make no mistake—these are smart, creative folks: to keep the balance sheet respectable and to manage risk, it will be an unavoidable temptation to package these loans into nice little bundles, and sell off the risk to other investors, and to multiply the dollars leveraged. It also made sense to lobby Washington, even getting former president George W. Bush, arguing for a "home ownership" society, helping create a climate that encouraged low or even no-down-payment loans. The big firms succeeded in getting approval to raise leverage by a threefold factor—a huge factor in the ultimate demise of the bank's capitalization structure. The other side of the aisle joined in, making it all a truly bipartisan effort, with U.S. Representative Barney Frank also touting the societal value of home ownership. And the Wall Street guys kept getting bigger and bigger bonuses. And, as one of the CEOs said, everyone kept on dancing. And all is well in fairyland until the economy, finally reaching a stress point from the unrestrained spending and economic mismanagement throughout the vaulted U.S. economic system, began to contract a bit. The first to fall were the sub-prime loans, made to those who had no margin for financial tightening. Default was in the air. The self-reinforcing downward spiral had been triggered. And the incredibly leveraged structure permitted in 2004 meant that things could go down much faster than they had gone up. And on Thursday night, September 18, it hit the tipping point for the world's most prestigious financial center—the businesses of the Wall Street banking firms were on the edge of collapse.

So, we need regulation. Today, as illogical as it seems, the huge derivative business—the credit default swap business and the hedge fund business—operate essentially without control. If you have a tiger in your yard, you better construct a fence that keeps the neighborhood secure and the kids safe. There are many ways of doing this, as all good managers know. It is a subject beyond the scope of this chapter, but a route that I favor is regulations that require a very high level of transparency of the business operations. In my judgment, it is the first line of "regulation" because it still allows for innovation and is less likely to become a disincentive to the businesses and services that the companies provide. Other critical issues that we face are the development of regulations that are adopted globally and deal with the "too big to fail" issue. Perhaps firms "too big to fail" should be broken into smaller entities, and if that is not feasible, for whatever reason, perhaps they are, by definition and practicality, a firm that needs to be "nationalized," or at minimum, become a quasi-governmental, tightly regulated entity. Obviously, reasonable regulations on debt to net-capital ratio, separation of commercial and investment banking, and the derivative shadow market need to be promulgated as soon as possible.

The current financial crisis demands that these issues be dealt with in a non-ideological manner and that wise decisions be made that restore the nation's economic health. These are issues that will define our future economic system. Loyalty to party or ideology versus loyalty to reality, wisdom, and understanding will, without question, result in our failure to establish a pragmatic regulatory framework to assure future stability.

The Unsustainable Security Net: Social Security, Medicare and Medicaid

Advanced, prosperous nations all strive to provide their people with a quality of life that is a mirror of how that nation sees itself in terms of being a caring, progressive, modern state. It is a measure and also a means of creating a vibrant national economy. *It's the nation's contract with its people: if you give us your sweat and blood, a sincere work effort, and your allegiance, we will, in turn, try to assure that you will always have the basic life needs— food, shelter, clothing and the care of your health—even if fate and circumstances do not treat you kindly.* This is a contract that has a moral and a business element. It speaks to the question of who we are and how we see ourselves. It speaks to the tension that exists between the merits of pure socialism and the merits of pure capitalism.

Although I have strong thoughts and opinions on the degree or depth to which our nation should provide this security network, it is my intent to focus on the question, not the answer. My objective is more elementary and more fundamental: It is simply to raise an awareness of the path that we are on and to suggest that this path represents an irresponsible position in terms of the moral contract that the nation has with its people, and with our long-term financial capacity to deliver. *Today, we are on a course that is not remotely close to being financially sustainable.*

We are again faced with an issue that will take an extraordinary amount of courage to address in a forthright manner. To date, the people or the political leadership has not had the courage or character to demand that we deal with the issue. So we continue on an unsustainable path, apparently with the idea of pushing the day of reckoning and tough decision-making off to our kids and grandkids, probably hoping that by some miracle of fortune, they will find the funds to keep the program going that we have blindly charted. The Obama administration, to its credit, has said that it is determined to address the issue. Representative Jim Cooper has said that it is "astonishing" that Obama has announced this intent. It is courageous in that, as George Will says, "there has been *bipartisan avoidance* of the predictable crisis coming to the big three entitlement programs—Social Security, Medicare, and Medicaid."

The critical point is that it is extremely unlikely that this issue will be dealt with in an adult manner by Congress. Unless ... unless ... the people demand that it be addressed. This is recognition of the fact that "leaders follow" rather than lead in most tough issues. The debate, if it can be raised to a true, serious national debate, will be brutal. It will be brutal because it raises moral questions as well as state-control questions, a few of which will be discussed to illustrate the magnitude of the issue.

The first point of reality to cope with is to recognize that the three entitlements, Social Security, Medicare, and Medicaid, now account for more than 40 percent of the total federal budget. *Newsweek*'s Robert Samuelson notes that in the 2006 federal budget of $2.7 trillion, we spent $544 billion for Social Security, $374 billion for Medicare, $181 billion for Medicaid, and $181 billion for food stamps, aid to the poor, and other welfare-oriented programs. Added together, this is on the order of 48 percent of the federal budget. For the most part, these are programs that rest on law and are not subject to yearly budgetary management.

As indicated, these programs represent a large portion of today's expenditures but are, as David Walker, former U.S. Comptroller General, put it, "penny ante compared to the fiscal disaster that is bearing down on America." The issue is the compound effect of the 78 million baby boomers who have just begun to collect benefits, coupled with the rapid rise in health care cost. Using Walker's analysis, "The U.S. Government Accountability Office (GAO), noting that the federal balance sheet does not reflect the government's huge unfunded promises in our nation's social-insurance programs, estimated last year that the unfunded obligations for Medicare and Social Security alone totaled almost $41 trillion. That sum, *equivalent to $352,000 per U.S. household, is the present-value shortfall* between the growing cost of entitlement and the dedicated revenues intended to pay for them." These numbers seem almost like a joke, but they are not, so I suggest you read them again. Still, they are absurd and cannot be delivered against financially without wholesale change in our financial structure and the United States economic system as a whole.

Deeply embedded in the financial quagmire are several very significant sub-issues important to our decisions on how to deal with the finance issue that these programs present:

• People take more risk and are more innovative when they know they have a security net underneath them. These qualities are critically needed for our nation to continue to be competitive in a global economy. To what degree do we want to foster this aspect of innovation?

• What is the moral obligation that we hold for assuring that our elderly have a comfortable, reasonably enjoyable existence?

And to what degree does this apply to those who have been less fortunate or were born with fewer skill gifts? Do we make sure we have well-staffed, clean, and cheery nursing homes for all in need? Do the benefits reach down to the assisted-living level?

• What level of financial assistance is appropriate for well-to-do individuals? Since these people have provided a disproportionate share of the tax that funds these programs, are they entitled to be recipients of the benefits, regardless of whether they have the means for self-payment?

• What level of medical care do we give the poor? To the irresponsible (smokers, alcoholics)? The lazy or indolent? The old and those approaching the end-of-life stage? Where are expensive medical procedures warranted and where are they not? How do we address the issue of multiple-birth pregnancies resulting from multiple embryos implanted during infertility treatment, knowing that multiple births result in a much higher level of premature and handicapped babies and that these children incur tremendous health care costs?

• Are we prepared to look at the alternative health care systems used in several European countries that deliver superior care at one-half to two-thirds the cost, or is the concept of universal single-payer an ideology that moves us down the path to a level of socialism that, overall, is detrimental to our economic well-being? Is the subject so contrary to our ideologies and the myths we hold that we cannot bear to acknowledge that there might be something to be learned?

• What is the process by which we resolve these issues? Is our government still capable of dealing with tough, difficult societal and economic issues? If not, what do we do?

As the above comments suggest, the Social Security, Medicare, and Medicaid issue are inextricably linked to the whole health care cost issue. We cannot deal with one without dealing with the other. Likewise, we will not resolve the deficit and financial issues without dealing with the health care and safety network issues. They are interlocked to a degree that simply demands that they be dealt with in a collective manner. And that is our challenge. It is truly an immense challenge.

Can a Nation Be Great with Great Income Inequality

Economists talk about this but, as best as I can tell, without much advice to offer. I think it's because it's one of those subjects that is confounded by so many factors—contempt for the lazy; the trade-off that people probably make between choosing a less-demanding lifestyle that may accompany a lower-paying job but that leaves more time for fishing; the fact that we are born with vastly different skills and abilities; the fact that some of us are born on third base, having affluent and well-connected parents; recognizing the element of luck, a major determinant of success, according to Gladwell's studies; that some societies seem to have a predilection for a caste system, whether determined by birth or achievement; the sense among some economists and politicians that the wealthy are the job- and industry-creators and hence, this disparity is needed for the good of all.

I cannot help but think of the maternal and paternal families that I grew up with. Grandpa Orlin and Grandma Gertie were the dynamic, hard-working, successful side. They were nose-to-the-grindstone people. I think this is the reason why Uncle Bud had a good relationship with his folks. He was of the same ilk. My dad, on the other hand, although he always had a job and was never on the dole, did not take a liking to the endless days of hard work. And if it was a day of hard work, he made it an 8:30 to 4:30 day. In that respect, he meshed well with Grandpa Fred and Grandma Maggie, my mother's folks. Nice, caring people, but not progressive. They lost everything during the Great Depression and carried the mark for life, but it seemed they had more fun. During the summer, my dad would finish up the farm chores early, my mother would pack a picnic supper, and we would head for Zumbro Falls, picking up Fred and Maggie on our way to "Red Bridge," a pasture below the power dam on the Zumbro River. That was our fishing hole, and we went so many times that I can still see the stumps on the bank where we sat holding our cane poles.

On Wednesday night we ate an early supper of lunchmeat sandwiches and made the twenty-minute drive to Zumbro Falls to see Fred and Maggie, all in time to see the outdoor traveling movie. We had to get there in time to watch the first part, which was a serial movie that carried over from week to week. If my mom felt rich that night, we might even end the evening with a bowl of chili. It was a social time. On Saturday night it was the same thing, only without the movie. Instead, the businesses of the town contributed a few bucks each, and at 10 p.m. there was a drawing in the outdoor bandstand. Top prize was a five-dollar bill. You had to be there to collect, or it went back into the kitty for the next week's drawing. Occasionally, a ladies aid group from one of the local churches would have a pie-fest after the drawing as a fund-raiser. Great cooks and delicious pies!

So when I look back, I have very mixed feelings. Clearly, and by a wide margin, I admire Grandpa Orlin's work ethic and achievements more than Grandpa Fred's. Inside, I would much prefer to be like Orlin, yet I had more fun with Grandpa Fred. But the real difference in my feelings toward them had nothing to do with their financial status, work ethic, or the fun times. Grandpa

Orlin, in some way, always let me know how important I was and that he sincerely cared about me and believed in me; that he'd always be there if I needed him. It was exactly the same with Bud.

The point of this is that income inequality is not like other fairness issues. It's there, but its importance to us, as individuals, is desensitized because we value other qualities more than wealth or income level. Grandpa Orlin was special to me, not because he was more successful and affluent but simply because he cared about me. But yet, income inequality is an issue that is very important to our nation for a number of broader societal and economic reasons.

One is that it has major bearing on economic well-being and stability. Beginning with President Reagan, the theory of supply-side economics was advanced as a core economic philosophy. It's not clear how this philosophy took route but the story, as yet not refuted, is that Arthur Laffer, an economist who anticipated none of the issues of the current financial crisis, sold the idea to a *Wall Street Journal* editor—the infamous back-of-the-napkin curve, showing how a reduction in the marginal tax rate among the wealthy would lead to increased investment and prosperity, and that this prosperity would "trickle down" to the masses. Jude Wanniski, the *WSJ* editor, in turn convinced Jack Kemp of the doctrine. At the time, Jack Kemp was contending for the Republican presidential nomination. Not long after, Kemp made an agreement with Ronald Reagan that he would drop out of the presidential race, but only under the condition that Reagan adopt the supply-side theory as a cornerstone for his economic policy.

Reagan readily and cheerfully adopted the idea. It was a rationale for cutting taxes for the rich and thereby gaining their financial support. Interestingly, the theory had no proven validity. Even David Stockman, Reagan's budget manager, acknowledged that the supply-side economic theory was a hoax designed to cut taxes for the wealthy and to set context for reduced spending on middle-class and low-income programs. The net effect, of course, is history: federal spending and budget deficits increased at unparalleled peace-time rates under the Reagan administration, the beginning of our irresponsible financial adventure that has been ongoing for most of the past thirty years. Of course, as we are all painfully aware, it has now come home to roost.

So although most of us are comfortable with the idea that some of our populace—even neighbors and family members—may be far more wealthy than the others, the issue of income equality has tremendous national significance in that it has major bearing on our attitude toward an equitable, economically sound tax structure. And from there flows the whole cascade of our economic policy. For example, back to the Reagan question: do you spur economic growth by lowering the taxes of the rich, who then invest; or, alternatively, do you lower the taxes of the lower- and middle-class folks, who then have more to spend, spurring the "demand side" of economics that produces economic growth.

Starting with the Reagan era, we have seen a tremendous move toward wealth and income being funneled from the bottom to the top. Since 1980, the effective tax rate for the richest tier has fallen from 60 percent to today's 34 percent. In 1980, the top 1 percent of families took home 10 percent of the nation's income; by 2004 the top 1 percent were taking home 22 percent. The richest 1 percent of Americans—those with incomes of $950,000 and up—now hold about 40 percent of all the nation's assets. The income of the top 10 percent is almost equal to the total of the remaining 90 percent. Perhaps more concerning, the rich are now getting richer, while the common people are losing ground: since 1980 the income of the bottom 95 percent has risen by less than 1 percent, while the income of the top 1 percent has increased 100 percent, and the income of the top 0.01 percent has gone up 500 percent. Real wages (that is, adjusted for inflation) of those employed in the manufacturing sector have actually fallen.

Bottom line: the rich control the nation's wealth, and the rich are getting much richer. Most of the tax cut under Bush 43 went to the rich and furthered their position of financial dominance. And with money comes power, both to influence government and to perpetuate family-member opportunity, status, and position.

Among the developed nations of the world, the United States has become the nation with the greatest level of income inequality. There are several ways of measuring this demographic. One simple way is to compare the income of the top 10 percent to the bottom 10 percent, giving a ratio number as measurement of the inequality. Using this metric, the United States has the highest level of inequality at 5.6; Japan is 4.1; Canada is 3.9; Germany is 3.2; and Sweden is 2.6. Another metric is a scale called the Gini coefficient, which sets 0 as absolute equality (all people have the same income), and 1 as absolute inequality (one person has the entire nation's income). A few of the countries noted in a 2007 report:

Japan	0.25
Sweden	0.25
India	0.33
United States in 1970	0.39
United States in 2005	0.47

It's critical to understand that a growing income disparity can reach a point where it becomes a self-reinforcing phenomenon. Wealth begets wealth. There is high potential for creating an income or wealth caste system in our nation if this trend is not reversed.

What are the manifestations of the income and wealth inequality issue before us? There are several, some of which I have alluded to:

- To what degree does the idea of having a "robust, healthy middle class" have impact on the long-term economic health of the nation? I would argue that a prosperous middle class is very important. (I also acknowledge that I have seen no hard data or reputable studies to support this view.)

- What are the moral implications of having a nation with a high level of income and wealth inequality? I would argue that this is not the nation that we want to be. Yet it is also true, as Seymour Martin Lipset, a highly regarded sociologist noted, that when you leave unequally endowed people free to achieve, you get unequal results.

- To what degree should income and wealth inequality be dealt with by creating "equal opportunities"—university-level education available for all, skilled labor retraining, universal health care, improved K–12 schooling, community college access?

- At what level and at what tax rate should there be an estate tax on extremely large inheritances? How do we ensure that this tax is communicated to the public in an honest manner, rather than being embedded in misleading propaganda? The so called "death tax," using a $3.5 million per couple exemption level, will, contrary to the impression created by many intellectually dishonest politicians, affect only about 1 out of every 200 people who die. (Due to a crazy budget-setting process, the exemption level has increased to where it is entirely eliminated in 2010, only to return to the 2001 level—a feature that Paul Krugman has called the "Throw Momma from the Train Act.") Are we walking the "all people created equal" talk of the Constitution? Is the concept of "people created equal" consistent with the concept of the creation of dynasty wealth? Is it good and just for society at large?

- What is our overall tax policy and structure, including the stimulus plan structure, given the growing level of income and wealth inequality? To what degree should the tax rate be progressive, and to what degree should it be structured to encourage investment by the wealthy? And does the latter theory have any demonstrated validity?

The decisions that we make on these issues will be critically important, not only in terms of our current economic crisis but also, assuming we are successful in digging ourselves out of the hole we are in, to the longer term health of our nation. The issue demands our concern and attention, our willingness to set aside ideology and consider the issue with open eyes, with the hope that we'll make wise decisions—decisions that are good for the nation we leave our kids.

Deficits: Living Beyond Our Means

By any consideration, our nation has had the opportunity during the past few decades to set the stage for continued prosperity and well-being. No major natural disasters, such as the droughts of the '30s, were encountered, and no major wars, such as WW II, were thrust upon us. The 9/11 attack in 2001 was a very significant event that made us realize that we had to make protection against terrorist attack part of our security strategy. With the world's goodwill response, we had opportunity to forge an international alliance of cooperation. Contrary to the administration's propaganda machine, the 9/11 terrorist attack had nothing to do with Iraq. That was a war of choice, and the true reason for our decision to invade and occupy this country remains unknown. We had issues of importance to face, but these were as much issues of opportunity as they were problems: education, stemming the growth in income inequality, global warming and environmental questions, health care cost containment, the energy question, and many others. Certainly big issues, but also issues that provided a huge opportunity for bringing together the nation's people and for creating a sense that our country was moving in the right direction and that we were all part of making the world a better place.

It was the perfect setting for asking the people to help create a solid, sustainable economy and to embark upon a national strategy that had the courage and discipline to build a stronger nation, one that was moving forward not only for the good of itself but also for the good of the world.

But we let this opportunity elude us. We somehow became self-absorbed and irresponsible. We failed to address the education issue in a meaningful way; we buried our heads in the sand on the energy issue; we stonewalled the global warming question. And, in a way that was almost symbolic of our irresponsible behavior, we made collective decisions to spend beyond our means. Occasionally, an economist or a business news commentator or a written editorial would speak to the issue. But for the most part, the people were quiet. Our financial institutions, which clearly have the expertise to see the problems that were building, said nothing, and in fact allowed their greed to dominate their interests. And our government and the politicians that we elected provided no leadership—to the contrary, they became major contributors to the problem.

Some in the Bush administration argued that deficits were not important. In a very narrow sense, that might (or might not) be true. A number of the developed nations of the world have higher deficit levels than the United States. What they failed to see, however, is a far more important metric. That is, the *rate of change*, a sense of what the shape of the curve looks like. It is seeing and sensing what the process means, where it will lead, and what other societal issues are accompanying this change. It means focusing on the question of what governance and societal changes will be required to change the slope of the line, rather than simply looking at a year-end number and concluding that it is in the tolerable zone. This is what vision and longer-term strategy is about; it's what competent management is about. We didn't have it, and now we are in a mess.

The deficit inflection point began in 1980 with the Reagan administration and implementation of supply-side economic theory and tax reduction, without a corresponding spending decrease. The balanced budget concept, where either spending was reduced enough to match revenues or tax increased enough to balance spending, was kicked down the road on the basis that economic growth and hence, revenue resulting from the supply-side stimulus would ultimately bring the budget into balance, setting the stage for sustained economic prosperity. We were beginning our journey down a path that replaced reality and substance and toughness with the delusional message that because America is the "shining city upon a hill," it was somehow entitled to spend far more than its income—that providence would intervene and protect our special status.

But that was just a beginning. We continued to meander, with a significant respite during the Clinton administration where, at the end of his term, very rapid economic growth actually created a surplus, allowing a reduction in the deficit. This was about to end in a decisive way, however, with the Bush 43 administration and a return to the ideology of supply-side economics and the support it engenders among the very rich. In 2000, the deficit stood at about $4 trillion; by 2008 it had grown to roughly $10 trillion, a 250 percent increase. Concomitant with this budget deficit increase was an increase in the current account deficit, the trade difference between the amount we sell internationally and the amount of goods that we buy. With the current financial crisis and President Obama's stimulus and recovery packages, the expected 2009 budget deficit is projected to add another $1.75 trillion to our deficit, a scary scenario yet one that most economists see as essential to bringing the economy out of its current crisis.

Much of this is the result of our economy's becoming more and more dependent on consumer spending. In 2008, consumer spending was 72 percent of the economy; it is now about 71 percent, a level far above the twenty-five-year 1975–2000 level of 67 percent. Almost a mirror image of this is the consumer savings rate, which actually became negative late 2007/early 2008, as we dipped into our savings simply to maintain our spending lifestyle.

Much of this consumer spending spree was made possible by three compounding factors—perhaps the perfect storm that has dug the deepest part of the financial hole that we are in. First was the greed factor, causing the financial institutions to give ever-more easy credit loans that put more short-term money in the borrower's pockets, which they promptly spent. The second factor was that Greenspan and associates kept the Federal Reserve interest rate far too low, bowing to the political pressures to keep the economy vibrant. And third, we had willing global lenders, particularly China, who used our gluttonous ways as a market for their goods and their economic growth, a symbiotic relationship that grew to huge proportions during the 2000–2008 period. But it was all unsustainable.

This constituted a generational change. As Michael Gerson, columnist for the *Washington Post*, pointed out. "Many Americans who struggled through the Depression adopted a set of moral and economic habits, such as thrift, family commitment, savings, and modest consumption, that lasted through their lifetimes—and have decayed in our own." Even some of our religious leaders have made note of this generational change. As Gerson noted, "Pope John Paul III warned of making 'people slaves of possession and of immediate gratification, with no other horizon than the multiplication or continual replacement of the things already owned with others still better.'" Bill Gross recently noted that "human nature means that institutions at some point lose their sense of mission." Institutions in this case include nations.

The result of our irresponsibility is the mess we find ourselves in. The president's plan, as I have mentioned earlier, is to reinvigorate and to stabilize the economy, and then to transition into a sustainable economy with responsible budget management. I also mentioned how difficult I see this transition being longer term—walking the Niagara Falls tightrope in a 50 mph cross wind.

The dangers are mind-boggling, so we have to be successful. President Obama's plan has to be successful. The danger is that we could easily enter into "stag-flation" (economic stagnation coupled with rampant inflation, the route many countries have gone down) or "stag-deflation" (economic stagnation coupled with price deflation, similar to what Japan has endured since the 1990s). A number of leading economists see the longer term outcome of our financial crisis being hyper-inflation. Clearly, there is a very high level of uncertainty on the ultimate outcome of this financial mess. One of the potential "tipping point" issues is the possibility of foreign nations becoming reluctant to loan the United States the funds needed to finance the huge deficit that the recovery program and future budgets will require. Almost 50 percent of the U.S. Treasury debt is now held by foreigners; it was 31 percent only eight years ago. Almost 80 percent of our new debt will need to be funded by foreign countries. At present, China is our largest lender and also holds the largest share of foreign-funded debt.

Gerson has commented, "It has always been a quiet fear of capitalists that the success of free markets would eventually undermine the moral basis for free markets—that decadent prosperity would dissolve values such as prudence and delayed gratification." The transition from a consumer-spending economy to a saving, low- or no-budget deficit economy will require a level of understanding, cooperation, and commitment of the people that we have not seen since the WW II effort. It is instructive to note that there are a limited number of options in resolving this huge deficit issue: The first is to live with it, which is not a sustainable option; the second is placing our hope on our being able to ignite an explosion of economic growth, producing a major increase in tax revenue; the third is to inflate the debt away, almost always a disastrous, chaotic economic path; and *the fourth is for the nation and its people to become fiscally and monetarily disciplined, tough-minded, and responsible.* Remember, while we are doing this, we have many the other serious issues that face the nation: education, energy, health care costs, global warming, foreign policy, etc.

But—and this is the biggest *but* one can imagine—it could be the most satisfying, enjoyable, fulfilling time in our nation's life … if we have the will. And if we have the courage. If we can set aside ideology and party loyalty and replace it with reality and a true concern about the nation's future.

The Nation and You

We have a chance, nationally speaking, to solve the financial issue but only if we, the people, become responsibly and intelligently engaged. This means letting the nation's leaders know that *we know* we face a huge problem, a huge challenge. It means letting them know that we expect their most sincere effort; that partisanship and self-serving pontification and unfounded and intellectually dishonest ideologies will not be tolerated. It means telling our elected officials that we are willing to sacrifice and look long term. It means telling them that we understand infrastructure investment, and investment in basic research to find a solution to our energy situation. It means telling them that we are not afraid of revolutionary change. Because that is what will be required.

But what if we collectively do not have the will or the courage? Then our nation will enter a chaotic decline. I mentioned that I saw a miniature version of this at Pillsbury. I was lucky and survived the layoffs, but many were not. Fortunately, the nation's economy was relatively prosperous at that time, so many were able to find jobs that were sufficient to maintain a reasonable life. A national decline today would be far more severe and could easily accelerate to a situation comparable to the Great Depression days. However, that was a time in our history when people had far less distance to fall. We drove less, lived in smaller communities, grew much of own food, and lived a life much less dependent on our financial status. Today, a fall to the Great Depression level would be life-shattering for a large segment of our urban-oriented population.

Yet there is a real chance that this can happen. When it might happen, and to what degree, and the mathematical likelihood of its happening is impossible to predict. But there is a chance. We have dug the hole so deep that we definitely are in danger of the "death spiral" that has destroyed many poorly managed businesses and many once-great nations.

So what do we do? We must do everything we can to prevent it from happening. It means becoming engaged with our national leadership. Individual passivity is equivalent to irresponsibility. It means that we look reality in the eye. It means having the courage to seek truth and understanding the financial mess, rather than relying on party dogma for answers.

For individuals, particularly the young people, the mess we are in makes it even more critical that we develop our personal skill base. It means developing skills that have robust value— meaning that our skills have value, even in a declining economy, or value in a different country, or value for a longer portion of our lives, allowing us to work, if needed, past traditional retirement age. It means having a willingness to retrain and to view skill development as an unending education process. The best insurance means developing professional skills that have global value. It means developing language and computer skills. It means seeing the entire world as an opportunity base.

It also means managing one's lifestyle so that it is not dependent upon as much income, living slightly below our means, rather than at the edge. It means appreciating and enjoying the smaller things in life—family, reading, a warm but more modest home, local music groups, honesty, friends, the new dog; it's all those things. Our happiness is determined far more by our attitude toward life, the quality of our inner character, by taking time to appreciate the wonders of our existence, and by how we treat others than it is by trying to satisfy insatiable material and ego demands and by denying the realities that have led us into this financial mess. My generation clearly forgot most of that message, and now we are in big trouble.

One of the great wonders of our existence is that we do not know what tomorrow will bring or the changes that will occur. Man has proven, time and time again, that he has the capacity to be resourceful and responsible. Because of that, we always have hope. And with sufficient effort and with the courage to be loyal to truth and reality, rather than being loyal to party or ideology, we will be able to crawl out of this financial hole and return our nation to financial prudence and stability.

CHAPTER 12

ENDING THE ISRAEL-PALESTINE CONFLICT WITH REALITY

"Peace is not an absence of war, it is a state of mind, a disposition for benevolence, confidence, Justice."

—Baruch Benedict de Spinoza

*"We must remember that hatred is like acid.
It does more damage to the vessel in which it is stored than to the object in which it is poured."*

—Ann Landers

Can an old farm boy from Oak Center, sitting in his little rented office in Hopkins, with no foreign-relations experience whatsoever, have anything to contribute to a conflict that has defied resolution for over sixty years? Five individuals have received the Nobel

Peace Prize, and although most of the leaders of the developed world have tried, including significant effort by at least four or five United States presidents—all have failed. So what thoughts can I possibly bring to bear on the issue that have not been considered by those far more capable than I?

My logistical approach to writing this book is a technique that I used for many years at Pillsbury. I earned my keep by looking at complicated issues, most of which nobody else wanted to address, then making an informed assessment and advancing a course of action. The end-product was often a concise, focused position paper that would move through management, the ultimate objective being to put the company in position to move ahead competently and confidently on a complex issue or opportunity. What very few people saw was the voluminous amount of working material that formed the background information and the pro-and-con arguments upon which these position papers were based. My approach was to organize hard-copy material in three-ring binders to facilitate in-depth study of the material. A few of my closest work associates were aware of my methodology, and Hans Zoerb, a work colleague and good friend still, refers to this approach as the "Rabe Three-Ring Binder Method."

So it was natural, I guess, for me to collect and organize the large amount of background material for this book in the same way. In fact, I sometimes feel a bit disappointed that a single paragraph in this book, often rather general in substance or in detail of position, is the meager sum or conclusion drawn from a couple of these three-ring binders. On the other hand, this approach seems to identify aspects of an issue that are, surprisingly, often not considered, not even by those who have been intimately involved with the subject. I have that same sense with respect to the Israel-Palestine conflict, and those perceptions—I believe, realities—are what this chapter will deal with. And most important and critical, it is my contention that only by acknowledging these realities can a sustainable peace be established.

The importance of the Israel-Palestine issue is well known and well understood by all our political leaders, and the media, and most of the informed public. Along with the issue of oil and energy, the Israel-Palestine conflict is central to the entire Middle East stability question and to the Muslim extremists/terrorists issue. The implications of the Israel-Palestine issue is totally out of proportion to the population numbers that are involved, roughly 5.5 million Jews and about an equal number of Palestinian Arabs. These numbers are slightly less than what would be involved if the people of Wisconsin were in conflict with the people of Minnesota. The rest of the world would surely yawn. Yet the Israel-Palestine issue is a huge consumer of our energies and, for many years, has been a major risk to world peace and to good relations throughout the Middle East.

The Three Realities

There are three major realities in the Israel-Palestine conflict that have not been dealt with but that are absolutely crucial to any form of resolution of the conflict:

- Confronting the ancient scriptural myth that God gave the Israelis a promised land.

- Acknowledging the reality that the Palestinians are the historical, indigenous people of the land.

- Recognizing that the solution must be one with which the conscience of the world can live long term.

The *first* is an issue undergirded by the thesis of this book: We will not be able to deal with problems unless we look at the problems through the lens of reality. In discussion of the Israel-Palestine conflict there are some considerations—realities that are "swept under the rug"—that are apparently deemed too sensitive to discuss. A key reason this issue is not discussed is because it opens the door to examination of parallel presuppositions held by people of other nations and religions. I am referring to the notion held by the Jews that they are a "chosen people" and that they have been given special rights by God to a geographic piece of land—"the promised land."

The *second* factor is to look at the international decision that led to the creation of the state of Israel and to the decision that it was justifiable to take land away from an indigenous people, the Palestinians, and give it to another. And further, to look at the outcome of this decision in terms of the well-being of the people that were displaced. This later point, the plight of the Palestinians, is a subject that has been discussed to some degree; the morality and the international law and justice aspects of the former point—the idea of "chosen people" being given a piece of land from a God—has hardly been discussed at all, at least in this country. Or if it has, it has not been at the depth required for significant influence in our foreign policy or decision-making.

The *third* factor is to recognize that any solution to the Israel-Palestine conflict, in order for it to be sustainable, will have to be a solution that the conscience of the world can live with long term. That means that the decisions made now or in the near future to resolve this conflict will have to withstand the moral and international law judgment of tomorrow's generation in order for it to be an enduring peace. This is an absolutely critical point for the Israelis to recognize: their nation will not endure long term if the eyes of the world see them as having an unjust presence in these ancient lands. All the proposals, including the extremely admirable efforts of former president Carter, which I have collected in my three-ring binders, fail in this regard.

Although recognizing that we are only one of the nations of the world that has interest in the Israel-Palestine conflict, our decisions will need to be made within the context of the three factors—call them realities—that I have noted, if we are to have any hope of resolving this problem. The decisions we make will also need to be pragmatic in the sense that "we are where we are." There is a critical difference, however, between acknowledging mistakes that have been made and the realities that have been denied, and sweeping them under the rug when we acknowledge "we are where we are." The following elaborates on these three realities and concludes with some thoughts on the decisions and position that we should encourage our government to make, so that our nation and the world, along with the Israelis and Palestinians, can focus energy on creating a decent existence for all people.

Confronting the Myth That God Gave
the Israelis a Promised Land

The foundational argument for the creation of the state of Israel is that God promised to Abraham and his descendants "everlasting possession" of these ancient lands. Orthodox Jews and Zionists believe that the Jewish people are a "chosen" people, and that they have a unique, special relationship with the creator. It is a conviction that is rooted in scripture and tradition:

> "Then and there the Lord made a covenant with Abram. He said, 'I promise to give your descendants all this land from the border of Egypt to the Euphrates River." (Genesis 15:18)

211

"Behold, I have given up the land before you: go in and *take possession of the land* which the Lord has sworn unto your fathers through Abraham, through Israel, and through Jacob." (Deuteronomy 1:8)

"Moses called together all the people of Israel and said to them, 'You saw the terrible plagues, the miracles, and the great wonders that the Lord performed. But to this very day he has not let you understand what you have experienced. For forty years the Lord led you through the desert, and your clothes and sandals never wore out. You did not have bread to eat or wine or beer to drink, but the Lord provided for your needs in order to teach you that he is your God. And when we came to this place, King Sihon of Heshbon and King Og of Bashan came out to fight against us. But we *defeated them, took their land,* and divided it among the tribes of Reuben and Gad, and half the tribe of Manassh. Obey faithfully all the terms of this covenant, so that you will be successful in everything you do.

"Today you are standing in the presence of the Lord your God, all of you--your leaders and officials, your men, women, and children, and the foreigners who live among you and cut your wood and carry your water for you. You are here today to enter into this covenant that the Lord your God is making with you and to accept its obligations, so that the Lord *may now confirm you* as his people and your God, as he promised you and your ancestors.'" (Deuteronomy 29:2–15)

"Samuel said to Saul, 'I am the one whom the Lord sent to anoint you king of his people Israel. Now listen to what the Lord Almighty says. He is going to punish the people of Amalek because their ancestors opposed the Israelites when they were coming from Egypt. Go and attack the Amalekites and completely destroy everything they have. *Don't leave a thing; kill all the men, women, children, and babies; the cattle, sheep, camels, and donkeys.*'" (1 Samuel 15:1–3)

In a core chapter of this book, "My First, Big, Enduring Myth," I set forth that I have come to conclude that the Bible—while a book that contains beautiful literature, wisdom, and life-decision truths—is a book of myth. As I indicated, the reasons that I came to this conclusion are many. One of the reasons, but only one of the many reasons, is that the Bible is totally inconsistent in its concept of God: is God cruel and angry, or is he loving and merciful? 1 Samuel 15:1–3 is not an isolated passage; consider "I will not pity, nor spare, nor have mercy, but destroy" (Jeremiah 13:14). This is quite at odds with "The Lord is good to all, and his tender mercies are over all his works," again one of many such passages (Psalms 145:8).

There is no historical record of the exodus. Nothing. Accordingly, there seems to be something very self-serving in the notion of God's picking out a "chosen people" and commanding that they kill off some of the others of his creation. One should also note that the verses above, which are the basis for the Jewish claim for these lands, come from the scriptures, which also have the world created in seven days, which loaded every species of animals on a boat, which have burning bushes talking to people, where some lived to 900 years before dying, and where living in the belly of a whale was possible.

My purpose here is not to provide a detailed theological or historical basis for concluding that it is a myth that the "chosen people" were given a "promised land." Many theologians and historians can—and have—argued this case far more effectively than I can. But for me, the story of Israel's being a "chosen people" and that they have some kind of a God-given right to a piece of the earth—the land between the Jordan River and the Mediterranean Sea—is ludicrous. If it were not for the Christian religion evolving from the Old Testament Israel story, the idea of a chosen people would be readily and widely rejected as mythology—a beautiful tale but of no historical validity and most certainly *not the basis for foreign policy*.

The crucial point, however, is that we have swept this aspect of the Israel-Palestinian conflict under the rug. I suspect that the reason, in part, is because the Christian myth is embedded in the Israel chosen people/promised land myth, and because the Islam religion is embedded with comparable myth. By raising the question of whether a central tenet of Judaism is myth, the door is opened to asking parallel questions about the Christian and Islam faiths. So there is silent agreement to avoid the most foundational issue of the conflict. For the United States to establish foreign policy that either implicitly or explicitly rests on acceptance of these myths is, at best, misguided policy, and at worse, policy that supports bigotry and increases human suffering.

I want to point out that there is an "Israeli people" factor that warrants thoughtful consideration. Religious mythology is not the only thing that binds people, which gives them a proud identity. There are cultural aspects such as heritage, music, language, and a deeply shared sense of community. But this is very, very different than claiming the right to a piece of land because someone believes that God picked a small group of people, out of the whole of mankind, and gave them divine right to occupy that land. My sense is that the European community, while not yet talking about it in the open, is considering this point in a quiet way and that it is having an influence on their position regarding the Israel-Palestine conflict issue.

I also want to make an important follow-up point: this issue does not, in my judgment, mean that Israel, as a nation, should not exist. We are where we are. But to achieve a lasting peace, the idea that God parcels out land to special people must be openly acknowledged as little more than ancient mythology. The conscience of the world will ultimately demand that this reality be addressed. It is an essential precondition to the creation of a lasting peace. It also needs to be acknowledged by the Israelis themselves. This means that the non-fundamentalist Jews will need to assert themselves; it is a fact of life that the far right Orthodox and Zionists, as well as the supportive far-right, fundamentalist Christians, have neither the courage nor capacity for true inquiry and the search of reality. But both groups can be reduced to minority players if those who have the courage to search for truth and understanding step forward. Encouragingly, there are many polls that suggest this movement is well underway.

It is also the prerequisite position that needs to be taken to address a parallel point authentically and to make a comparable declaration that we believe that the Islam religion is mythology-based. While most Muslims will disagree, they will also respect our sincerity and honesty and impartiality.

In summary, Israel does not have a *divine right*—a decree from God—to the piece of Earth that, until 1947, was called Palestine. This candidness is crucial to meaningful dialogue and any realistic hope of resolving the conflict. It is perhaps the most foundational issue and cannot be avoided—one either agrees or disagrees. It is not an option to pretend the question does not exist. And it needs to be the cornerstone topic for true dialogue and resolution of the Israel-Palestine issue.

The Palestinians Are the Major Historical, Indigenous People of the Land

The argument that the people of Israel are the major historical inhabitants of the land is not a true statement. The pre-BCE biblical record, as discussed, is mythological. (This does not mean that there are not elements in these stories that have a factual historical or geographical basis; even fictional novels often have a recognizable historical or geographical setting.) Most historians believe that the Israelis were small, wandering tribes, living among the other indigenous people of the land. It is generally believed by historians that during the first half of the first century—two thousand years ago—the Jews were probably in the majority. By the fifth century, they were in the minority, with the Christians probably predominating, and by the twelfth century, the Muslims predominated. Following is a numerical estimate of the Jewish population beginning in the 1500s to the date of the United Nations formation of the State of Israel in 1948:

	Jewish %	Christian %	Muslim %
Early 1500s	3	4	92
Late 1600s	1	5	94
1800	3	8	89
1890	8	11	81
1914	14	10	76
1922	11	9	78
1931	17	9	74
1947	32	7	60

This table is intended to point out that there is simply no basis for believing that the Israelis are the "rightful" occupants of the land or that they are the historical inhabitants. What is clear, from a historical perspective, is that this has been the homeland for over forty generations of Palestinians. Following the growth of the ancient Christian religion, and because these lands were conquered by several empires over time, the Jewish people left these lands and dispersed throughout foreign lands, including Russia, Spain, Germany, and many other countries—the Diaspora. A remarkable sense of community and the depth of their religious faith held them and their descendants together. Among the Orthodox, the sense of being "chosen people" with a "promised land" gave them unity, a strong identity and hope.

In the chapter on "Evil," I discussed the most evil episode in history, the Holocaust, the systematic extermination of six million Jewish people. It is the most revolting, repulsive act imaginable, something so awful that it has an element of being a Twilight Zone phenomenon—something almost unbelievable. Yet it happened. The structures of Auschwitz and Dachau and other extermination camps still stand in mute testimony to the depth of evil that man is capable of committing. At various times, when thinking about this, I have gone to the Minnetonka Ridgedale Library and spent afternoons perusing the library's books for an explanation for the degree of hatred that could perpetuate such an act, and which could involve the participation of many, many German people. I shared with you some of the thoughts of social scientists on this matter, including the thoughts of Jewish survivors.

While the Holocaust was unparalleled in the depths of its atrocity, for centuries the Jewish people have been persecuted time and time again in many different countries. It is reasonable and perhaps instructive to ask why. I believe that a clue for the answer to this question can be found in what is now being called the "Catastrophe," the umbrella term used to describe the horrible treatment that has been inflicted upon the indigenous Palestinians by the Jews after creation of the Israel state.

At the risk of being racial, in an upside-down sense, I believe it is accurate to say that the Jewish people are an exceptional people; they are a very intelligent people—creative, industrious, family-focused, educationally driven, disciplined, and bound together by admirable traditions, culture, community, and—probably most important—by their religion. I have known many, have worked with many, and have traveled with some, and invariably I sense their bond and their exceptionalness. I admire them and wish that more people had these qualities.

But there is also a concerning element that I suspect is tied to their religion—the belief and inner sense of their being a "chosen people" with a land "promised" to them by God. This is the sense of having a unique hold of truth; *a relationship with God that other people do not have.* From this, it is an easy, almost logical step to a belief or sense of superiority, and a belief in entitlement, certainly with respect to the "promised land." The three Abraham religions all have this problem; they are religions of absolute truth claims, giving the faithful the "right" to put their perception of God-given direction ahead of all other considerations. It becomes a license to dominate and to subjugate others because they have convinced themselves, albeit without anything close to serious inquiry, that it's the will of God. It is putting themselves and their beliefs before the beliefs and needs of others.

This may begin to explain—but certainly not to excuse—why nation after nation has persecuted the Jewish people, rendering them an immense amount of pain throughout history, and ultimately, the unconscionable suffering to which millions of Jewish men, women, and children were subjected during the Holocaust. When a people believe that they hold the truth and believe that they have been given special status with God, these people acquire a reputation and identity—"marked" to use a biblical term—by the others of mankind; they are viewed by others as being self-absorbed, arrogant, and with a feeling of superiority to others. Eventually, I believe it became a mark upon the Jewish people and from there, they became the target and lightning rod for all the problems of the day, a most useful tool for an evil political organization.

The efforts by Zionists to establish the Israel state go back to the early 1900s, perhaps farther. The movement is intertwined with the history of the land, with its conquerors, with the Ottoman Empire, with WW I, with the British mandate, with WW II, and with the efforts of the League of Nations and United Nations—international governing bodies created to help maintain world peace. For the purpose of this discussion, it will suffice to transcend the earlier years and move to the definitive point in history, the decision by the United Nations in 1947 to partition the land into an Israel state and a Palestinian state, with Jerusalem and Bethlehem as international areas, concomitant with the 1948 departure of the British forces that had occupied the area. Israel declared its independence as a nation, with conflict between the indigenous Palestinians and Israeli Zionists beginning immediately. Historians are divided on who perpetrated the conflict, but hard-to-refute records show that as soon as the United Nations made the decision to create an Israel and Palestine state, there was a very deliberate, carefully calculated, effort by the Zionists, called Plan Dalet, *for the ethnic cleansing of the Palestinian people from their native land.* After a year of conflict, a cease-fire was negotiated, with the Israel partition increasing from about 55 percent of the area to 77 percent, with the boundaries becoming known as the "Green Line." But most revealing is the history of the past sixty years, which shows the relentless separation and settlement effort by the Israeli Zionists to produce a pure Jewish nation that occupies what they claim—based on their ancient scripture—is the "promised land" given to them by God.

It is often cited, correctly, that there was a movement to create an Israeli state well before the 1947–48 period; the Balfour Declaration in 1917 proposed an Israeli homeland for the Jewish people. But in 1939 Britain placed severe restrictions on Jewish immigration, which raised questions as to the depth of international commitment to the creation on an independent Israeli state. Revelation of the horrors of the Holocaust after WW II, however, drove home the plight of the Jewish people in a mind-boggling way. Neither apologies, nor retribution, nor anything else could address the horrors that the Jewish people had endured. The only meaningful response that would assuage the guilt of the Gentile world, even to a small degree, would be the creation of a homeland in Palestine called Israel, the promised land.

One could not have expected what followed, not from a people who had known the horrors of Auschwitz. More than 700,000 Palestinians were driven from their ancestral homeland, and hundreds of their villages were razed. If they did not move voluntarily, they were forced out. Israeli historian Ilan Pappe wrote: "On 10 March 1948 ... veteran Zionist leaders, together with young military Jewish officers, put the final touches to a plan for the ethnic cleansing of Palestine." The Jewish people, at least the far-right Zionists, justified their acts by believing selected verses of man-composed ancient scripture.

To this day, the Palestinians are treated inhumanely by the Israelis, instead of being treated with dignity and as equal human beings. In a very systematic manner, the Israelis have taken more and more of the land that the United Nations portioned to the Palestinians. *Always, the political rationale is that the Palestinians present a security threat.* It borders on ludicrous that Israel builds settlements in the Palestinian territories and then cries "foul" when the Palestinians respond with anger. Although it is a stretched argument and most would disagree, perhaps a case could be made that Israel has the right to annex "buffer" land for security reasons, *but it is beyond any reasonableness of argument that building settlements in these lands is for "security" purposes.*

According to international observers, the West Bank now looks like Swiss cheese, with no practical way for the Palestinians to develop an authentic, functioning state of their own in the area. Less than a year ago, *The Economist* offered a brief description (also contained in President Carter's 2009 book) of the everyday conditions imposed upon the Palestinians:

> "Around 5m [five million] Palestinians live in historic Palestine, under Israeli control. In the West Bank, Israeli settlements and military zones take up 40 percent of the land ... Israel has laced the territory with walls, fences and checkpoints that box its 2.5m Palestinian residents into dozens of largely separate enclaves. Since the Islamist party, Hamas, took control of Gaza last June, its 1.5m people have been confined within the strip's 146 square miles, kept alive on a drip-feed sustenance of international aid.
>
> "The 1.1m Palestinians inside Israel are far better off, though they have long suffered legal and economic discrimination. They are increasingly isolated from their brethren; Israel bars them, as citizens, from traveling to

Gaza or to most Arab countries and their cousins in the occupied territories are unable to visit them since Israel, to keep suicide bombers out, has cancelled most permits ... Small wonder that in a recent poll 62 percent of them expressed the fear that Israel would one day expel them. The 250,000 Palestinian residents of East Jerusalem, which Israel annexed in 1967, have Israeli resident permits. But if they move to the West Bank or travel abroad to work, they risk losing forever their right to live in the city of their birth."

Following a visit to the area, Joe Kline describes his impression of the Israeli occupation as "inhumane and outrageous. Palestinians are imprisoned behind a barrier wall that does not conform to the 1967 lines; they are forced to endure hundreds of Israeli checkpoints and roadblocks whose purpose seems humiliation as much as security; their lands are slit by highways that only settlers are allowed to use; the settlements, populated by the extreme Israelis, have doubled in size since 1993 Oslo accords." And it continues. As I write, 2,500 more settlement housing units are under construction and 455 more are scheduled to begin.

It has become crystal clear that the strategy of the leadership of Israel is to make the land between the Jordan River and the Mediterranean the "promised land" of Jewish religious myth, and that this "promise" gives them the moral, God-given right to persecute the Palestinians in any manner that ultimately leads to the fulfillment of this dream. It is a religious and political ideology that is designed to move from the current practice of "as much apartheid as you can get away with" to the ultimate establishment of Israel as a pure Jewish nation, reaching from the Jordan River to the Mediterranean Sea, a nation that would be a model for the world. Some Jewish theologians argue that this does not include Gaza, the area of the ancient Philistines, non-Semitic "sea people, and that therefore it is not part of the promised land," the united monarchy land of King David and King Solomon. This may explain Israel's decision to relinquish control of the region, even though there continues hatred and economic persecution of the Gaza people.

The international community has, on many occasions, taken the stance that the indigenous Palestinians have comparable right to this area as their homeland. But it has been a position taken with no teeth, even though the international community (primarily via UN decisions) holds ultimate responsibility for the Palestinian *nakba*, or catastrophe. There are two pragmatic reasons, in contrast to the broader denial reasons, that the international community has not taken action to rectify the historic injustice done to the Palestinian people.

The two reasons are related. The first is that the international community—practically speaking, the United Nations—has become non-functional in matters where major world parties are in conflict. Any of the major powers can essentially prevent the UN from taking meaningful action in conflicts of even lesser significance to peace and human justice.

The second reason—the main reason but inextricably linked to the first—is that the United States supports the conduct of Israel, either by our outright economic and military support, or by our acceptance of Israel's conduct, which includes the inhuman treatment of at least three million Palestinian people, all under the pretense of the "security" issue, and the outright, flagrant, and repeated violation of international law. In the eyes of the global community, including Europe and both the Arab and non-Arab

Muslim world, the image of Israel is inseparable from the image of the United States. Regrettably, this is not an absurd view for them to hold.

Historians have written that it was a difficult decision for President Truman to support the creation of the Israel nation, in essence annexing the Palestinian homeland. Numerous advisors recommended against it, including General George Marshall and future Secretary of State Dean Rusk. Truman had concerns about the far right, Zionist element of the Jewish people; he wrote in his personal diary:

> "The Jews, I find, are very, very selfish. They care not how many Estonians, Latvians, Finns, Poles, Yugoslavs, or Greeks get murdered or mistreated as DP [displaced persons] as long as the Jews get special treatment. Yet when they have power, physical, financial, or political, neither Hitler nor Stalin has anything on them for cruelty or mistreatment to the underdog. Put an underdog on top and it makes no difference whether his name is Russian, Jewish, Negro, Management, Labor, Mormon, Baptist, he goes haywire. I've found very, very few who remember their past condition when prosperity comes. Look at the Congress attitude on DP—and they all come from DPs."

Despite this apprehension, Truman made the international community tipping-point decision in favor of the creation of the state of Israel, setting the stage for sixty years of growing support from the United States.

The right-wing Zionist stance that characterizes the actions and decisions of Israel does not reflect the will of many of the Jewish people, both Jews in Israel and Jews in the United States and elsewhere. Various polls, in fact, show the moderates are in the majority. These Jews envision a different Israel, one marked by compassion, morality, and justice for all people. This division is very remindful of the division between the far-right, fundamentalist Christians and the moderate Christians. While I am not as informed about the Islamic religion, many experts have indicated that the same is true among the Muslims; that the extremists constitute only a small, albeit powerful, vocal faction. Moderate Jews would say, I believe, that they see more truth in the verses of the Torah that talk about love than the verses that talk about the "chosen people" or "the promised land":

> "When an alien lives in your land, do not ill-treat him. The alien must be treated as one of your native-born ... You are to love these aliens as much as you love yourself ... because you were aliens in Egypt." (Leviticus 19)

This is an admonishment made more than thirty-six times in the Torah.

I have repeatedly made the point that "we are where we are." The crux of the issue is no longer whether the state of Israel exists or does not exist. Instead, the crux of the issue is to acknowledge and deal with the truth that the creation of Israel was a historical injustice committed against the Palestinian people, a tragedy and injustice magnified each of the past sixty years by Israel's and the United States' lack of courage and moral character to acknowledge this reality. If decisions are to be made that lead to a sustained peace, it will be because the will of the people—the Israeli Jews and the United States citizens—demand that this reality be openly acknowledged and imbedded in these decisions, a solution that confers justice, dignity, and opportunity to all, both Israeli Jews and Palestinians.

The Solution Must Be One with which the Conscience of the World Can Live Long Term

Polls show that the moderates—the Jews in Israel and in the United States, and Christians in the United States—have increasingly moved to favoring a peaceful settlement and toward giving the Palestinians the dignity of being equal human beings. Europe is far ahead in this respect. To the degree that the previous two points are acknowledged—the first point being that the "promised land" is Hebrew scriptural mythology, and the second that historically, this is the true homeland of the Palestinians—the conscience of the world will demand that the historical injustice done to the Palestinians be assuaged. It will be increasingly recognized that two wrongs—the persecution and Holocaust of the Jews, followed by the historical injustice and denial of dignity to the Palestinians—do not make a right.

Going against the conscience of the world is like fighting an incurable cancer. An assertive, aggressive defense of the Zionist position may hold the injustice at bay for a while, maybe even for an extended time, but eventually, truth and realization of this injustice will rise to the surface. Sooner or later, truth will prevail and world opinion will change. The bogus rallying cries, such as the Iran nuclear danger, will no longer rally the masses or delay the world's sensing of the reality of the injustice. It will be seen for what it is: that Israel represents the greater nuclear threat because they have the nuclear arsenal, and if they used it, the United States would be immobilized in terms of any meaningful action against Israel, even if the United States saw it as a horrible, illegal, unjustified act of war. Conversely, if Iran—which does not now possess a nuclear arsenal, while Israel is believed to have a secret store of forty to two hundred nuclear warheads—were ever to mount a nuclear attack on Israel, the United States and Israel could quickly turn their country into an ashtray. Iran may want nuclear capabilities but only for political influence and to be treated as a regional "power" and as a determent against Israeli aggression.

The war-mongering by the Israeli leadership is, as in the past, little more than psychological strategy to keep the foundational issue of their right to a biblical land and the injustice done to the Palestinians from rising to the surface. Ultimately, the United States will have to come to grips with the fact, despite all the rhetoric, that Israel is not a true democracy, as the fundamental tenet of a democracy is fair and equal treatment of the people. The United States will have to acknowledge that Israel, under current leadership, has the goal of being a "democratic theocracy"—a Jewish nation occupying the promised land. The United States will have to face the reality that the Zionist leadership believes it has a God-ordained right to use any means available to achieve this mythology-inspired goal.

The conscience of the world will not live with this long term. Each day and each year of denying the reality of these circumstances will make it only that much more difficult to bring a peaceful settlement to this sixty-year-old conflict. Already, many highly qualified and knowledgeable authors, historians, and governmental leaders believe that the two-state solution, given the degree to which the settlement strategy has already been implemented, has passed the point of being an achievable objective. It may well have passed, because of the refusal to acknowledge reality. Even if they are wrong, their worries indicate that time is running out and that the opportunity for a two-state solution may pass in short order.

I am slightly more optimistic. The global community is seeing what avoidance of reality in the financial sector can do to the economic health of the world. The status and the role of the United States in this financial crisis are being questioned. It is a crack that may continue into other avenues of international affairs, including the status of the Israel-Palestinian conflict and the United States support of Israel. Without U.S. support, Israel's belligerent stance against the Palestinians would crumble. I am slightly optimistic because the moderate Jews, both in Israel and in the United States, may sense the very survival of Israel is at stake, and that there is a different way for the twenty-first century Jewish community to think about themselves.

Moderate Jews see a vision of themselves as a "nation" of people, a community, held together by their Hebrew heritage, their exceptional dedication to education and health, their care for one another, and the bond that is possible only by a people who have experienced the suffering and evil that man is capable of committing. The Israel nation, so defined, has so much to give the world; it would, in fact, be a world model.

Conclusion

These three realities need to be addressed openly. They are crucial to establishing the foundational context for developing a just and lasting solution to the Israel-Palestine conflict. The exact nature of the plan would be determined by negotiations between the non-fundamentalist and non-literalist Israelis and Palestinians. Once the realities become acknowledged, the doors will open wide for the establishment of an economically sound, proud, and viable Palestinian nation, and a secure, progressive, peace-promoting Israeli nation.

To address these three realities will take unprecedented courage. At the risk of being redundant they are:

- *Confronting the ancient scriptural myth that God gave the Israelis a promised land.*
- *Acknowledging the reality that the Palestinians are the historical, indigenous people of the land.*
- *Recognizing that the solution must be one that the conscience of the world can live with long term.*

Witness the volumes and volumes that have been written on solution of the conflict, with none hitting these issues head-on. It is very much like dealing with an alcohol problem. We can talk forever about job performance, family dysfunction, car accidents, and so forth, but until we address the foundational issue—the addiction to alcohol—we have no hope of solving the problem. In the same way that alcohol addiction is addressed, we can address the three realities that prevent dealing with the conflict in a substantive manner: it would have to be dealt with honestly, with complete candidness, with integrity, and by treating the people—all of them—with dignity. It is unconscionable for the United States to contribute to an ideology that has, as its goal, the ethnic cleansing of an indigenous people. But that is what we have been doing for decades. We have given over $60 billion in federal aid to Israel during the past decade. As recently as October 2009 in an interview with *Newsweek*'s Lally Weymouth, Israel Prime Minister Benjamin Netanyahu repeated, "*the Palestinian-refugee problem should be resolved outside Israel's borders. Jews come here and Palestinians will go there.*" This is a continuation of the ethnic cleansing program of the Zionists. These realities must be acknowledged.

The international community, having significant responsibility for the genesis of this conflict, should—and I believe will—be prepared to assist in the economic development of both nations, and particularly the Palestinian nation, which is now in utter shambles because of the injustice and persecution they have endured. Imagine the model this would be for the Middle East, the nation of Israel, and the non-Arab Muslim world!

It is my hope that the non-fundamentalist/non-literalist Jewish and Christian people will rise to the challenge of bringing reality and understanding to the forefront and that the decisions we make will be decisions that prove to be good for all our kids and grandkids, Jewish and non-Jewish. I find it hard to believe that the God of the Torah or the God of the New Testament or my spiritual, incomprehensible Higher Power would not want us to follow this path.

CHAPTER 13

SURVIVAL: THE CONFLUENCE OF GLOBAL WARMING, POPULATION, AND ENERGY

"Mother Nature is just chemistry, biology and physics. That's all she is."

—Bob Watson

"And Mother Nature always bats last, and she bats a thousand."

—Thomas L. Friedman

Many of the immense challenges that we are facing, including those in the title of this chapter, are inextricably linked. The decisions that we make will require that we synthesize many separate sub-decisions into a holistic, overarching governance objective. And the decisions we make on global warming, population management, and energy are a perfect example. These issues are separate yet inseparable in impact; together, they have potential for catastrophic consequences for the habitability of Planet Earth.

These challenges and the decisions that will be made are difficult for a number of reasons beyond the fact that they are inextricably linked. The first is the "cliff" issue. We may know, perhaps even with a high degree of probability, that a particular issue will become a major problem, but we don't know when. The "cliff" that we are racing toward might be 100 yards away, or it might be 100 miles away. Being the human beings that we are, we allow the distance to the "cliff"—or at least our perception of that distance—to unduly influence our decision-making, usually by avoiding the issue or with procrastination in acknowledging the issue. It does not seem to matter what the impact or depth of the issue is; if it's a ways off, we simply get a lot less excited about the ramifications. The three issues of global warming, population, and energy all share this problem.

Another problem that characterizes these issues is that we may not know, with any degree of certainty, the exact ramifications that will result if we do nothing; for instance, will global warming be a human disaster, or will it be a development that we will be able to manage as it unfolds? As a populace, we do not deal intelligently with probability issues. This is particularly true for that segment of the population that does not have an understanding or appreciation of science. We want the issue neatly packaged, with a definitive answer on whether it's going to happen, and if so, a concise prognosis of the ramifications. Until we "feel" that level of certainty, we tend not to treat the issue with urgency. For example, a slowly evolving yet catastrophic issue combined with a low probability of its happening has a very hard time gaining serious public attention. And unscrupulous politicians play this weakness in human decision-making by telling their constituents that there is no basis for concern. Even though the issues noted— global warming, population, and energy—will have major impact on our kids and grandkids, we have trouble making them front-and-center issues, in part because of this lack of certainty and the "cliff" problem.

An additional problem is that these challenges become lost in the immediacy of today's problems. It is hard to focus our energies on global warming, for example, when we have a financial crisis to resolve. There's an old saying: it's hard to drain the swamp when the alligators are biting at your ass. We always have "immediate" or "today" issues to resolve, so we drift without clear acknowledgement of the "future" problem ... and miss the opportunities and sense of accomplishment that may accompany our working toward a solution.

Sometimes the solution to an issue requires the creative destruction of an entire industry. History has shown, time and time again, that instead of facing and addressing reality in a forthright manner, industries and politicians will dig their heels in and do everything possible to protect status quo. Corporate boards and senior management, by and large, have demonstrated very little vision and entrepreneurial creativity when faced with the need for transformational change. The tobacco industry and the U.S. automobile industry are excellent examples of denial and proactive resistance that becomes corporate and industry strategy, rather than acknowledgement of reality and the opportunities that more a farsighted management would have pursued.

Closely related is that we are afraid of "sinking the ship" if we focus on the big-picture issues. How do we keep the economy humming as we tackle the global warming issue? Short of mobilizing for war, governments and economies find it difficult to make transformational change or to change course rapidly or decisively. This is particularly true when the change necessitates that some aspect of today's economy will need to undergo transformational change. For example, it will be difficult to move to alternative energy sources when it means that the coal companies and their workers will be displaced. Creative destruction and transformational change are popular economic terms, but they are not popular political concepts.

Contributing to the problem are global issues. And we do not have an effective mechanism or institution for dealing with issues that demand a global-scale solution. The one organization with global reach, the United Nations, has not been effective, even in far less demanding challenges. Mobilizing the populace of one nation is extremely hard; mobilizing the international community in a collaborative effort might be close to impossible.

Last, we have the "will and capacity" question. This is the gnawing sense that even if the issue represents a major concern, we will not have the political "will and capacity" to deal with the problem. It can be argued that transformational problems will be too big, too tough for our bureaucratic, politically driven governance system. Our experience with major issues suggests that we simply will not be able to get everyone on the same page, so we "tinker" with change—we kick the can down the road. We become immobilized by the realization that any transformational proposition will be torn apart and used as partisan ammunition, rather than as a starting point for understanding and serious discussion.

Combine these constraints, and it is easy to see why it is so hard to deal with issues such as global warming, population pressures, and energy needs. So given the magnitude of the challenge, should we even try? That, of course, is the first-order question. It is a question that will tax our courage to search for reality and our decision-making capability. Yet avoidance is not a morally acceptable option.

My primary objective here is to show that global warming, population pressures, and energy represent an immense challenge and an *immense opportunity*. These issues demand that we invest the energy to understand them as best we can, and that we have the courage to look at them through the lens of reality; that we make decisions that are responsible and that are considerate of the next generation. It should also be noted that many scientists believe we are nearing the point of no return on global warming—the point where it becomes a self-reinforcing phenomenon, the point where man can no longer influence the magnitude or the rate of the warming that will occur.

This is the huge difference between past issues that have confronted mankind and the current global warming/population/ energy issue. We may be facing a situation that demands that we act immediately and in a truly transformational way, even though the scientific information is incomplete. The reason: if the global warming/population/energy issue prove to be as real and as urgent and as disastrous as many of the world's best scientists believe, we may be approaching the point where catastrophic damage to human existence can no longer be prevented.

There are two decisive, fork-in-the-road decisions that we will be making, either by responsible, thoughtful thinking ... or by default. These two decisions carry immense ramifications. The first decision: is the global warming/population pressures/energy issue a real and true risk to the very existence of the earth as we know it? The second decision: if we conclude that the threat is real—ultimately, a collective global decision—then what are we going to do about it? This is an important and tough issue, for if we decide that the risk is real, the "tinkering" that we have done to date and the extremely modest changes proposed to date are totally inadequate, given the risk we face. Individual, governmental, and

societal changes completely outside our experiential framework
will be required. So, my friends, we have some tough decisions to
make. The worldview response options are limited:

- That after very thoughtful, responsible consideration, we decide
  that the risk is not "substantial" (meaning that the problems
  to mankind that result from the global warming/population/
  energy issue will evolve slowly and in a limited way and are
  "manageable," without making transformational change, and
  that the odds of disastrous non-linear, abrupt climate change are
  so low that we do not need to act).

- That regardless of the ramifications or the odds of these problems
  happening, we do not have the will or capacity, pragmatically
  speaking, to mount the global-level transformational changes
  that would be needed; that mankind is simply not up to the task.
  We can get to this decision either by thoughtful consideration
  or we can get to it by default (that is, by denying or simply not
  dealing with the issue).

- That we make the decision that global warming/population/
  energy constitutes a very real risk to the well-being of mankind
  and the earth as we know it, and transformational change is the
  only responsible decision that man can make.

The global warming/population/energy issue is a monstrosity;
man has never been faced with an issue of this magnitude. But
it's an issue that we have before us, whether we like it or not.
And there is an up side: if we have the will and the creativity and
inventiveness and character and toughness, we can turn this global
issue into the greatest opportunity that man has ever experienced.
So it's not only transformational in terms of the technology and
world order with which we are dealing; it's also a transformational
opportunity for the happiness and well-being of ourselves, our

kids, and our global brethren. This opportunity is the ultimate in being a big-time, exciting, and wonderful adventure—living life to its fullness! And if there is a God or an incomprehensible spiritual power embedded in our existence, I think he/she would be very pleased that we chose the courageous, responsible course!

Global Warming

Global warming is an issue that every one of us faces, because it has potential to impact us all. Some of us do not believe that it's a real problem; that it's something the climatology geeks and tree-huggers have invented; that it is environmentalists-created mythology. Some of us believe that the questions surrounding global warming are still in hot debate; that while many of the scientists believe it's an issue, other equally competent scientists do not. Or we believe that the scientific understanding is still too incomplete to draw any meaningful conclusions. Others, however, believe the data and scientific understanding have reached a point where it is known, with a high degree of probability, that man is altering the climate of the earth in a way that may be very dangerous to our existence and to Planet Earth as we know it.

This type of uncertainty is the nature of all complex issues; it is *not* the foundational problem. The foundational problem is that we have many uninformed people, yet they voice firm opinions on the issue. Their position on the issue is not drawn from any meaningful understanding of climatology science but rather from gut feeling, ideologies they hold, or a trust in a mythology-based religion that sees the world as something created in seven days by God, and that the earth continues to be under the divine supervision of that God. In this mental context, what man does to the earth is, comparatively speaking, irrelevant because of the plan God has for the world. By and large, this group will continue to play in their sandbox of denial. Within this fundamentalist group, only those individuals who marshal the courage for inquiry will break the bond of this addiction and begin to look at the global warming issue objectively and with reality. Distortion and the dissemination of false information by organizations sponsored by the coal and petroleum companies, a tactic borrowed from the tobacco companies, provides the ideological sound bites for these uninformed denial groups.

Among the open-minded and scientifically astute, there is little I can add, technically speaking, to the debate that has not been discussed in a more authoritative way in many books or in-depth reports of large, highly competent international research groups that have been commissioned to study the global warming issue.

I do believe, however, that it would be useful to paint a broad picture of some of the issues, with the idea of drawing in those who have not, for whatever reason, given the subject serious thought. My hope is that these points will stir enough interest within this group to cause them to give the subject the serious consideration that it warrants. I have mentioned several times that in my judgment, leaders follow rather than lead. If average folks, collectively, come to the view that global warming constitutes a potential risk to mankind and that there is a way to reduce this risk, it will be our collective "will" that becomes manifested in national action and worldview. What ultimately happens with respect to global warming, at least in the United States, will depend on the collective decisions that we make as individuals. It is up to "we, the people"; our Congress has shown it does not have the will, vision, or capacity to lead the way.

With that said, what are the points that I feel need to be brought to the forefront for further consideration and which are important in our decision-making? The first is the necessity of recognizing the robust yet fragile nature of the earth and life, its awesomeness and uniqueness in the universe. Contrary to what our Christian upbringing instilled in us, the earth is not unchanging. It is true that in all of the history of mankind, until perhaps the last hundred years (250 years at the most), man has never had enough influence to substantially change the earth. On a geo-climate scale, 100 or even 250 years, is an *extremely* short span of time. But we have changed the planet profoundly in this very short period of time: the best estimate is that 10,000 years ago, the beginning of the current interglacial period, there were only five million people on the whole planet. We have that many in Minnesota today. It was not until the Industrial Revolution, starting about *1750*, that man existed in a great enough numbers and had the means to have measurable or meaningful impact on the earth. This was only 250 years ago! So, ever since the last ice age, 10,000 years ago, the climate of the earth, other than for some regional mini-events, had been essentially unchanged.

But the earth has been around for a much longer period of time. By the use of various scientific methods, including ice core analysis, tree rings, pollen deposits, and ocean sediment, it can be shown that during the past 600,000 years, the climate of the earth has been far from constant. *It is clear that major changes do happen. Some of these major shifts have happened quickly— a few decades or less.* Global warming skeptics point to this as being evidence that there are other controlling factors, other than mankind's influence, that are responsible for climate change. Most scientists, however, interpret and draw a very different conclusion from this data. Their conclusion is that this is *evidence that the earth's climate is, in fact, in delicate balance.* Some rather modest changes, such as the earth's small orbit changes, which occur every 20,000 years, have the capacity to initiate an ever-accelerating

239

positive feedback loop, whereby relatively small changes (for example, the ratio of sun's energy reflected by ice and snow to the amount absorbed by land and oceans, or the amount of carbon dioxide or methane in the stratosphere) produce larger and larger climatic changes, until reaching a new "steady state," a climatic condition that lasts many thousands of years before new forces build that cause the climate to move to a different state.

One of the great thinkers of our time is James Lovelock, a scientist from England. In the 1970s, Lovelock (along with American biologist Lynn Margulis) began to advance the Gaia theory. The publisher of one of Lovelock's books defines it this way:

> "Gaia theory tells us that the entire Earth functions as a single living super organism, regulating its internal environment much as an animal regulates its body temperature and chemical balance. But now, says the theory's founder, James Lovelock, that organism is sick. It is running a fever born of the combination of a sun whose intensity is slowly growing and an atmosphere whose greenhouse gases have recently spiked due to human activity ... this is a call to action to address a major threat to our collective future."

Lovelock's view of the earth, while built on in-depth scientific understanding, has, for me, a spiritual dimension. He speaks to our intimate relationship with Planet Earth in a way that a child looks to its mother. She is strong, and yet she is fragile.

Many measurements in the scientific literature indicate that we will reach the point where an ever-accelerating, runaway warming condition could be initiated (some scientists are fearful that we have already reached this point). Recent research, indicating that the rate of warming is double that predicted a few years back, is, alarmingly, consistent with the earth's entering the beginning part of the positive feedback curve. The pre-industrial (1750) concentration of CO_2 in the atmosphere was roughly 280 parts per million by volume. Since then, it has increased to over 380 ppmv, *much higher than at any time during the past 650,000 years.* Concentrations are increasing by about 2 ppmv per year. Other greenhouse gases—methane, for example—are increasing as well. Modeling studies indicate that CO_2 concentration will likely rise to 500 ppmv within three or four decades, and to 550 ppmv by the end of the twenty-first century, with some predicting an even higher level. The average estimated global temperature change by the end of the century, as a result of the increase in greenhouse gases, ranges from 2 or 3 degrees to as high as 8 Celsius degrees (14 Fahrenheit degrees).

Essentially, all climatologists, agriculturalists, oceanographers, and water scientists agree that a global temperature increase of this magnitude would result in significant economic and human life disruption. The rate at which it would occur is very important, in that it would have large impact on the capacity of affected nations to cope with the resultant problems, such as regional droughts, severity and frequency of storms, drinking water, agricultural/ food production, sea level increases, and disease propagation. As the warming progresses, perhaps by the end of the century, ocean coral reefs would become extinct; the Amazon rainforest would disappear; sea levels would rise and coastal flooding would be extreme; rainfall and weather patterns would be changed; and major areas of currently productive farmland would not be able to grow food.

The most concerning issue, in my judgment, is not a linear temperature change—*as important as that may be*—but the possibility of a non-linear climate change. This is the concern that we will reach a tipping point—the point at which conditions establish an ever-increasing positive feedback state—with a resulting exponential increase in temperature. This has happened to the earth before, albeit a long, long time ago. The earth entered a prolonged heat wave (it lasted over 50,000 years) about 55 million years ago. It was most likely caused by a sudden doubling or tripling of CO_2 and other greenhouse gasses in the atmosphere. The temperate rise was 10–12 Fahrenheit degrees. Such a change would assuredly result in major, catastrophic harm to mankind and Planet Earth.

As an old chemistry guy, the mechanics of non-linear or rapid temperature increase reminds me of the principle of activation energy and accelerating feedback mechanisms, a concept that has similarities with enzyme-driven reaction rates. This is a property of chemistry that is well known but extremely difficult to model mathematically, particularly when several interrelated variables control the system. Similarly, there are many climate-forcing factors that we now know are at play in control of the earth's temperature. Perhaps it will suffice to simply list some of these, with the hope that you will see intuitively, when all factors push (force) in the same direction and reinforce each other, that this can result in rapid, ever-increasing changes, until the system depletes itself of the forcing mechanisms, or some other counter-controlling factor becomes dominant. Here are a few of the most important forcing factors that could result in our entering an ever-increasing positive feedback loop. The combined reinforcing effect of two or more of these factors could produce a granddaddy feedback state—this is the risk of most concern:

- A factor often discussed in the media and easiest to understand is "albedo" feedback. Snow-covered ground reflects a high percentage of the sun's energy, while dark-colored earth and water absorbs a high percentage of the sun's energy. As this balance or ratio changes, this becomes a positive feedback loop in and of itself.

- Of the several greenhouse gases, one of the most important is methane. Methane, although it has a much shorter life in the atmosphere, is twenty-four times more potent on a methane molecule versus carbon dioxide molecule basis. The tundra contains huge amounts of vegetative carbon, and when the permafrost thaws, microbial digestion of this vegetative material has the potential to produce large amounts of methane. More thawing means more methane; more methane means higher temperatures; higher temperatures mean more methane, and so the feedback loop progresses at an ever-increasing rate.

- The solubility of carbon dioxide and methane (and other gasses) decreases as water is warmed. The oceans hold huge amounts of water that warms very slowly. However, they also hold huge quantities of carbon dioxide (about fifty times the quantity contained in the earth's atmosphere) and methane. As warming occurs, more and more of these gasses are released to the atmosphere, again setting the stage for a potential positive feedback condition.

- Ocean algae are great consumers of atmospheric CO_2, a negative "pumping down" forcing factor. Algae are sensitive to temperature, however, and when the ocean temperature rises above the threshold level of 10–12 degrees Celsius, the vertical flow pattern of the water is changed, and the nutrient supply for the algae is reduced, and their capacity to consume CO_2 decreases markedly. Some highly regarded scientists believe that the impact of losing the pumping down of algae could have major impact, creating a potential feedback cycle.

243

- Although the greenhouse gas mechanism has been raising global temperatures, fairly recent research indicates that pollution particulates, produced by the same industrial sources that produce CO_2, are creating a cooling effect. These particulates reflect solar radiation, a condition termed "global dimming." The best estimate at this point is that the "global dimming" effect has slowed global temperature increase by 30 to 40 percent. Ironically, as industry moves to cleaner systems (clean-burning technology to reduce smog, for example), the temperature "negating" effect will be lost.

- Tropical forests also consume large quantities of CO_2. But they, too, are temperature-dependant. The earth has many regional examples of forested areas that have become scrub land as a result of changing temperature and rainfall conditions. Large-scale loss of the tropical forests would likely contribute significantly to a positive feedback phenomenon.

Again, two key points: the first is that these potential forcing factors are inextricably linked and, very important, reinforcing of each other; the second is that it is extremely difficult to model or predict the temperature rise curve that could result from multivariable feedback loops that occur simultaneously.

The correlation between atmospheric carbon dioxide and methane concentration and global temperature is well established. Most of man's history has been with a CO_2 level of about 280 ppmv, but with the conversion of fossil fuel into CO_2 and energy, current concentrations are in excess of 380 ppmv. And it is currently increasing at a rate of 1.9 ppmv per year. Because of the tremendous growth of energy requirements in the rapidly developing countries—China and India being prime examples—it is almost certain that the rate of CO_2 addition to the atmosphere will increase. The increase could be substantial and occur fast.

I should note that skeptics often make the argument that global warming, resulting from some other forcing mechanisms, is the cause of the CO_2 increase. They note that the research studies of previous climate changes (ice core analyses going back 650,000 years) indicate that global temperature increase begins to occur ahead of the CO_2 increase, suggesting to them that CO_2 increase is not the cause of the temperature increases that have occurred during the previous climate changes. Most climatologists interpret this data differently, explaining that in the past cycles, the initial rise in temperature was an "initiating event" that resulted from forcing factors, such as the earth's orbital changes that occur every 20,000 years. After this triggering event, CO_2 and methane increased and produced the positive feedback condition, which resulted in the bulk of the temperature increase. It is exactly this understanding that is the basis for concluding that the earth's climate—at least the climate friendly to mankind for the past 10,000-year interglacial period—is really more fragile and susceptible to triggering events than realized a generation ago. Hence, the concern that the current increase in atmospheric CO_2 concentration may trigger a positive feedback cycle, which will result in a global temperature increase that will be very harmful to mankind and the earth.

The most critical question of the global warming issue, I believe, is whether global temperature increase will be gradual and long term and thus, more manageable, or if it will be a triggering event that produces *abrupt* climate change. There is high probability, in my judgment, that we will have a gradual global temperature increase. The question is how fast and to what extent will it be before we reach a new steady-state condition (that is, no further increase in concentration). A number of climatology scientists have rendered the opinion that 500 ppmv CO_2 concentration may represent the tipping point that we must stay below in order to avoid disastrous, non-linear climatic and environmental change. While this may sound like a good option in light of the "cataclysmic abrupt change" possibility, it will be extremely difficult to achieve. In fact, with continued global development and with the non-substantive reduction efforts under global discussion, maintaining a CO_2 concentration of less than 500 ppmv is very close to impossible.

Scientists cannot assign a probability of abrupt change occurring as a result of the forcing of a positive feedback loop. What is known is that abrupt change has occurred in Earth's history. It is also known that we are in uncharted waters with respect to CO_2 concentrations; they are far above anything that has occurred during the past 650,000 years. But there are so many variables that are interlocked, and with positive feedback potential, that it is beyond scientists' ability to model the abrupt-change scenario with any degree of reliability. The odds of a climate change of this magnitude may be far greater than what the average citizen believes, or it may be fairly low. We don't know. This is a reality not to be taken lightly; we may be talking about the very existence of most of mankind. To paint this picture as accurately as possible, consider the comment taken from a National Research Council and the National Academies of Science assessment:

> "Abrupt climate change refers to sudden (on the order of decades), large changes in some major component of the climate system, with rapid, widespread effects. The potential for abrupt climate changes cannot be predicted with confidence; however, abrupt climate changes are an important consideration because, if triggered, they could occur so quickly and unexpectedly that human or natural systems would have difficulty adapting to them."

"Greenhouse warming and other human alterations of the Earth system may increase the possibility of large, abrupt, and unwelcome regional or global climatic events. The abrupt changes of the past are not fully explained yet, and climate models typically underestimate the size, speed, and extent of those changes. Hence, future abrupt changes cannot be predicted with confidence, and climate surprises are to be expected."

Writing about global warming almost demands that I state my personal position on whether the global warming concern is "real" or—as some have suggested—the greatest hoax of modern times. The first point to make, and one that can be made with certainty, is that the greenhouse gas warming science is extremely difficult, complex, and technically demanding. Hundreds of our most gifted scientists—chemists, physicists, climatologists, engineers, oceanographers, mathematicians—are studying the issue. Without disrespect for the credentials of any reader, the hard-core scientific theories and research data underlying the conclusion (of the vast majority but not all scientists) that global greenhouse gas warming is "real" and anthropogenic (that is, due to man's acts) are beyond understanding by the lay person. We seem to accept this concept of "beyond understanding by the lay person" when, for example, we get diagnosed with cancer and therefore seek an expert oncologist for treatment. Another example of our acceptance of this concept is when we trustingly get on an airplane with a sense of assurance that the engineers who understand mechanical force and fatigue equations know their business and have done their job, even though we have no in-depth understanding of these scientific disciplines.

It is accurate to say that essentially all (I know of no exception) of the major, creditable research bodies—the Intergovernmental

Panel on Climate Change (IPCC), the National Climate Data Center, the National Research Council, or any of the other international research bodies—agree that global warming is real and that it constitutes a risk to the earth's health. There are individual scientists who disagree, but they are in the vast minority. The fact that we are in midstream of an evolving scientific issue (as with most scientific issues under study) means that we have to accept and understand that we are dealing with probability.

For anyone to say that global warming is a hoax is, quite frankly, absurd and a demonstration of ignorance. It may, however, be reasonable for someone who has studied the issue thoughtfully and with some expertise to come to the conclusion that the risk we face is acceptably low.

My position on whether global warming is "real" rests on two considerations. The first and most important is the expert judgment from the science community; the second is the common-sense test, the judgment we all make, even without the technical background or expertise to understand the scientific detail or theory.

With respect to the first, what are the experts saying? The answer here, as I have indicated, is that the overwhelming majority of the knowledgeable scientists have concluded that global warming is occurring and that it is man-made. For most of these scientists, it is only a question of how fast and to what degree the warming will be, and in that respect, they deal with probabilities. Some very highly regarded scientists believe we are moving ever closer to a catastrophic climate change condition, probably within a time span measured in decades rather than centuries.

With respect to the common-sense test, the following thought process says to me that it would be wise to take global warming very seriously:

- It is known conclusively that CO_2 concentrations have increased, from 280 ppmv at the beginning of the Industrial Revolution, to over 380 ppmv today. It is also clear that this is a much higher level than at any time within the past 650,000 years.

- It is known conclusively that during the past 650,000 years, the temperature of the earth has had a number of temperature cycles strong enough to produce ice ages, followed by moderately warm interglacial periods (as now); and that during these cycles, *CO_2 and temperature are very highly correlated.* Correlation does not prove cause and effect. But common sense says to me, even if all aspects of cause and effect are not known, that the next time CO_2 concentrations go up, I should be thoughtfully concerned. And up they are; CO_2 concentrations are beyond anything we have experienced in 650,000 years and, very important, they are still rising … and rising rapidly.

- The theory behind global warming, at least at a physical chemistry 101 level, makes sense. And more important, the physical and chemical mechanism of positive feedback forcing systems (as noted, there are several) makes sense to me and my scientifically trained colleagues.

- There is very good evidence that the earth has undergone large and abrupt temperature changes in its geological past. This says that the climate of the earth is in delicate balance and subject to change when forcing factors occur. This is an indication to me that the possibility of major climate change aberration should not be disregarded. It seems logical and reasonable, from a science standpoint, that the CO_2 increase that results from the burning of fossil fuel and the accompanying forcing factors could produce another climate aberration (warming) of a degree that modern man has never experienced and which could prove catastrophic for billions of the earth's inhabitants.

Consideration of these points lead me to believe that global warming needs to be considered "real," and that it has substantial odds of reaching a dangerous level within the lifespan of my grandkids. Perhaps even more concerning to me is that abrupt climate change, although of a lower probability, constitutes a finite risk. This is enough for me to conclude that global warming is one of the immense challenges we face, and that it is imperative that we deal with it through the lens of reality.

It's an awesome thought that during the entirety of time that mankind has been living on Earth, and most certainly for the past 10,000 years, during which time we have gone from 5,000,000 people to 6,500,000,000—a 1,300-fold increase—the earth's climate has been relatively constant and unchanging. In fact, that is how we think of the earth's climate—as being constant, rather than a home that has its own regulating mechanisms, not unlike our bodies—robust, yet very fragile if we abuse it beyond its limits. And it's an even more incredible thought that for the first time in mankind's history, we are at a point where our growth and "progress" has put the earth in jeopardy, with the risk that we will change it in a way that it will no longer be a good home for much of the human race. Lovelock titled one of his books around this thought, *The Revenge of Gaia*.

I mentioned earlier that we have three general options for dealing with the global warming issue, but there are actually four, the fourth being avoidance or denial of the issue. For many, that has been the course of action to date. The decision to do nothing is acceptable to me if that decision is based on careful thought. But it is not a moral position if made in ignorance or if it stems from ideology, mythology, laziness, or selfishness. We have responsibility to all the kids and grandkids of the world to face the question of the earth's health as intelligently as our abilities permit. You and I are not only unique human beings, but we also have been given a place on Earth at a unique time—the first time that man has to make a decision on the global warming phenomenon and the habitability of Planet Earth.

Population Pressure

An integral element of humankind survival and a key part of the global warming challenge is population pressure. I find this a fascinating part of our thinking, probably because of some grade school memories. My folks moved to the farm that they bought, with the financial help of Grandpa Orlin, a mile and a half north of Oak Center and just east of the fence line of Orlin's farm. It was 160 acres, with a set of old buildings in poor condition. We moved from Grandpa Fred and Grandma Maggie's house to the farm when I was about two years old. The old farmhouse was huge—nine bedrooms, with no electricity or running water. I don't know the history, but it was obviously built for two large-sized families. We lived in the west half of the house. I remember the kitchen floor being a point of interest—about half of the floor, the south half, had sunk a good three inches. So when you were in the kitchen, you walked on a slope half of the time. The kitchen area was heated by an old cooking stove that burned wood that was cut from the oak trees in the pasture between Grandpa Orlin's place and ours. After a few years, my folks were able to "modernize" the kitchen by buying a white porcelain cooking stove, fueled by two hundred-pound propane tanks that sat outside. It was modern, with pilot lights for lighting the four burners, and a pilot light for the oven!

251

But once in a while, the pilot lights didn't work. So it happened on a warm summer afternoon that my mom was going to start the oven and bake something for dinner. But she failed to note that the pilot light did not ignite the oven burner. After fifteen minutes or so, and seeing that the stove was not getting hot, she realized that the oven burner was not burning. Being skeptical of the pilot light's working as it should, she decided to light the burner with a wood match.

It was a dandy explosion. I was sitting in a chair maybe ten or fifteen feet from the stove, and I still remember the force of the blast. It surprised me, in that it seemed to compress my body from all sides, yet it slid me across the floor. A niece who was visiting also went sliding across the floor. My mom, quite surprisingly, was only shaken and singed; her eyebrows were gone and the hair line on her forehead set back an inch or so. But she had no serious injury, not even a doctor visit was needed.

But the old house! On the east side of the kitchen was a big, long, three-seasons porch with at least twenty feet of full-sized windows. The explosion blew out every one of them. Even the door to the outside was barely hanging on. She also blew out all the kitchen windows, frames and all. My memory of the scene is much like the pictures in the newspaper of homes that have been hit by a tornado. My mom told me to find my dad as quickly as possible. I knew he was working in a field near the one-room school I attended, so I jumped on my bike and headed off to get him. The more I peddled, the funnier the explosion, with all the windows blown out of the house, seemed. By the time I got to my dad, I was bending over in laughter. "Hey Dad, Mom wants you to come home right away. She blew up the house a few minutes ago." He never did see it as being funny.

Sorry for the roundabout way to get to the one-room school that I attended and the real point of this story! I remember we had a world history subject with a red textbook that had great pictures of African pygmies. (When I say "we," I mean our class of two— Nancy Haglund and me.) I remember our writing a report on the population of the world—how many, and who lived where, and why there were differences in population density; a rather neat subject for a ten-year-old. And I still remember from that report that the population of the United States was 145,000,000 people. That was sixty years ago. Since then, we have more than doubled.

While this whole story may seem disconnected from the issue at hand, it is meaningful to me in the sense that it allows me to appreciate a broader context of the population pressure issue. In one sense, it brings home the arithmetic of exponential growth, something even Einstein said he found hard to appreciate on a day-to-day basis. We will have grown from 2.5 billion people in my grade school days to probably 7 billion or so by the time I cash in, coupled with each of us using far more resources than we did when my family lived in the old house that my mother blew up. And in an additional sense, it speaks to the insidiousness of steady, compounded growth—we don't really sense the magnitude of the change when it steadily occurs. Then one day, we look back and realize that between grade school times and now, the population in our country has doubled, and worldwide, even more so, and that our consumption levels have increased by an even greater multiple. But what we don't appreciate or recognize, we ignore.

While this short section won't offer anything really new—at least not for anyone awake and breathing—I hope to instill a gut-level recognition or sense of the importance of the confluence of global warming issues and population growth, which are soon to be joined by recognition of the energy factor. So let's start with a brief refresher of a couple elementary concepts—numbers and curves—all with the idea of looking at the world and the livability, perhaps even survivability, that it will provide for our kids and grandkids.

The first concept is simple—the idea of "total load" on the earth's capacity for livability. Some social and physical scientists have a related term that stems from this: the "carrying capacity" of the earth, meaning simply that the product of the number of people times the average resource needs per person, gives us a metric for discussing the question of how many people the earth can provide for on a sustained basis. The amount of global warming greenhouse gases, added to the atmosphere, is simply the population times the amount emitted per person. First, a couple of numbers on world population:

Year	Population
1750	0.8 billion
1950	2.5 billion
2000	6.1 billion (2009 estimate is 6.7)
2050	9.2 billion (estimate is 8.0 to 11 billion)

In very rough terms, we will see a 50 percent increase in population in the next forty to fifty years. This number can be managed to the low side, somewhat, by making family planning and woman's health care services available to all, but because of the high number of young people in many of the developing countries, the die is set for major population growth—it is only a question of degree. Most important, however, is recognition that in terms of the impact that population has on the earth, we are dealing with only the very recent tail end of exponential growth. Here is the curve, showing that population pressures only began to "take off" at about the same time as the Industrial Revolution began—roughly speaking, 1750. Not very long ago on an earth-life scale.

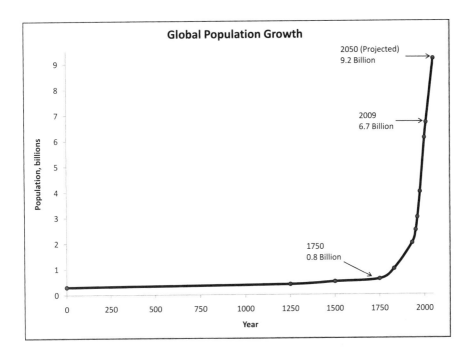

These numbers are concerning, but not nearly as concerning as the numbers that emerge when we add "per person consumption" growth on top of population growth. If we are worried about greenhouse gases and global warming as being a scientific possibility, these numbers get scary fast. This is because we live in a developing world. The people of the lesser developed nations want to enjoy the quality of life they see the folks of the developed world enjoying. And their governments, rightfully so, are trying to deliver. No reasonable person would argue that these people are not entitled to the same pursuit of well-being that you and I enjoy, so it is almost inevitable that per-person consumption will rise in these countries, again perhaps exponentially. And with increased consumption is the corresponding increase in energy needs, with the concomitant increase in greenhouse gas emission from the fossil fuel plants that produce this energy.

The big increase will, of course, come from the Asian countries. China has on the order of 1.3 billion people, four times the population of the United States. Per capita consumption for each person in the United States is currently somewhere between eight and eleven times the consumption of the average Chinese person. The numbers are similar for India. And the rest of the non-Western world is looking to improve their living standards as well. Assuming that there is sufficient fossil fuel to meet this energy need (a questionable assumption, but let's assume it for the sake of argument), the greenhouse gas emission impact would be absolutely huge.

Jared Diamond, a professor of geography and one who is concerned about the future health of the earth, has converted some of these numbers into a useful metric for thinking purposes. His metric is simply to express the carrying capacity load on the earth in terms of a "population number," using the present United States per person consumption level. Here is the shocking result of this arithmetic: if China and India, *alone*, were to come up to the U.S. consumption level, the result would be equivalent to a world population level of 72 billion people. I suggest you read that last sentence again.

Obviously, this level of population growth, coupled with consumption growth, and hence, fossil fuel use and greenhouse gas emission growth, is not an achievable or sustainable state. But even trying to get there could be disastrous. Students in elementary biology classes often perform a lab demonstration in which an organism (a bacterium, for example) is placed in a closed system (hence, having limited resources), where the organisms are encouraged to multiply (that is, some food, a comfortable temperature, and a pope telling them to multiply fruitfully). There is no check on the number of organisms produced or control over the resources available. At first, the number of organisms grows very rapidly, and then, within a short period of time, the resources are depleted and the system becomes poisoned, resulting in the abrupt destruction of the colony. A lesson?

Homo sapiens have evolved a long way, but we are still carrying the procreation genes of our less developed ancestors. The only thing that will keep us from a fate similar to the bacteria is the hope that the rational thinking process and decision-making genes evolve fast enough to manage man's natural procreation drive. An earth that has overloaded its carrying capacity will assuredly be faced with water and energy shortage, pollution, species extinction by destruction of natural habitat, quality of life reduction, environmental degradation, and a whole lot more. And all these outcomes would be made far worse, and possibly encountered far sooner, with climate change stemming from global warming. All of this is very possible within the lifetime of our kids and grandkids!

No one seems to be sure how to deal with the emerging challenge of global warming, population pressures, and energy requirements. What I know is that if there is any hope, we need to take off the blinders, embed the concept of exponential growth in our heads, and muster the courage to address reality. It will not be achieved by clinging to the mythology-based thinking of the pope, or the Religious Right, or the Islam extremists, or the impotent congressional electorates, or a backward-looking media. No, it will take a courageous, heroic effort by grassroots folks who are willing to consider transformational change. Transformational change sounds like a political sound bite—as if we have heard it before—but this time it's the future Earth that is at stake, so maybe it's time to get serious. The next section has thoughts on how it can be done. Come along.

Energy

Say the word energy and you have opened the door to hundreds of sub-topics:

• The impact of four-dollars-per-gallon pump price.

• The question of whether corn-derived ethanol takes more energy to produce than it provides, and whether the whole idea is a subsidy sham.

• The amount of CO_2 and other greenhouse warming gases that are emitted by the hundreds of new coal-fired electrical plants being built in China.

• The question of whether windmills and solar energy are a distraction or part of a meaningful long-term solution to clean energy.

• Whether battery-powered cars or hydrogen fuel-cell-powered cars are the answer to tailpipe emission concerns.

• If oil was the real reason for invading Iraq.

• Whether Tom Friedman, *New York Times* columnist and author, has a point in his relentless effort to get people to recognize, as he believes, that there is a critical link between foreign policy and our ever-growing dependency on oil from the countries run by dictators, who have a fundamental dislike for the U.S. culture.

If we dig more deeply into these issues, we will reach the point of common foundational realities that undergird meaningful discussion and decision-making on the energy subject. If we avoid these fundamentals, we risk getting caught up in tangential issues and lose focus on the big, controlling issues that will determine the future of our kids and grandkids. This is certainly not to say that the sub-topics are not worthy and important issues, because they very much are. Yet at the end of the day, we have a few realities that will control the big picture and the ultimate direction that we will have to take. What are these controlling points?

- We are going to run out of affordable oil. The oil industry experts are not in agreement on when this will happen, but they do agree that it's coming. Actually, what will happen is that the price-elasticity curve will move northward, making oil ever more expensive, eventually reaching prohibitive levels for high-quantity consumption. The time scale of this curve is a much debated subject.

- Coal-fired electrical power-generating plants are a huge contributor to greenhouse warming gasses. If we ever take the global warming issue seriously, conventional coal-fired plants will have to be shut down. At present, developed and developing countries are bringing large numbers of conventional coal-fired plants on stream, with many more in the "shovel ready" stage. While "clean coal" technology is frequently discussed in scientific and academic circles, there are no serious plans for commercialization of the technology. In fact, "clean coal" technology in a commercial sense has not been proven to be a practical, viable concept. Most of the coal-fired plants currently being built or planned will not be able to be retrofitted with "clean coal" technology because of design, construction, and location reasons, even if it is eventually proven commercially feasible for some new construction location sites.

- Alternative energy sources, such as wind power, solar, hydrogen, algae-synthesized hydrocarbons, bio-fuels, etc., hold some promise, and the technologies involved should be pursued and advanced as fast as possible. But they offer no reasonable hope—repeat, no reasonable hope—of producing the CO_2-free energy needs that will be required to meet world energy requirements. As with clean-coal technology, the alternative energy ideas, while good and worthwhile, carry the risk of distracting us from the immensity of the energy issue.

- *The only possibility of achieving CO_2-free energy is through worldwide adoption of nuclear power—nuclear power from a particular reactor design. Fortunately, this is a "doable" approach; almost all the technology exists and has been demonstrated commercially feasible, but the political problems are enormous.*

Just to recap: we have a CO_2 greenhouse gas concentration of 386 ppmv and rising. We have grown the world's population at an exponential rate, with huge differences in living standards. And now the have-nots want what the haves enjoy, meaning our energy needs and greenhouse gases from fossil-fuel burning will increase, perhaps dramatically. Our best scientists note that we are already in uncharted waters—we have an atmosphere unlike any that the earth has seen in 650,000 years—and they caution against going over 450–500 ppmv CO_2 lest we risk the habitability of much of the earth. That's the big picture. We dare not lose sight of it by clouding it over with detail.

The magnitude of the energy/population/global warming challenge is so immense that I fear that the human response will be to deny the issue, to let our eyes glaze over, and to move on with today's tasks, or to move the furniture while the house burns—let tomorrow take care of itself. And, subconsciously at least, we will continue to hope that there is a fatal flaw in the global warming theories, or that the energy-need numbers are off by four or five zeros. I confess that I share a bit of this mind-set, and I have to keep telling myself that if we are going to ignore the reality of the situation, it would be more responsible to do so after some careful thought.

Sharon Begley, *Newsweek* science editor and author, has cited some energy-consumption numbers to put the issue in perspective. I don't know if her numbers are exactly right (they are not easy to compute), but I have compared them to some other sources, and they are definitely in the ballpark. Total world energy consumption is roughly 14 trillion watts per year. She has assumed that the world's population will level off at 9 billion people by 2050 and that the world's economy will grow by 1.6 percent (the have-nots would take issue with this number, saying it's too low) and that we will make *major* energy-efficiency improvements. Cranking through these numbers, our 2050 energy needs will grow to 28 trillion watts. (Without the energy efficiency improvements, the number is 45 trillion watts.) She goes on to point out that given the current 386 ppmv CO_2 level, 26.5 of the 28 trillion watts would have to come from zero-carbon energy sources, if we want to keep the CO_2 concentration below 450 ppmv.

That presents an energy problem that is not solvable with our current technology trajectory. With our increasing dependence on coal, it is *completely* out of the realm of being achievable. Following is a brief table showing today's sources of energy:

Oil	37%
Coal	25
Natural Gas	23
Nuclear	6
Hydro	3
All other	<6 (wood, solar, wind, geothermal, etc.)

The bottom line is that twenty-first–century man finds himself between a rock and a hard place if the global warming issue is real and dangerous. At least 85 percent of our energy comes from fossil fuel, and the carbon that has been immobilized and stored for eons in the bowels of the earth continues to be released during the energy conversion process. This carbon is either absorbed by the oceans, or it becomes part of the atmosphere that envelops and controls the climate of the earth.

But while global warming might be fairly judged as the all-important consideration, it is not the only factor that should be considered in our decisions; there are two other big factors. The first factor is economics. Oil supplies are of concern. We have seen $150-per-barrel oil and $4 per gallon at the pump and travel-stopping airfares. Again, we are in uncharted waters with respect to the longer term supply-demand curve and the economic impact that might result. The second factor is that oil has become a major foreign policy factor. As mentioned earlier, Tom Friedman writes about this often and in pointed terms: the dollar we spend on oil "ends up with the mullahs who build madrasas that preach intolerance—that dollar would have gone to our own Treasury to pay down our own deficit and finance our own schools."

I mentioned that there is a glimmer of hope out of this rock-and-hard place problem. But it will also take incredible courage to make the transformational changes necessary to move, within a reasonably responsive time frame, to nuclear energy. Preparing for this book has led me down some paths that I did not fully expect. The need and the opportunities and the reasonableness that nuclear energy could be the salvation of Planet Earth and the entrée to a new world order of international peace and justice was not something I expected.

I would like to say just a bit about the courage required. This may seem a strained connection, but I'm going to share a story about two people who, if they were alive today, would have far more courage than they did in their lifetime. Psychologists have studied old people and have asked the question of what would they do differently if they had the chance to live their life over. Almost invariably, they answer that they would have taken more risks, been more adventuresome, been more courageous.

Somehow, we need to move this learning to an earlier point in our lives, to become courageous before it's too late. I'm certain the two people I'm thinking of would be the perfect example. Diane and I got a phone call from my close high school friend, who later became my brother-in-law, Ralph Meyer. He called to tell us that he had been diagnosed with colon cancer and that surgery at the Mayo Clinic was scheduled. He was fifty-four years old. Following surgery, his doctor said the cancer was extensive and would be terminal. Six months later, we got a call that my sister, Phyllis, Ralph's wife, was being transferred from the local hospital in Lake City to the Mayo Clinic because of abdominal pain that the local hospital had been unable to diagnose. After surgery at Mayo, she was quickly given the bad news that she had an advanced stage of ovarian cancer.

The saddest scene I have in my entire memory occurred a couple of months later. Phyllis had a second surgical procedure, and Diane and I drove to the hospital in Rochester a day later to visit her. Shortly after getting to her room, the door opened and they wheeled Ralph in to see Phyllis. Two people who were close to me, both younger than me, husband and wife, my only sister and brother-in-law, wonderful and caring people, faced the reality that they were soon going to leave their earthly existence and their two kids, Tom and Sue, and most likely knew that their final days were going to be filled with agony and pain. Ralph died a month later. Phyllis passed away six months after Ralph.

There are important "take-aways" for me: count your blessings; enjoy your days because they might be unexpectedly numbered. But most important, be everything that you can be—live your dream of being compassionate, caring, and courageous. And that is why I shared this story. We need to be courageous before it's too late. This is something that we will not want to say on our deathbed: "I wish I would have ..." The earth we leave our kids and grandkids strikes me as something we will wish we had done well and with courage, including the courage to shed mythology, ideology, and the fear of taking a bold step.

And here is the exciting possibility—the bold step—that I have learned exists as I did research for this book during the past couple of years. Nuclear energy, for the most part, is a here-and-now technology that generates close to carbon-free energy. It is the only realistic possibility we have that will allow us to meet the energy needs of the world without adding a very risky level of greenhouse gasses to the atmosphere. There is the possibility that we are already too late, but we are where we are, and maybe we can survive the transition period that would accompany the move from a global fossil-fuel economy to an essentially unlimited, carbon-free-energy world economy. Revolutionary—you bet. Transformational—to say the least. This is an opportunity to take mankind to the next evolutionary level and to plant the seed for a level of peace and justice that has always eluded man, to give mankind a reasonable chance for a sustainable future. Now, if that doesn't wet your whiskers, I don't know what would. And yes, I know the problems. The political challenge is absolutely immense. The level of courage required is greater than anything our nation or the world has ever faced. And, yes, it is possible that we cannot get the conversion to nuclear energy done before the atmospheric greenhouse gas concentration produces an uncontrollable positive feedback, the tipping point.

The core technology that we are talking about is the Integral Fast Reactor (IFR), sometimes denoted by different names, including the Advanced Liquid-Metal Reactor. Much of this book has been brewing in my mind for at least four or five years, but Integral Fast Reactor is a concept I did not fully appreciate until only a year or two ago. And that is what is so surprising to me. In fact, it has caused me to be somewhat cautious in accepting what I have now come to understand. I still cannot reconcile the fact that it has received essentially no discussion in the media or among environmental advocates. Tom Blees, author of *Prescription for the Planet: The Painless Remedy for Our Energy and Environmental Crises*, provides one of the better sources of information on fast breeder reactors understandable to lay people. His explanation of why it's the best kept technical secret (actually, it's never been a secret but simply never broadly understood by those outside the nuclear physics world) is that any term that has the world "nuclear" in it is immediately put in the "don't touch with a ten-foot pole" box. He may have a point. People like John Kerry and Bill Clinton were instrumental in stopping United States research on the technology, their argument based on erroneous technical information. My good friend and former work associate, Jay Morgan, and I were discussing this, and Jay pointed out that irradiation, as a way to assure the microbiological safety of meat, has suffered from a similar, decades-long misunderstanding of the technology and safety issues.

The breeder reactor is a nuclear-powered device that, in a sense, creates more fuel than it uses. The physics of this phenomenon have been understood since the early days of nuclear research that led to the development of nuclear bombs and to "conventional" nuclear power plants that now generate about 6 percent of the world's total energy needs and 15–20 percent of the world's electrical energy.

Nuclear breeder reactor technology is confronted with three huge problems, all three of which have prevented rational thinking and decision-making about the economic and quality-of-life benefits that it could provide for the earth's growing population; the most important benefit is that it offers the potential to eliminate the risks that accompany global warming. We are now, however, in a race against time. With some luck that the magnitude of future global warming is on the low side of the projection range, and with a truly "transformational" effort by the international community, there is a glimmer of hope that we can reduce the risk of causing serious damage to the habitability of Planet Earth. Following are the three issues that have prevented the development of unlimited CO_2-free energy from breeder reactors:

- Political resistance fostered by the fossil fuel gas, oil, and coal companies, industries that would be impacted by major development of an alternative non-fossil energy source.

- Security concerns that the material used and produced by breeder reactors can be more easily converted into nuclear-based weapons by terrorists or by rogue nations.

- Safety concerns undergirded by a general "fear factor" within the populace of anything that is "nuclear."

Regrettably, *none* of these issues should have been show-stoppers. To help address these issues, it would perhaps be helpful to discuss the design and operational characteristics of the Integral Fast Reactor.

The IFR is the latest, most advanced nuclear power-generating device yet designed. Because of the technology employed, it can utilize a very high percentage of the potential energy that is contained in uranium ore. Native uranium ore contains only a very small amount of the form of uranium that will react in a conventional nuclear reactor. This usable form is an isotope called U235 (termed a "fissile" form), and it constitutes only about 0.7 of 1 percent of the uranium ore, the primary constituent being a form called U238 (termed a "fertile" form). For use as a fuel in a conventional reactor, the concentration of the U235 has to be increased to 4 percent or more.

The "fissile" U235 form of uranium has two important properties: first, it's a radioactive material that "emits" neutrons, one of the components of the uranium atom; and second, if an adjacent U235 atom absorbs a neutron (the nuclear physicist term is "capture"), it is fairly likely to split apart, releasing heat and additional neutrons. Under carefully controlled conditions, packages of U235/U238 are organized in such a way that if the neutrons emitted are not absorbed by something else, a self-propagating chain reaction will result. When this condition is reached, the physicists say that a "critical mass" has been achieved. In practice, one of the techniques for keeping the reaction progressing at a steady, carefully controlled rate is to control the amount of the neutron-absorbing material placed between the U235/U238 fuel packages. (The absorbing material is in containers called "control rods.") Very substantial amounts of energy can be manufactured via this process: France, for example, produces 60 percent of its electrical needs by this process. This type of reactor is often referred to as a "thermal reactor" or a light water reactor (LWR) and is the most common reactor in use. They are also referred to as "slow" reactors, meaning that water is used to moderate (slow down) the neutrons that are emitted by the U235. This is done because a natural property of U235 is that it captures slow-moving neutrons better than fast neutrons and therefore, is more likely to split and release energy.

These reactors, however, have inherent design and physical chemistry limitations. The first is that they use only a small percentage of the potentially available energy in the uranium ore (most of the U238 is not utilized) and because of this, there is a substantial amount of nuclear waste material. In practice the reaction in the reactor is terminated when the level of undesirable reaction products, the "poisons," build up to a level where further energy production is severely limited. At this point, the spent fuel, which is of a type that is radioactive for a very long time, has to be removed and replaced with a new U235/U238 supply.

Most of the U238, which is 96 percent of the starting fuel load, has not been used. That is to say, by and large, it did not absorb the neutrons that were keeping the reaction going because in this type reactor, the neutrons are traveling relatively slowly. (In contrast to U235 which captures slow neutrons more readily, U238 captures fast neutrons more readily, forming P239.) But a few atoms of U238 *do* absorb a neutron, resulting in the production of plutonium 239. P239 is also a fissile material that will sustain chain reaction, but some P239 remains in conventional thermal reactor waste, an important point to note because, when separated, it's a superb fissile material for producing nuclear weapons. I mention this because it is the basis for an important misunderstanding about the Integral Fast Reactor.

The IFR has very substantial design differences and takes advantage of nuclear physics in a way that the thermal reactors do not. Most fundamentally, the IFR employs a design concept whereby the energy level of the neutrons is high or "fast"; the neutrons are not moderated and slowed as they are in the conventional thermal reactor. Under high-energy neutron conditions, the probability is much higher that the U238 atom will capture a neutron, producing P239, which works as well in the heart of the reactor as does U235. The "integral" part of the reactor design is a sub-system within the reactor assembly, where undesirable "poisoning" reaction products are removed and the fissile material is concentrated and reformed into new fuel packages, with the advantage that almost all of the U238 can be converted into fissile fuel. As a result, the U238, which constituted the bulk of the original fuel mixture, can now be transformed into heat energy. *Because of this efficiency of energy extraction, the IFR design has potential to provide the earth's inhabitants with an essentially unlimited supply of energy.* And it leaves only a small amount of nuclear waste.

The nuclear physics and the metallurgical and the chemistry and the engineering of the IFR are complex; make no mistake. The U.S. research on the IFR, begun during the Carter administration, was centered at the Argonne National Laboratory, and a highly successful small-scale unit was developed and tested. Included in this testing was the concept of "passive" safety. This is a concept (now available for use in conventional thermal reactors as well) whereby the fission process "shuts down" if temperatures exceed a design point. Walt Deitrich, Argonne reactor safety expert who helped develop the passive safety concept, explains it this way:

> "Modern safety design is to provide this protection by relying on the laws of nature, rather than on engineered systems that require power to operate, equipment to function properly and operators to take correct actions in stressful emergency situations. We call this approach, which relies on the laws of nature, 'passive safety.'"

One component of this design concept (there are a couple of others) is having nuclear fuel packages that expand if temperatures exceed a design point, with the result that the fissile material is no longer at "critical mass." The Three Mile Island incident or the Chernobyl accident would have been *impossible* if they had incorporated the passive safety design concept.

The last remaining technical step for demonstration of the entire IFR system was the "integral" process for removing small amounts of undesirable reaction products and reforming the fissile materials into new fuel packages for recycling back into the heart of the reactor. This process is termed the "pyroprocessing" step, proven to work on a small-scale basis. A very similar electro-refining process is already used in commercial non-nuclear industrial applications. This process would be adapted to the IFR concept by developing a robotic handling system. A very important design consideration is that the "pyroprocessing" step would be contained *within* the IFR containment system, and because the fuel material being reprocessed is very highly radioactive at this stage, it is inherently too reactive for anyone with ill-intent to handle. This is a critical advantage in terms of security.

Regrettably, because of the three issues mentioned earlier, the research at the Argonne National Laboratories was stopped in 1994 during the Clinton administration. Key players arguing to stop funding the research were Energy Secretary Hazel O'Leary and Senator John Kerry. Review of Kerry's chamber statements indicates clearly that he did not understand the technical aspects of the IFR concept. The key Argonne research scientists have retired or moved to different assignments, with the result that the United States has lost at least fifteen years, probably more, in progressing to energy independence and having a CO_2-free, unlimited source of power. This is particularly regrettable for those who remember Richard Nixon's declaring, "Our best hope today for meeting the nation's growing demand for economical clean energy lies with the fast breeder reactor ... [with] commitment to complete the successful demonstration of the liquid-metal fast breeder reactor." The Joint Committee on Atomic Energy of Congress concurred. *That was in 1970.*

The advantages of the IFR are many, and given today's concern about global warming, they are of immense importance. Following are the key advantages:

- The major source of fuel would be the spent fuel (the nuclear waste) of conventional reactors and decommissioned nuclear weapons. This supply of fuel would supply the *total* world's energy needs for the next 100 to 300 years. And there is enough uranium ore to be mined to power the world for many thousands of years if we capture its intrinsic energy, which the IFR concept does.

- The security concerns erroneously held by the public and political leaders—that the IFR concept makes it easier to pilfer/ steal P239, a preferred fissile material for nuclear weapon—is based on a serious misunderstanding of the IFR technology. A very important security advantage of the IFR is that the fuel reprocessing system is an integral part of the reactor complex. The fuel for recycling is secured within the system and is so radioactive that there is no reasonable way a terrorist or a rogue nation could remove it without receiving a lethal dosage of radiation themselves. In addition, the fuel being recycled in the pyroprocessing system could not be used in weapons without further refinement, using a process termed PUREX (essentially, the same process used for obtaining weapons-grade material from conventional thermal waste). Because the chemical elements differ, it is more difficult to concentrate IFR waste into weapons-grade material than thermal reactor waste.

- The radioactive waste from conventional thermal reactors and the fissile material from decommissioned weapons could be used as fuel in the IFR, eliminating the disposal issue that has remained unresolved for decades. The waste from an IFR is very small compared to the waste from thermal reactors and is radioactive for about 200 years, versus tens of millions of years for thermal reactor waste.

- Economic analyses indicate that the economics of the IFR would not be prohibitive. Clearly, conversion to IFR production of energy would incur a high capital cost for construction of the facilities. The cost per KW of energy produced now favors conventional thermal reactors, but this is because long-term disposal cost for the nuclear waste is not being included and because uranium ore is currently low in cost—a situation that will not endure long term, given the inefficiency of thermal reactors and the amount of uranium ore available for mining.

- The passive safety concept makes the IFR system extremely safe. It is also instructive to note that radioactive nuclear waste and radioactive materials for many purposes are being handled and transported safely every day by many countries.

- The physical size of an IFR electrical power-generating facility is not huge. The system concept also lends itself to standardized, modular construction and in some cases would allow a partial retro-fit concept to use the steam-powered turbine-electrical generator sub-systems of existing or planned coal or thermal nuclear facilities.

Steve Kirsch, a software developer who has become an advocate for the IFR, has summarized the potential of the technology: "The Integral Fast Reactor (IFR) is a fourth-generation nuclear design that provides a clean, inexhaustible source of power, cheap, with virtually no waste, inherently safe (if you remove the cooling, it shuts down rather than melts down), and the added benefit that it consumes the nuclear waste from other nuclear plants that we can't figure out how to get rid of." Kirsch adds: "To get rid of coal plants and have any hope at all on controlling climate change, you must come up with a power plant capable of 24 x 7 operation ... such an invention could, quite literally, save the planet from destruction. It would be the 'holy grail' in the fight against global warming. It would arguably be the most important invention in history."

At this point it is appropriate to acknowledge something that is probably and rightfully bothering you. If the IFR concept does what I have described, why have we not heard more about it? Good point. A fair number of people are now asking the same question. Earlier I mentioned that I only became aware of the practicality of the IFR within the past couple of years. Having been associated with the field of chemistry for a long time, I was aware of breeder reactor theory. But I did not know that it had been developed, with the exception of the pyroprocessing/electro-refining step, to the commercial design stage. In view of this skepticism, I sought other published sources of information, including published interviews with Charles Till, the director of the Argonne National Laboratory program; a report by the Nuclear Engineering department at the University of California, Berkeley; Manuel Garcia Jr., a retired nuclear physicist; Tom Blees, author of *Prescription for the Planet*; James Hansen, the highly regarded climatologist from the NASA Goddard Institute for Space Studies; and General Electric Nuclear Energy. A substantial number of other experts in the nuclear physics field are knowledgeable advocates of the technology.

It should be noted that the breeder reactor concept is being pursued by other countries. (It is not clear if any of these developments incorporate an integral, sequestered fuel reprocessing system.) The countries reported to be developing breeder reactors include France (reported to be in the start-up phase), Japan, China, and India. It is disturbing that the United States has fallen behind in the commercialization of the breeder concept. On the other hand, it can be argued that it is encouraging that the international community has a sense of the opportunity and need for breeder technology, which suggests that an international cooperative program might be politically feasible, with the right leadership from the major industrial nations, including non-partisan support from the United States.

Clearly, we cannot talk the issue of energy—the need for CO_2-free energy because of the global warming risk; the concerns emerging with respect to oil supplies; or the foreign policy ramifications of our oil dependency—without addressing the global implications. I have skirted over the huge issue of how this technology might be commercialized, particularly global commercialization, as it relates to the political questions and the international cooperation and control that would be required. Al Gore, at least to date, has not been an advocate of IFR technology. Some believe it is because he is not technically informed, and that he has unfounded concern regarding the security risk, and that he sees the political issues as being insurmountable. He has, however, been a strong advocate of a Global Marshall Plan to cope with the global warming risk. Tom Blees has proposed, as a starting point for serious thinking, the formation of a Global Rescue Energy Alliance Trust (GREAT), initiated with a focused effort by the Group of Eight (G8) nations. Others, in a more general sense, have urged the development of a Manhattan Project or, using a more recent example, the Apollo program, where the nation makes a major, committed effort to the development of CO_2-free energy.

Certainly, the Manhattan or Apollo concepts need to be considered for development of the final pyroprocessing/electro-refining step and for the development of standardized, modular construction techniques.

It is important to note that most experts believe the most difficult technology developments associated with the IFR concept have been successfully completed and that the remaining technical development, the pyroprocessing/electro-refining step, is eminently "doable," given commitment of engineering resources.

The reality is that IFR technology is the only practical answer to our energy needs and to the global warming risk. That is not to say that we should not pursue other alternative forms of energy production, including clean-coal technology and aggressive energy conservation measures; we very definitely should. In part, the reason we need to pursue these avenues is that IFR commercialization will take many years, probably two to three decades, at minimum, before it could replace coal-fired electrical plants or provide the energy consumed by the growing, more energy-demanding population. But the hard truth is that none of the alternatives being talked about—wind power, solar, clean coal, hydrogen, etc.—have any realistic hope of solving the energy crisis, and actually make the matter worse by distracting us from the reality of the issue.

Focusing on Reality and Decision-Making

This chapter, "Survival: The Confluence of Global Warming, Population, and Energy," deals with one of the monumental challenges that we face as the people of the earth. But very few people have made an effort to become even baseline knowledgeable on the global warming/population/energy subject. The opinions usually expressed are either intuitive or a reflection of ideology. This will not do; we are facing issues that have the potential for catastrophic consequences for the habitability of Planet Earth. To summarize:

- The risks associated with global warming are real. A linear rate of warming is almost assured. The probability is very high. Only the rate of temperature rise and the new point of steady state are really in question. Many of the very best climatologists believe we will increase surface temperature by 9 to 11 Fahrenheit degrees by the end of the century. Major climatic change would almost assuredly accompany this temperature increase and cause suffering for many millions of people. Of lower odds, but having some element of probability, is the possibility of rapid, abrupt, non-linear climate change due to the unpredictability of self-reinforcing positive feedback mechanisms. This would be catastrophic for most areas of the world. The issue before us is that we need to make responsible judgment regarding these risks. Burying our heads in the sand is hardly a responsible position. Honest, adult discussion and policy-making are required.

- Population growth and per-person resource demands have been the primary cause of the earth's health question. The die has been cast for this problem to become much worse as the lesser-developed world increases consumption. Worldwide family planning and a reevaluation of material needs are rational endeavors to keep this from making matters worse.

- Energy generation from fossil fuel burning and the concomitant emission of CO_2 and methane will need to be reduced drastically in order to hold atmospheric CO_2 concentration at levels where the risks associated with global warming have a reasonable probability of being more moderate and more manageable. All CO_2-free energy alternatives and energy conservation

276

techniques need to be pursued, but the reality is that only CO_2-free energy production from nuclear reactors has realistic potential to solve our energy needs. Current interest in wind power, solar, hydrogen, and other CO_2-free energy will, in fact, be counterproductive if they distract us from the essence of the issue. With a focused, international, high-priority effort, the incredible efficiency and practicality of Integral Fast Reactors could be the salvation of Planet Earth.

The decisions we make and our collective will to deal with these issues will determine the future of Planet Earth. And the health of Planet Earth will determine the future for our kids and grandkids. Only by facing reality and by summoning an unprecedented level of courage can we meet this challenge.

PART III

A Deliberate Walk
in the Woods

CHAPTER 14

THE BIG PICTURE

*"Beware lest you lose the substance
by grasping at the shadow."*
—"The Dog and the Shadow"

*"One does not discover new
lands without consenting
to lose sight of the shore."*
—Andre Gide

I realize this is a complicated, convoluted book. The first part of this book was my attempt to address the humanness that embeds all of us. It was also to share with you my belief that each of us is an awesome, unique individual. It was also to ask that you take time to reflect on the mysteriousness of your existence. By any metric or by any philosophical measure, it is an incomprehensible "miracle" that you are here at this time and at this place. In fact, not only are you unique, but the time and place in which you find yourself is also unique. The state of the world that exists today never existed before, and the state of tomorrow's world is yours to imagine and design.

Your uniqueness and wonder should be precious to you. My hope is that you see your existence as a grand adventure. As hard as it is, we should treasure the newness of each day and the opportunities and challenges that each day holds. Your unique existence says that you owe nothing to anyone, but at the same time, you owe everything to everyone. I think that is what Bishop Spong means when he talks about the freedom to love. Your uniqueness means that the universe has given you a wonderful chance, albeit only one chance, to experience its awesomeness and wonder. Perhaps there is something eternal about our existence. Most of us hope there is, but the hard fact is that *we do not know*. Man finds this hard to accept and to many of us, it is such a disturbing reality that we find ourselves easy prey for someone who claims to have the answer.

We also know that there is hurt and suffering in this world. It, too, is part of our existence; it unquestionably comes with the territory of life. No one has an answer to why there is so much hurt in life and in the world. Some theologians have come to the conclusion that suffering negates any possibility of a loving God. The evolution purists see it as simply part of the process. Maybe they are right. I'm less sure. I hold out the possibility that there is a greater dimension to our existence than what we see, but that is a guess, and it's beyond human capacity to come to a definitive answer.

We do know that hurt is instructive. Because we have seen it and because we have felt it, we can relate to all the other folks on the planet. It's like holding hands with everyone else. Perhaps most important, it gives real purpose to life. It becomes the grand goal of our existence. We want to make the world better, not only for ourselves and our kids, but also for the occupants that we have never met but know, and for the generation yet to be born.

We also know that our Earth home is like a living body. It is robust yet fragile. We understand that the history of the earth has been long, but that man's slice of existence on this planet is very short, and that for most of his history on Earth, man's activities have had no lasting effect. But we also know that this has changed. Within the very short span of 250 years—and mostly during the very tiny span of the past 100 years—man has developed the capacity to change the face of the earth profoundly. And we must ask what this means, because now, for the first time ever, our *decisions* will have immense, long-term impact on Planet Earth and mankind.

Our unique existence on the earth, as twenty-first century beings, means that we have more history to educate us than ever before. If we have the will, we can look at the nonsensicalness of some of the things that man has spent his energies pursuing—war, subjugation of others, material trappings, supremacy, hatred. If we choose, we can study the basis for evil, learning how to recognize it when it's taking form.

If we have the courage, we can ask ourselves why myth and ideology control our beliefs and conduct, and why we permit this without inquiry. We can ask whether these are the primal, tribal genes that still override the rational thoughts of a more highly evolved mankind to which we are hopefully advancing. It should be asked whether deference to these myths and ideologies will allow man to cope with a world of nine billion people, an atmosphere of 500 ppmv CO_2, and tribes believing they hold moral superiority and special status with God. For that is the world in which the next generation is destined to live.

We can even begin to ask ourselves, including the common folks living in Minnesota and Wisconsin and the rest of the country, what the future holds for our nation. We can ask the serious question of whether we will continue to be a leader in the world's affairs or if the downhill slide will progress further ... and further. Is General Motors the United States, or has the United States become General Motors? We can even ask the tough questions of whether our vaulted dog-eat-dog capitalistic economic system needs rethinking; whether honesty and ethics are important and whether unbounded greed is tolerable; whether income disparity will lead to a nation of haves and have-nots; and whether the promised but unfunded entitlements will lead to financial chaos. We may need to ask whether *Newsweek International* editor Fareed Zakaria has a point, as he suggested, that we need to take a very hard look at "a Washington establishment that has gotten comfortable with the exercise of American hegemony and treats compromise as treason and negotiations as appeasement ... [that] the only way to deal with countries is by issuing a series of maximalist demands"; his conclusion being "this is not foreign policy; it's imperial policy."

Never before have we been faced with such immensely challenging issues and questions. They are more challenging than ever before because of their potential impact on our lives. To be legalistically accurate, perhaps there was one comparable period of time. That was during the post-WW II cold war period when the Soviet Union and the United States had 20,000 deployable nuclear weapons, with thousands ready to be launched within minutes. But that was a different kind of challenge. The day-by-day control, if not the evolvement of the cold war stalemate, was managed by rational thinking and easily understood mutual destruction concerns. The challenges we now face are vastly different. The profound, multifaceted issues we now face require moving from myth and ideology to reality. Asking ourselves whether our beliefs and ideologies represent truth and reality will require a level of courage never before demanded of mankind. Being the strongest and most dominant will no longer be the answer.

My walk-in-the-woods story began a number of years ago. I retired from Pillsbury, and Diane retired from the Veterans Administration Hospital. Retirement means a big change in your life. You have time to do things that you couldn't do while working. I know the rat race; I allowed it to consume me. With retirement came the opportunity and freedom to explore things of interest that could be given substantial commitments of time and energy. It's a very enjoyable time of one's life.

There was an unexpected downside, however. The more I read, and the more I studied, and the more I observed, and the more I talked with some close friends, the more concerned I became about not only the direction of our nation but also about some of the global issues that pose catastrophic risk to Planet Earth's people. And most important, along with this concern came the recognition that many of the challenges we face are due, in large part, to the fact that so many of our beliefs are based on myth and unfounded ideologies. These myths and ideologies consume us and control our decisions. And it became apparent that, in large part, these are beliefs that we have never subjected to substantive inquiry. It became painfully obvious that we live in a world of denial, without the courage to view the world and our existence through the lens of reality.

I could sense in myself a growing discomfort. I was certain that I had made a valid assessment of the challenges facing us— the evidence is overwhelming—but I felt powerless to do anything about it. Simply telling some of my friends that their belief system is based on superstitious mythology or on unfounded ideology, and with them saying, "Thanks for telling me," does not accomplish much or provide much comfort. Humorist Franklin Jones was right: "Honest criticism is hard to take, particularly from a relative, a friend, an acquaintance, or a stranger."

Perhaps this helps explain why belief systems based on superstitious mythology or unfounded ideology are rarely challenged in the media. When, for example, was the last time you read about someone's taking issue with the foundational proposition that God came down and told a small, select group of people that they had divine right to a certain piece of land on the eastern edge of the Mediterranean, particularly when it's based on ancient writing in which, a few pages later, there is a description of how the color of goats could be controlled by placing peeled tree branches in front of the mating pair. We don't demand reality, and we resist engaging in substantive inquiry.

Instead, we follow the herd. I realized that I also, on occasion, had followed the herd; that I had allowed myself to be captured by group-think. Hence, my sharing with you the "My First, Big, Enduring Myth" story as a personal example of not pursing truth and reality, not thinking for myself in a substantive way.

The decisions we have made in the past, many of them nonsensical decisions, have resulted in incredible pain and have hurt many people; one only needs to think of the wars, poverty, and hardships man has endured throughout the ages. But survival of a habitable earth and the well-being of *billions* of people were never at risk.

That is the difference between the past and the present. It is a huge difference, yet we continue to deny reality. We cling to the false security net of myth and ideology. We have yet to recognize that the challenges of the scope we face cannot be met unless we are willing to acknowledge reality, to look it in the face. Only if we change our allegiance from party and ideology to understanding and reality will there be any chance for mankind to escape catastrophe and to progress to a better world.

It was the frustration of not knowing how to respond to this realization that led me to the idea of this book. I do not have the oratory skills or public relations abilities or the charisma to motivate people to cope with the evolving dilemma. So writing this book has been my way of dealing with these concerns. It gives me some peace of mind because it allows me to conclude that it's the best that I can do, given my abilities.

I share this because of the obvious question that this book precipitates; the question that I was faced with: what to do? This is an important question for two very important reasons. The first, if you take my conclusions seriously, is that we must find a way to build support for the transformative changes required. A corollary question is a more personal one. This is the question of how I live at peace with myself if the transformative changes prove to be unachievable, politically or from lack of courage and the will of the populace. I dealt with this question by writing this book. But a massive grassroots movement "for the people, by the people" that demands that we address reality will be required.

This will be difficult; most people already have more demands on their time and energies than they can handle. They are not retired grandpas. Work, the house, and the dogs, the kids in school, the car that needs fixing, the effort to keep the errant-prone teenager on course, the budget that always seems to have more debits than credits, TV time, the request to coach the Little League team, hair salon appointments—the demands go on and on and on. They would say, "Fat chance that we have time for deep thinking or walk-in-the-woods contemplation." Anyhow, isn't this what we pay our politicians and the universities and all the research organizations funded by our tax dollars to do? Been there. Understand it. Can't argue.

But unless there is a grassroots movement to abandon myth and ideology, we will continue to make uninformed decisions; we will continue to be at the end of politically driven propaganda strings; and we will continue to deny the realities that have gotten us into the jam that we are in. And make no mistake—it is a jam of proportions that man has never before faced. That is a strong statement, made only after some long, hard thought by this grandpa. But as I have said over and over again, we are where we are. It's only the decisions that we make going forward that have relevance.

As dire as this all sounds, the challenges we face also present us with the greatest opportunity ever offered mankind. We are at a place in history that man has never been before. The opportunity to create a new world order is before us. Being part of raising mankind to this next level of development holds immense reward, satisfaction, and happiness for those who dare to have the courage to become engaged. Although scary, it is an adventure that we should enter enthusiastically. It's the greatest gift we could possibly give to the next generation. That, too, is a reality; it is perhaps where the courage to be counted will come from.

CHAPTER 15

IMAGINING A NEW
WORLD ORDER

"Wisdom begins in wonder."

—Socrates

*"We know what we are, but
not what we want to be."*

—William Shakespeare

*"Not everything that is
faced can be changed,
but nothing can be changed
until it's faced."*

—James Baldwin

There is a useful tension between pragmatism and idealism. I would argue that in most cases, idealism is more often relegated to the dream world, with the prevailing view that the real doers are the pragmatists, those who actually get something done. This view undoubtedly has some merit. But at the same time, I think we have to admit that our nation's founding fathers placed tremendous importance on idealism. Their vision of what a nation might be was transformational in every sense of the word. Anyone who doubts that the Constitution or the Bill of Rights or the Declaration of Independence are documents of idealism and vision, perhaps even unrealistic imagination, should re-read them.

During the 1980s it became popular for companies to develop a mission statement. This was often a prolonged, thoughtful exercise to state succinctly the purpose of the institution and, most important, the key characteristics or principles that the institution believed it must live by to accomplish this purpose. Interestingly, most of the institutions that developed mission statements were not new institutions. They were, instead, institutions that were asking themselves what their vision should be now—today—given that time had changed the world in which they were operating. It was a marriage of reality, or pragmatism, if you will, and idealism, the overarching principles that describe purpose and guide conduct.

So the question is: if the earth and world have changed during the past 250 years, and mostly during the more recent 100 years, should we review our purpose of being—the idealism part—and the operating principles or tactics that enable us to move toward this ideal? I am not suggesting a total rewrite of the Constitution, by the way. What I am suggesting is that we need to consider, in a thoughtful, deliberate way, what the changed world means in terms of societal conduct, including our *personal response*. Following are a few ideas to *illustrate* what I am thinking about with respect to the argument that the world that has changed and that "idealism" needs to be revisited and become a part of our growth journey:

A Nation That Focuses on People Development: Rethinking What Growth Means

The current economic problems have made all of us aware of the materialistic bent that has dominated our lives in recent decades—bigger houses, statement cars, more exotic vacations, larger engagement diamonds, ever more elaborate weddings, kids sporting teams with equipment that rivals the pros, the latest operating system and fastest computer in the home office; the list is long. And insidiously, it is this materialism that has become the metric that defines who we are. It has become the measure of our status in the world, not only in terms of how others see us but also how we measure the "worth" of ourselves. Sociologist, writers, psychologist, clergy, and many others more attuned to what it means to be a wholesome, healthy individual have warned us of this danger for many years. But the warnings were not heard. It has taken the economic crisis to cause people to question what the holy grail of materialism really means to them.

Combined with this is the fact that the world has become extremely complex. Consider today's world of computer and telecommunication technology, medical science, nuclear physics, robotic manufacturing, molecular genetics, the myriad laws governing individual and organizational practice, material chemistry, international trade, financial derivatives—the list is daunting. During the past few decades, the education requirements for us to perform our jobs have grown exponentially. We struggle to keep up. We rightfully feel that we do not have enough time or energy to stay on top of all the things deemed important to our lives and job.

Ironically, the economic answer for lifting ourselves out of the current economic crisis is to encourage ever more consumption, ever more materialism, even though it was this materialism and spending obsession that was one of the fundamental causes of the financial crisis. We now have a world that has more production capacity than is needed, and at the same time unemployment and under-employment. We dug a hole and our answer, at least for now, is to dig it deeper until we can figure out a better answer.

This is an extremely abbreviated and incomplete description of the personal and economic problems that we are facing. My hope is simply that this brief discussion is sufficient to cause us to think about the fundamental illogic, the irony and senselessness of the path we have been taking, personally and as a nation.

I am sure that we need to consider more fundamental change. For example, perhaps we need to consider, for at least a significant portion of the work force, a four-day workweek—a four-day work week *coupled* with a fifth day of substantive skill and knowledge development. This could have diverse and multiple objectives— training for the next more technically demanding job; equipping ourselves with the knowledge to make informed decisions on the immense challenges that we face as a nation; lifestyle and health maintenance education to lower heath care cost and improve quality of life; making it possible to obtain graduate school degrees while on the job; exposure to the arts for those of us who focused on science, and vice versa. The possibilities are endless. My thinking is this would be a disciplined and committed societal effort for development of our most precious resource—people. We now live in a different world and we need to think differently, in a very fundamental sense, on what this demands of us in terms of personal growth and the nation's growth, and what constitutes true happiness and quality of life.

My belief is that such an endeavor would make us a better people. It would give each of us a rewarding sense of growth and accomplishment. It's a rethink of what the word education means in today's world. It would be a great example for our kids and grandkids, saying that education and growth does not stop at the end of high school or college but that it is an ongoing process that leads to an ever higher level of individual development and fulfillment.

With an increasing population and the demands this will place on the earth, do we not have to think of "growth" in a more substantive way—personal, business, and societal growth versus unlimited material growth? The answer needs to be part of our imagining a new world order.

Challenging a First-Order Myth: Religion Myths

With a church or synagogue or mosque at the corner of many of our intersections, it is difficult to envision there being a meaningful change in how the members of these congregations see truth. Serious inquiry about the validity of their faith and core beliefs is not on the table. One could easily conclude that "no way" will this happen.

That is true for almost all the members, probably the vast majority. But I suspect there is 1 percent who harbor some questions, some concern about the conclusion that they are the sole possessors of truth. Perhaps there is 1 percent who ask themselves what belief in being the sole possessors of truth means in terms of world peace and how this absolutism is perceived by the rest of mankind. In a 500-member church (or synagogue or mosque), that's five people.

Five people can have amazing impact. Simply as example, let's say the five people write a letter to the church's leadership group (it was called the Council in the Lutheran churches I belonged to) with a list of some of the questions I shared with you in an earlier chapter, "My First, Big, Enduring Myth." This note could ask that a faith study class be formed for those who are having faith questions, a request that one would think the church would take seriously. Along with the Bible, it could be suggested that a few of the books that raise serious question about the validity of the Bible also be used as discussion material. Or it could be suggested that a biblical scholar who has concluded that the Bible has a mythology core be invited to share the basis for this view.

I have little doubt where this process would end. For many—those who have the courage to look at reality—the result would be the recognition that Christianity (or Judaism or Islam) is a man-made, mythology-based religion. The books underlying these faiths contain beautiful verses, are instructive in understanding the human condition, and have much wisdom to share but nevertheless rest on man-made mythology. It would be an all-important step in encouraging our brothers and sisters to look at their existence through the lens of reality. Ultimately, it could change the way we view the rest of the world and allow us to see how strongly myth and unfounded ideology control mankind's thinking.

Is there 1 percent with this courage? Is there 1 percent with the inner strength to accept the risk that inquiry might show that the ideologies and myths they hold may not have merit, that there is a greater truth? In some parts of the world—Europe, for example—it is already happening. So perhaps there is hope that other parts of the world will also begin to seek religious truth rather than clinging to false comfort offered by cult mentality. It is not easy. I know. But it can be done.

Climate and Energy Development

The odds are high that the earth's health is at significant risk because of the global warming phenomenon. *Many of the world's best minds believe this is the most crucial issue ever faced by mankind.* Although the Western industrialized nations have produced two-thirds of the increase in CO_2 atmospheric concentration, it is now a problem of international scope, given the ever-increasing amount of greenhouse gasses produced by developing countries, and simply because the effect of global warming transcends national boundaries.

Short of some unexpected, miraculous discovery, nuclear energy, specifically integrated breeder reactor technology, is the only realistic alternative for meeting the world's CO_2-free energy needs. All other alternative energy concepts are good and should be pursued aggressively, but they also carry the serious risk of being a distraction that prevents us from focusing on the foundational opportunity. In reality, the alternative forms of energy being discussed—wind power, solar, etc.—cannot eliminate or even significantly reduce the global climate risk. But nuclear energy carries proliferation and safety risk. The situation demands that we develop an international Planet Earth Energy Cooperative to control and manage the world's energy needs, and that this institution implement a Marshall or Apollo type plan for moving to breeder reactor production of all the world's energy needs. The magnitude of this challenge is, of course, mind-boggling, yet it may be the only realistic alternative we have for avoiding a climate change catastrophe. And that is what our very best science minds are telling us will be the outcome if we do not move to a CO_2-free energy source. An international program of this nature is hard to imagine, but then again, never in the history of mankind have we been in this situation.

Effective Governance

The United States has a governmental system that no longer works. It is controlled by lobbyists, funding sources, special-interest ideology voting blocks, and the lust for power. Our government avoids the serious, long-term challenges and instead, occupies itself with sound-bite posturing. Politics has become loyalty to party and ideology rather than loyalty to truth, understanding, and reality. It is imperative that we consider changes that address the fact that our system is corrupt, that it is controlled by greed, special interests, and lust for power.

The immobilized state of government demands that two relatively straightforward yet far-reaching changes be made immediately. *The first is to move to a single-term limit for the Senate and House of Representatives.* This change would have profound impact in restoring our Congress to a functioning body and would have profound impact on the incumbent—no energy would be expended in re-election campaigns, no courting of special-interest groups would be necessary. The legacy left would be by what he or she accomplished, not how long he or she served. *The second far-reaching change is to restore the military draft system with essentially no provision for deferments.* The volunteer system has made "going to war" a far too easy decision. It destroys our sense of prudence in thinking about military action and its purpose. Only when it's our own son or daughter, grandson or granddaughter, who might be called upon to take the risk of making the ultimate sacrifice will we examine, deeply and carefully, the decision to engage in war and the appropriate level of investment in the military. Both of these fundamental changes are critically needed; together, they would produce an immediate and profound impact on our need for more effective governance of our nation.

The lobbying system that now controls Washington needs to be regulated closely. It needs to be changed, by law, into an information system that is totally transparent and that provides no campaign funding or personal support. In addition, a general information mechanism that's readily available to the entire populace, now quite feasible through the Internet system, should be established, with oversight and presentation of the information by an appointed, non-partisan board—an information system for the nation *not controlled by viewer ratings or subscription numbers*. The challenges that we face will require the support and involvement and sacrifice of the people. A mechanism for greatly increasing the *inform*ed engagement of the public will be essential in order to gain public support for the transformative changes required to meet the huge challenges we face.

I believe it is important that we consider the establishment of an independent body, separate from the executive and legislative bodies, for establishing the nation's annual budget proposal. The current process is fundamentally flawed in that it is a political process controlled by re-election interests and efforts to establish party dominance. This independent body—*The Economist* journal has suggested calling it the "fiscal council"—would be charged with responsibility for development of a balanced budget and presentation of strategy for dealing with our massive unfunded commitments. It could be charged with the development of a budget that links financial budget numbers with clear communication of national objectives. It would even be possible to send each taxpayer a "statement report," showing how his/her tax monies have been allocated, with the explanation and rationale for why these dollars are being spent. Some local governments already do this, albeit in a limited way. This would go a long way in placing burden on the legislative bodies to approve a visionary, substantive, and responsible budget that engages the populace.

In place of blind allegiance to party, we will need to consider more fundamental questions, such as where on the pure capitalism/pure socialism continuum we need to be for effective governance of our nation. Where is the balance point? As a practical matter, it is not reasonable to believe that we can function on the extreme end of either side. Governance and discussion forums of this magnitude are required for the nation to reestablish credible leadership and compete in the global economy. Politically, one can even imagine a new "Reality Party" that has honesty, reality, and vision as its purpose; a party that has no candidates of its own but instead focuses on substantive discussion of issues and a willingness to confront irresponsible behavior of candidates. Or we may have reached the point where a new party of responsibility and reality with its own slate of candidates can take root.

Foreign Policy for Tomorrow's World

U.S. foreign policy, certainly as conducted during the past three decades and particularly during the past decade, is not reflective of the economic changes that have occurred globally, nor is it cognizant of the fact that our world influence, compared to what we enjoyed in the second half of the twentieth century, will be less. A significant segment of our nation's population is still mired in an idea of world order that tries to legitimize arrogance and self-centeredness. There is a vocal segment of the populace, particularly the far right, that confuses patriotism with nationalism. Nations are people, and they do not like others who are conceited and unwilling to confer dignity onto others. This, too, however, is a grassroots issue. The nation's posture will be the posture of its people.

There are interesting and creative ways to make our populace more understanding of the world. My "new order" proposal is that everyone be encouraged to travel overseas, visiting with the real people of other countries. Diane and I and our travel friends have discussed many times how travel changed our perspective; the world is filled with wonderful people. Everywhere we have gone, the common folks have been welcoming and generous. We have seen the common goals we share. Travel makes it more difficult for our media and politicians and religious leaders to demonize the people of other nations.

The mechanics of this proposal would be that there is a one-time tax credit for a one-time trip to a foreign country. There are many excellent travel organizations that would be happy to make this a truly educational, mind-opening adventure. Think of a whole nation of people who now have seen the people of another nation, close-up—large numbers of people meeting face-to-face with the Chinese, Malaysians, Koreans, Iranians, and Russians. Think of the conversations this would create when the people return. Think of the contribution this might make toward the conduct of international trade, the understanding of humanity, to peace efforts, and toward nuclear disarmament.

Financially feasible for the nation? Think of it this way: we have seriously contemplated the expenditure of one trillion dollars for the purchase and operational expenses of a new fleet of jet fighter planes. For a comparable amount of money, we could send 100 million people—one-third of the nation's population—on a $10,000 trip to a foreign country, where they could begin to understand the people of that country; where they would be seen as ambassadors from our nation. Thinking of it another way, if we reduced the defense budget by 20 percent, we could send 100 million ambassadors—probably half of our adult population—on this $10,000 trip during the course of a two-term president.

Which one would foster personal growth? Which one would allow you to see reality? Which one would have the most impact on world peace?

Ending Poverty

Our conscience should not allow us to proceed with business as usual in the face of the one billion who live in abject poverty.

Poverty is terribly hard to eliminate. It is not solved by handouts or charity. It cannot be eliminated by creating dependency. Real poverty alleviation is education, business development, infrastructure development, access to credit, family planning and health care facilities, and hard-nosed pressure for the development of competent governance. It is the conveyance of dignity and recognizing the desire that all people have for being self-reliant and self-directing.

The conscience of a nation is the conscience of its people. I had some experience while at Pillsbury in the role a corporation can play in poverty alleviation. What I found is that when the values of the corporation are in harmony with the values of the employees, a tremendously powerful force is unleashed. I am certain the same is true for a nation: when the values of the nation are in harmony with the inner values of the people, a tremendous force can be unleashed. Combining a specific percentage of our GDP—for example 0.7 percent, the Millennium Project goal—with a hard-nosed administrative program would produce results that would allow all of us to feel we are being considerate of the needs of the world's most unfortunate. I find it hard to believe that the people of our country would not readily endorse such an effort.

A Final Comment

Admittedly, these are examples that strain the sense of practicality; they are meant only to be illustrative of a broader concept. Many other transformative concepts worthy of serious consideration are possible: a health care system redesigned from the bottom up, where the medical community is compensated for keeping people healthy, not for the number of procedures done; a military/police system designed for today's security needs, rather than fighting yesterday's international wars; a system that gives people the right to vote by passing a basic knowledge test on governance issues, perhaps similar in concept to the trade licensing process that assures a reasonable level of competency and judgment.

Although visionary and perhaps seemingly radical, these ideas and other ideas of comparable scope are not absurd if we think of them in the context of the challenges that we face, *and if we think of them in the context of being our generation's equivalent of the courage and foresight that were embedded in the ideals of our founding fathers.* We have no choice: it will require acceptance of transformational changes of this magnitude to deal with the challenges we face.

CHAPTER 16

THE WONDERFUL, MAGNIFICENT OPPORTUNITY OF TOMORROW

*"When we are unable to find
tranquility within ourselves,
it is useless to seek it elsewhere."*

—Francois de La Rochefoucauld

*"Hope has two beautiful daughters.
Their names are anger
and courage; anger at the way
things are, and courage to see
that they do not remain the way they are."*

—Augustine

I called this part of the book "A Deliberate Walk in the Woods" because, if I have succeeded at all, that is where the book will end for you—with a walk in the woods. I'm hoping that your take-away will be that you want to do some thinking; that you feel a long walk in the woods is needed to sort through your thoughts.

We have covered some big, heavy topics. Things like religious faith, global warming, and capacity to do evil are substantive stuff! Admittedly, each of the topics that we have discussed in the previous chapters is very much a subject within itself. Each requires its own contemplation and decision. Each of the topics is extremely important, but there are many more, and those that we have covered are, at best, illustrative and representative of others—at least, this was the intent.

The overarching purpose, however, was to encourage a more foundational way of thinking about these topics; that we will look for the underlying reality and truth that embeds these issues; and that we will rigorously ask whether we are viewing these issues and topics through the lens of reality or if we are only seeing them through the lens of myth and ideologies. That is the question that I am suggesting is the all important one and which, I hope, gives you pause for serious thought.

I have come to believe it is our primal human nature that has led us down the path of seeing the world through the lens of myth and unfounded ideologies. For many reasons, we find it easy and emotionally comfortable to follow the herd and allow our intellect to be a product of where we were born, rather than embarking upon an adventuresome, individualistic, more demanding search for truth. As I have shared, some of us have to become a grandpa before we have the courage to do this. Before the industrial age, and even perhaps during the first 150 years of the industrial age, viewing the world through the lens of myth and ideology was perhaps problematic at times but not catastrophic.

So now, after only a very short hundred-year slice of historical time, the tremendous growth of the world has put us in a place where man has never been before. We have always been unique human beings, but we are now in a unique place in the history of mankind as well. With the progress of the late-industrial age, there has come an explosion in population and the consumption of fossil fuel, which together are profoundly changing the face of the earth. We now know, with a high probability, that the climate of the earth is in delicate balance, and because of our population growth and energy needs, we are altering this balance in ways that risk the earth's ability to sustain its inhabitants.

Interestingly, the industrial age also corresponds time-wise with the history of the United States. It has been a fascinating, unparalleled historical journey. The nation became the world's symbol of progress and effective governance. My generation has seen it at the pinnacle of its stature—mighty and magnificent and blessed with resources and talented, hard-working people. But the capitalistic economic system that produced unparalleled prosperity for its people has developed serious cracks. Greed, arrogance, and irresponsible behavior have put the future and well-being of the nation's populace in uncharted waters. What the conclusion of this folly will be has everyone guessing.

Because of our human nature, we have difficulty internalizing the fact that we are now living in a world that is profoundly changed from only a hundred years ago. The earth of one hundred years ago—just three or four generations ago—was, in most ways, viewed fundamentally unchangeable. It was logical to see the earth as being very robust, and any influence by man would be local and rather insignificant to the earth at large. For the first time in mankind's existence, this is no longer true.

The uniqueness of these times also demands that we examine ourselves from the outside in. Where does leadership come from? Is our nation capable of committing evil? Is our economic system effective and just? Do we have a sustainable financial future? Are our religious faiths true? And to what degree are our beliefs on these issues based on mythology and unfounded ideology?

Society has always faced difficult questions. Still, I think when the very existence of a habitable earth is in question, and when we have serious, well-meaning people asking whether the world's greatest economy needs fundamental change, we are in unique times.

These are immense challenges.

But it is exactly these challenges that offer the most wonderful opportunity imaginable, for all are solvable with individual courage and will. Man is a funny creature. We are not at our happiest when coasting along. We are happy and feel good when we are being constructive and when we are solving problems. We are the happiest when we are building for a better tomorrow. We are happy and at peace with ourselves when we have a sense of personal growth. It's that simple.

Admittedly, it will take a tremendous amount of courage to embark on our search for reality, truth, and understanding. It means leaving the protective womb of myth and ideology and entering a world that is authentic and substantive and where our understanding of the essence of our self may be changed. My experience has been that when we make this leap, it becomes the most extraordinary, wonderful experience possible—the inner sense and confidence that we have become whole; true adults who reason for ourselves and who can be truly appreciative of the wonders of our existence. It is not a giggly, euphoric, "everything is great today" happiness, but rather something far, far deeper and more satisfying—that we are being honest with our existence; that we no longer need to deny reality. And at that point, we may rightly conclude that we are not only awesomely unique but that we have reached a wonderful level of contentment and peace of mind. It is the ultimate celebration of life. And if there is a Greater Power, I think that would be in accord with the grand plan of the universe.

It was inescapable that I would reveal my own views and concerns and even my own prejudices. But my purpose was not to convince you of any ideology but to encourage you to walk your own path of inquiry. The challenges you face are immense. The demands are great. And the times are unique. But you are, too! You have a wonderful, magnificent opportunity for a grand adventure! Be not afraid.

With unending love and affection and gratitude for all you have given me,

Grandpa

EPILOGUE

Desmond Tutu was asked in a recent interview, "Are you really as optimistic as your book *Made for Goodness* [published March 2010] says you are?" Archbishop Tutu's response to the question was "I'm not optimistic, no. I'm quite different. *I'm hopeful.*"

I can relate to that answer. Much of *"Through the Lens of Reality"* was written during the winter of 2009, probably when Tutu was writing his book. I watched a fierce presidential campaign, culminating in the election of the first black president of the United States. It was also a period of unusual turmoil. I have suggested that September 18, 2008, will be a date noted in history because it was the date that the Secretary of the Treasury and the Chairman of the Federal Reserve called an urgent evening meeting with the president and a small group of the most powerful members of Congress to tell them that the United States banking system was on the precipice of collapse and that the mighty United States economy was facing imminent meltdown.

The nation was already overburdened with an array of immense issues, most of a nature and magnitude that the nation had never before faced, several of which I discussed in this book. It would have been an easy, even a rationale, attitude to be pessimistic, given the circumstances.

But I was optimistic. Perhaps I was simply caught up in the "Audacity of Hope" of the newly elected president. I was reasonably confident that the division and partisanship and anger that were displayed during the campaign would disappear, and that given the immense challenges, Congress and the populace would put the nation ahead of party and ideology.

But I was wrong. The inane shrillness has continued, perhaps it has even intensified. National figures have continued to show no shame when making intellectually dishonest accusations. It is commonplace, as journalist Bob Herbert has said, to see "foaming-at-the-mouth protesters scream the vilest of epithets" with no regard for civility or common decency. We are still seeing loyalty to party and unfounded ideology and self-righteousness trampling truth and understanding and cooperation.

I am truly puzzled and bewildered and do not understand what drives this mania. What is it that drives this fear and anger? Perhaps those who are wiser than I and who understand human nature more intimately will eventually answer the question.

Yet I continue to be hopeful because I know that within each of us is a unique, special, transcendental being, capable of making transformative change. But it will require a grassroots "we, the people" movement to lead us away from the abyss to which the nation's inexplicable rage is carrying us ever closer.

As I write this closing note in March 2010—about eighteen months after I started this book—I, too, have a more guarded sense of optimism. I see the anger in the nation and the blind allegiance to party and ideology, and it is reasonable to ask whether reality, truth, and understanding will ever prevail and allow us to meet the challenges we face. Like Nobel Laureate Tutu, my optimism is shaken. *But I'm hopeful.*

ACKNOWLEDGMENTS

The two people most influential in my early life were Uncle Bud and Grandpa Orlin. Both believed in me and cared about me in the sincerest of ways. Yet they always encouraged me to find my own way, to follow my own conscience.

As a kid and teenager, I worked with Bud more than anyone else. He knew me; I knew him. Our many conversations were authentic and with trust and honesty. His counsel was always given in a quiet way, one-on-one. It was with his advice and encouragement that I left the farm to go to college and pursue a different career path. Bud loved farming, so it was not that he was trying to steer me away from that life; rather, it was his sense that I'd be happier doing something else with my life. He was as wise and as decent a human being as any I've known. I have wondered many times why he took as much interest in me as he did. But I am extremely grateful.

Grandpa Orlin was the ultimate encourager. Until he died, there was never a day that I didn't know that he was someone I could turn to if I really needed help, even if it was because I had messed up, big time. He was interesting and spirited. He had the charisma and presence that many of us long for. He was successful and an independent thinker. He was smart, hard-working, and tough. Having someone like that believe in you and care about you is as great a gift in life as can be given.

Bud and Grandpa, I'm not sure where we go after death—if anywhere—but I sure hope we can hook up again when we are on the other side.

And in my adult life I have been blessed with a wonderful companion, soul mate, and compass. Diane has provided guidance, encouragement, and unflinching love for forty-plus years. Fate smiled on me the day we met. Love you bunches, Diane.

These are the three people who have been most influential in my life. They are people of character. I hope I have returned their trust and love, as they have given theirs to me; this book stems from their ideals as much as mine.

FURTHER READING

I am sometimes asked for the title of some of the books that I have found to be particularly instructive on some topic. Following is a short list of books that I have found to be informative:

Your Awesomeness and Uniqueness

A Short History of Nearly Everything by Bill Bryson

You are Here: A Portable History of the Universe by Christopher Potter

The Nation's Decline in Moral Character

The Way of the World: A Story of Truth and Hope in an Age of Extremism by Ron Suskind

War Is a Force That Gives Us Meaning by Chris Hedges

American Fascists: The Christian Right and the War on America by Chris Hedges

The True Patriot by Eric Liu and Nick Hanauer

Idiot America by Charles Pierce

Ending Poverty

The End of Poverty: Economic Possibilities for Our Time by Jeffery Sachs

The Question of Evil

Ordinary People and Extraordinary Evil: A Report on the Beguilings of Evil by Emil Katz

When Religion Becomes Evil by Charles Kimball

Global Warming and CO_2-Free Energy

The Revenge of Gaia by James Lovelock

Gaia's Last Warning by James Lovelock

Prescription for the Planet by Tom Blees

Storms of My Grandchildren by James Hansen

Israel and Palestine

Palestine: Peace Not Apartheid by Jimmy Carter

We Can Have Peace in the Holy Land by Jimmy Carter

The Ethnic Cleansing of Palestine by Ilan Pappe

The Economic Mess

Where Does Your Money Go: Your Guide to the Federal Budget Crisis by Scott Bittle and Jean Johnson

Financial Armageddon by Michael J. Panzner

The Christian Myth

Liberating the Gospels: Reading the Bible with Jewish Eyes by John Shelby Spong

The Sins of Scripture by John Shelby Spong

Rescuing the Bible from Fundamentalism by John Shelby Spong

The End of Faith by Sam Harris

The Power of Myth by Joseph Campbell with Bill Moyers

Biblical Nonsense by Jason Long

Stealing Jesus by Bruce Bawer

The Jesus Mysteries by Timothy Freke and Peter Gandy

The Lost Goddess by Timothy Freke and Peter Gandy

The Gnostic Gospels by Elaine Pagels

The Origin of Satan by Elaine Pagels

The Jesus Puzzle by Earl Doherty

Why I Became an Atheist by John W. Loftus

A History of God by Karen Armstrong

The Battle for God: A History of Fundamentalism by Karen Armstrong

The Orthodox Corruption of Scripture by Bart D. Ehrman

Lost Christianities by Bart D. Ehrman

Why I Am Not a Christian and Other Essays on Religion by Bertrand Russell

ABOUT THE AUTHOR

Gerald Rabe—better known as "Jerry"—was born in southeastern Minnesota. He spent his early years on a dairy farm near the small town of Oak Center, a mere widening of the road with a country store, a farm equipment dealer, a creamery and a dance hall. Shortly after high school, Jerry joined the local U.S. Army Reserve which was activated during the Cold War's Berlin crisis. After returning to the farm, Jerry made a life changing decision to leave the family farm and pursue a college education in chemistry. He met his future wife, Diane, while an undergraduate student at the University of Minnesota; they were married while he was a graduate student at Cornell University in Ithaca, New York. His first employer was the Procter & Gamble company in Cincinnati, Ohio where he worked as a food research scientist. Several years later he accepted a technical management position with The Pillsbury Company where he was employed until retirement. His primary work interest was incorporating technology into the strategic plans of the corporation, and understanding the role of diet in chronic disease development.

Jerry and his wife continue to live in the house they built in 1975 in a western suburb of Minneapolis. They spend much of the summer at their cabin on an island in Lake of the Woods in northern Minnesota, and have traveled many foreign countries. They have two children and four grandchildren...and one dog.

After retirement, Jerry began the study of how people form the beliefs they hold and how these beliefs mold their decisions. It is this interest, combined with his view on the uniqueness of our times, which is the basis for his first book, *Through the Lens of Reality: Thoughts from a Maturing Grandpa*.